Acclaim for

P. J. O'Rourke's

GIVE WAR A CHANCE

"In the world of contemporary American humorists, O'Rourke is the experimental scientist....*Give War a Chance*...[is] the kind of book that takes a long time to finish because you're constantly reading parts of it to whomever happens to be around."
—*Newsday*

"O'Rourke is smart. He's funny. He can write like hell. He's opinionated and not afraid to say so....Go ahead and laugh at *Give War a Chance*; just watch out for the cruel undertow."
—*Seattle Times*

"O'Rourke is an effective propagandist with an astute insight into the dark side of the id of the sixties generation."
—*The Nation*

"The literary Prince of Venom...the man of a million mean words."
—*Cleveland Plain Dealer*

"O'Rourke has a sharp eye for incongruity...a tough and interesting mind.... What's in his closet isn't liberalism but common sense, and when he lets it out he's first rate."
—*Washington Post Book World*

P. J. O'Rourke

GIVE WAR A CHANCE

P. J. O'Rourke is the best-selling author of *Modern Manners, The Bachelor Home Companion, Republican Party Reptile, Holidays in Hell,* and *Parliament of Whores.* He writes for *Rolling Stone* and lives in New Hampshire and Washington, D.C.

GIVE

WAR A

CHANCE

Eyewitness Accounts of

Mankind's Struggle

Against Tyranny, Injustice

and Alcohol-Free Beer

P. J. O'Rourke

VINTAGE BOOKS

A DIVISION OF RANDOM HOUSE, INC.

NEW YORK

First Vintage Books Edition, May 1993

Copyright © 1992 by P. J. O'Rourke

All rights reserved under International and Pan-American Copyright Conventions.
Published in the United States by Vintage Books, a division of Random House, Inc.,
New York, and distributed in Canada by Random House of Canada Limited,
Toronto. Originally published in hardcover by The Atlantic Monthly Press,
New York, in 1992.

Library of Congress Cataloging-in-Publication Data
O'Rourke, P. J.
    Give war a chance: eyewitness accounts of mankind's struggle against
tyranny, injustice and alcohol-free beer / P.J. O'Rourke.
      p. cm.
    Originally published: New York: Atlantic Monthly Press, 1992.
    ISBN 0-679-74201-8 (pbk.)
    1. World politics—1985–1995—Humor.   2. United States—Social
conditions—1980– —Humor.   3. Persian Gulf War, 1991—Humor.
I. Title.
D849.076   1993
956.704—dc20   92-50591
CIP

Manufactured in the United States of America
10 9 8 7 6 5 4 3 2 1

Like many men of my generation, I had an opportunity to give war a chance, and I promptly chickened out. I went to my draft physical in 1970 with a doctor's letter about my history of drug abuse. The letter was four and a half pages long with three and a half pages devoted to listing the drugs I'd abused. I was shunted into the office of an Army psychiatrist who, at the end of a forty-five-minute interview with me, was pounding his desk and shouting, "You're fucked up! You don't belong in the Army!" He was certainly right on the first count and possibly right on the second. Anyway, I didn't have to go. But that, of course, meant someone else had to go in my place. I would like to dedicate this book to him.

I hope you got back in one piece, fellow. I hope you were more use to your platoon mates than I would have been. I hope you're rich and happy now. And in 1971, when somebody punched me in the face for being a long-haired peace creep, I hope that was you.

ACKNOWLEDGMENTS

"The Death of Communism," "Springtime for Gorbachev," "Return of the Death of Communism, Part III," "The Piece of Ireland That Passeth All Understanding" and most of the Gulf War section of this book originally appeared in *Rolling Stone,* where I am the "Foreign Affairs Desk Chief," a title given to me because "Middle-Aged Drunk" didn't look good on business cards. I would like to thank Jann Wenner and the staff of *Rolling Stone,* especially Bob Wallace, Eric Etheridge and Robert Vare for good editing, better ideas and best paychecks.

Although the Gulf War dispatches appeared in *Rolling Stone,* it was ABC Radio that actually sent me to Saudi Arabia. The General Manager of News Operations, my friend John Lyons, called me from Dhahran and said, "I noticed your bylines on the Kuwait invasion story were Jordan and the U.A.E., and this tells me you haven't been able to get a Saudi visa." John got me one and got me a job, too (my first real one since 1980), doing commentary for his radio network. The "Gulf Diary" entries and much of the material in the *Rolling Stone* dispatches are drawn from my radio pieces. I know nothing about radio, and John was a patient boss—though his patience was sorely tried when I wound up, briefly, as the only ABC Radio reporter in liberated Kuwait City and was sending back live reports such as: "Uh, uh, uh, uh . . . oh my gosh, blown-up tanks." Many thanks go

Acknowledgments

to John and to the equally patient real ABC Radio reporters in the Gulf, Linda Albin, Chuck Taylor and Bob Schmidt.

"Return of the Death of Communism," "Fiddling While Africa Starves," "The Deep Thoughts of Lee Iacocca," "The Very Deep Thoughts of Jimmy and Rosalynn Carter" and "Mordred Had a Point—Camelot Revisited" all appeared in the *American Spectator*, as did "Notes Toward a Blacklist for the 1990s." This last was expanded, with the aid of the *Spectator*'s readers, into a book-length proscription called *The New Enemies List*. Copies are available from *The American Spectator*, P.O. Box 549, Arlington, VA 22216. My thanks to R. Emmett Tyrrell, Jr., Wladyslaw Pleszczynski, Andrew Ferguson and the rest of the staff of that fine publication.

"Second Thoughts About the 1960s" was originally a speech, given in October 1987 at the Second Thoughts conference in Washington, DC. Second Thoughts was a gathering of former New Leftists and other people who had successfully recovered from the sixties. The conference was put together by Peter Collier and David Horowitz, and we all had a great time chastising our former selves. Part of my speech was published in the *New Republic*, then under the brilliant (even if he does call himself a liberal) editorship of Michael Kinsley. The entire text was printed in the book *Second Thoughts*, edited by Collier and Horowitz and published by Madison Books (Lanham, Md.) in 1989.

The Second Thoughts conference was organized with the help of Jim Denton, Director of the National Forum Foundation, one of Washington's more thoughtful think tanks. The National Forum Foundation has worked hard and even successfully to aid pro-liberty forces in Central America and Eastern Europe. It was Jim Denton who convinced me to go to Nicaragua for the 1990 elections. Jim even went so far as to claim Violeta Chamorro might win.

"A Serious Problem" was commissioned by the intelligent and beautiful Shelley Wanger, then Articles Editor of *House and Garden*. But Ms. Wanger left, *House and Garden* became *HG* and my piece was judged to contain too few photographs of celebrity bed linen.

"Studying for Our Drug Test" appeared in *Playboy*, assigned by

Acknowledgments

sagacious Articles Editor John Rezek. "The Two-Thousand-Year-Old U.S. Middle East Policy Expert" was published in *Inquiry* at the behest of its excellent Managing Editor, Jack Shafer. "An Argument in Favor of Automobiles vs. Pedestrians" saw print in *Car and Driver* when that doughty publication was being run by the as-doughty or doughtier David E. Davis, Jr. And "Sex with Dr. Ruth" came out in *Vanity Fair,* Executive Literary Editor Wayne Lawson being the only person on earth who could convince me to go see Dr. Ruth, let alone admit it later.

Additional thanks are due to Morgan Entrekin, my editor and publisher, who paid me again for all these articles even though I'd been paid for them already, and to Bob Datilla, my agent, who made Morgan do that. And I must sincerely—though sincerity is not my forte—thank my wife. She had been my wife for only a month when the air war started in the Gulf and I headed there for the duration. She didn't cry, she didn't complain, she didn't let the car insurance lapse. And, when she heard about the way I almost set off a booby trap by fooling around with a box of Iraqi ammunition, she said—in even, measured tones—those words which elucidate so well the content and the style of all my journalism work: "P.J., that was really stupid."

"... and from the nothingness of good works, she passed to the somethingness of ham and toast with great cheerfulness."

—Charles Dickens
BARNABY RUDGE

CONTENTS

Contents

Contents

INTRODUCTION

Hunting the Virtuous—

and How to Clean

and Skin Them

This book is a collection of articles about—if I may be excused for venturing upon a large theme—the battle against evil. Not that I meant to do anything so grand. I was just writing magazine pieces, trying to make a living, and evil is good copy.

Various types of evil are battled here. Some are simple. Iraq's invasion of Kuwait is a case of bad men doing wrong things for wicked reasons. This is the full-sized or standard purebred evil and is easily recognized even by moral neophytes. Other malignities— drugs in America, famine in Africa and everything in the Middle East—are more complex. When combating those evils people some- times have trouble deciding whom to shoot. And in this book there is at least one evil, involving the kill-happy Irish, which is being fought whether it exists or not.

Anyway, it's a book about evil—evil ends, evil means, evil effects and causes. In a compilation of modern journalism there's nothing surprising about that. What does surprise me, on rereading these articles, is how much of the evil was authored or abetted by liberals.

Now liberals are people I had been accustomed to thinking of as daffy, not villainous. Getting their toes caught in their sandal straps, bumping their heads on wind chimes—how much trouble could they cause, even in a full-blown cultural-diversity frenzy? (I mean if Euro- peans didn't discover North America, how'd we all get here?) But

Introduction

every iniquity in this book is traceable to bad thinking or bad government. And liberals have been vigorous cheerleaders for both.

"Liberal" is, of course, one of those fine English words, like lady, gay and welfare, which has been spoiled by special pleading. When I say *liberals* I certainly don't mean openhanded individuals or tolerant persons or even Big Government Democrats. I mean people who are excited that one percent of the profits of Ben & Jerry's ice cream goes to promote world peace.

The principal feature of contemporary American liberalism is sanctimoniousness. By loudly denouncing all bad things—war and hunger and date rape—liberals testify to their own terrific goodness. More important, they promote themselves to membership in a self-selecting elite of those who care deeply about such things. People who care a lot are naturally superior to we who don't care any more than we have to. By virtue of this superiority the caring have a moral right to lead the nation. It's a kind of natural aristocracy, and the wonderful thing about this aristocracy is that you don't have to be brave, smart, strong or even lucky to join it, you just have to be liberal.* Kidnapping the moral high ground also serves to inflate liberal ranks. People who are, in fact, just kindhearted are told that because they care, they must be liberals, too.

Liberals hate wealth, they say, on grounds of economic injustice—as though prosperity were a pizza, and if I have too many slices, you're left with nothing but a Domino's box to feed your family. Even Castro and Kim Il Sung know this to be nonsense. Any rich man does more for society than all the jerks pasting VISUALIZE WORLD PEACE bumper stickers on their cars. The worst leech of a merger and acquisitions lawyer making $500,000 a year will, even if he cheats on his taxes, put $100,000 into the public coffers. That's $100,000 worth

---

*It was that talented idiot Percy Bysshe Shelley who first posited this soggy oligarchy when he said, "Poets are the unacknowledged legislators of the world." Modern liberals are no poets, however, and are hardly satisfied with legislating in the unacknowledged manner. Today's liberals love politics as much as they love disappearing rain forests, homelessness and hate crimes, because politics is one more way to achieve power without merit or risk.

of education, charity or U.S. Marines. And the Marine Corps does more to promote world peace than all the Ben & Jerry's ice cream ever made.

Liberals actually hate wealth because they hate all success. They hate success especially, of course, when it's achieved by other people, but sometimes they even hate the success they achieve themselves. What's the use of belonging to a self-selecting elite if there's a real elite around? Liberals don't like any form of individual achievement. And if there has to be some, they prefer the kind that cannot be easily quantified—"the achievement of Winnie Mandela" for example. Also wealth is, for most people, the only honest and likely path to liberty. With money comes power over the world. Men are freed from drudgery, women from exploitation. Businesses can be started, homes built, communities formed, religions practiced, educations pursued. But liberals aren't very interested in such real and material freedoms. They have a more innocent—not to say toddlerlike—idea of freedom. Liberals want the freedom to put anything into their mouths, to say bad words and to expose their private parts in art museums.

That liberals aren't enamored of real freedom may have some-thing to do with responsibility—that cumbersome backpack which all free men have to lug on life's aerobic nature hike. The second item in the liberal creed, after self-righteousness, is unaccountability. Lib-erals have invented whole college majors—psychology, sociology, women's studies—to prove that nothing is anybody's fault. No one is fond of taking responsibility for his actions, but consider how much you'd have to hate free will to come up with a political platform that advocates killing unborn babies but not convicted murderers. A callous pragmatist might favor abortion *and* capital punishment. A devout Christian would sanction neither. But it takes years of therapy to arrive at the liberal point of view.

Since we're not in control of ourselves, we are all vulnerable to victimization by whatever *is* in control. (Liberals are vague about this, but it's probably white male taxpayers or the Iran-contra con-spiracy). Liberals are fond of victims and seek them wherever they go.

Introduction

The more victimized the better—the best victims being too ignorant and addled to challenge their benefactors. This is why animal rights is such an excellent liberal issue. Not even a Democratic presidential candidate is as ignorant and addled as a dead laboratory rat.

The search for victims of injustice to pester explains why liberals won't leave minorities alone. "The minority is always right," said that pesky liberal Ibsen. And, when it comes to minorities, there is none greater—or, as it were, lesser—than that ultimate of all minorities, the self. Here the liberal truly comes into his own. There is nothing more mealy-mouthed, bullying, irresponsible and victimized than a well-coddled self, especially if it belongs to a liberal.

Liberal self-obsession is manifested in large doses of quack psychoanalysis, crank spiritualism, insalubrious health fads and helpless self-help seminars. The liberal makes grim attempts to hold on to his youth—fussing with his hair, his wardrobe, his speech and even his ideology in an attempt to retain the perfect solipsism of adolescence. He has a ridiculous and egotistical relationship with God, by turns denying He exists and hiding in His skirts. Either way—as God's special friend or as the highest form of sentient life on the planet—liberal self-importance is increased. The liberal is continually angry, as only a self-important man can be, with his civilization, his culture, his country and his folks back home. His is an infantile world view. At the core of liberalism is the spoiled child—miserable, as all spoiled children are, unsatisfied, demanding, ill-disciplined, despotic and useless. Liberalism is a philosophy of sniveling brats.

There! It was good to get that off my chest. Now that I've had my say, however, you may be wondering—don't I sometimes get called a Nazi? Yes, name-calling, in which conservatives such as myself are so loath to indulge, is a favorite tactic of the liberals. I have often been called a Nazi, and, although it is unfair, I don't let it bother me. I don't let it bother me for one simple reason. No one has *ever* had a fantasy about being tied to a bed and sexually ravished by someone dressed as a liberal.

THE BIRTH,
AND SOME OF
THE AFTERBIRTH,
OF FREEDOM

THE DEATH
OF COMMUNISM

Berlin, November 1989

A week after the surprise-party opening of East Germany's borders people were still gathering at the Berlin Wall, smiling at each other, drinking champagne and singing bits of old songs. There was no sign of the letdown which every sublime experience is supposed to inspire. People kept coming back just to walk along the freshly useless ramparts. They came at all sorts of hours, at lunch, dawn, three in the morning. Every possible kind of person was on promenade in the narrow gutter beside the concrete eyesore: wide hausfraus, kids with lavender hair, New Age goofs, drunk war vets in wheelchairs, video-burdened tourists, Deadheads, extravagant gays, toughs become all well-behaved, art students forgetting to look cool and bored, business tycoons gone loose and weepy, people so ordinary they defied description and, of course, members of the East German proletariat staring in surprise—as they stared in surprise at everything—at this previously central fact of their existence.

Even West Berlin's radicals joined the swarms. West Berlin had the most dogmatic agitators this side of Peru's Shining Path, but that was before November 9th. Near the restored Reichstag building I overheard a group of lefties amicably discussing nuclear strategy with a half dozen off-duty U.S. GI's.

"Ja, you see, tactical capability mit der cruise missiles after all vas not der Soviet primary concern . . ."

"Sure, man, but what about second-strike capability? Wow, if we hadn't had that . . ."

All in the past tense. A British yob, who certainly should have been off throttling Belgians at a football match, came up to me apropos of nothing and said, "I fucking 'ad to see this, right? I 'itched 'ere from London and got these chunks off the wall. You think I can't pay for the fucking ferry ride back with these? Right!"

At the Brandenburg gate the East German border guards had shooed the weekend's noisy celebrators off the Wall. But the guards weren't carrying guns anymore and were beginning to acknowledge their audience and even ham it up a bit. Somebody offered a champagne bottle to a guard and he took a lively swig. Somebody else offered another bottle with a candle in it, and the guard set the candle on the wall and used a plastic cup to make a shield around the flame.

The people in the crowd weren't yelling or demanding anything. They weren't waiting for anything to happen. They were present from sheer glee at being alive in this place at this time. They were there to experience the opposite of the existential anguish which has been the twentieth century's designer mood. And they were happy with the big, important happiness that—the Declaration of Independence reminds us—is everybody's, even a Communist's, inalienable right to pursue.

The world's most infamous symbol of oppression had been rendered a tourist attraction overnight. Poland's political prisoners were now running its government. Bulgaria's leadership had been given the Order of the Boot. The Hungarian Communist Party wouldn't answer to its name. Three hundred thousand Czechs were tying a tin can to the Prague Politburo's tail. And the Union of Soviet Socialist Republics was looking disunified, unsoviet and not as socialist as it used to. What did it mean? The Commies didn't seem to know. The Bush administration didn't either. And you can be certain that members of the news media did not have a clue. Ideology, politics and journalism, which luxuriate in failure, are impotent in the face of hope and joy.

*   *   *

I booked a hotel room in East Berlin. When I arrived at the West Berlin airport a taxi dispatcher said the border crossings were so busy that I'd better take the subway to the other side. The train was filled with both kinds of Berliners, and stepping through the car doors was like walking into a natural history museum diorama of Dawn Man and his modern relations. The Easterners look like Pleistocene proto-Germans, as yet untouched by the edifying effects of Darwinian selection. West Germans are tall, pink, pert and orthodontically corrected, with hands, teeth and hair as clean as their clothes and clothes as sharp as their looks. Except for the fact that they all speak English pretty well, they're indistinguishable from Americans. East Germans seem to have been hunching over cave fires a lot. They're short and thick with sallow, lardy fat, and they have Khrushchev warts. There's something about Marxism that brings out warts—the only kind of growth this economic system encourages.

As the train ran eastward, West Berliners kept getting off and East Berliners kept getting on until, passing under the Wall itself, I was completely surrounded by the poor buggers and all the strange purchases they'd made in the west. It was mostly common, trivial stuff, things the poorest people would have already in any free country—notebook paper, pliers and screwdrivers, corn flakes and, especially, bananas. For all the meddling the Communist bloc countries have done in banana republics, they still never seem to be able to get their hands on any actual bananas.

The East Berliners had that glad but dazed look which you see on Special Olympics participants when they're congratulated by congressmen. The man sitting next to me held a West German tabloid open to a photo of a healthy fraulein without her clothes. He had that picture fixed with a gaze to make stout Cortez on a peak in Darien into a blinking, purblind myope.

At the Friedrichstrasse station in East Berlin, passport examination was perfunctory and the customs inspection a wave of the hand.

I walked outside into a scene of shocking, festive bustle. Though, to the uninitiated, I don't suppose it would look like much—just squat, gray crowds on featureless streets. But there are never crowds in East Berlin. And the crowds had shopping bags. There's nothing to shop for in East Berlin and no bags in which to put the stuff you can't buy. Taxi drivers saw my luggage and began shouting, "You want taxi?!" "Taxi, ja?!" Imagine shouting that your services are for hire in East Berlin. Imagine shouting. Imagine services. I heard laughter, chatting, even giggles. I saw a cop directing traffic with bold and dramatic flourishes. I saw border guards smile. It was a regular Carnival in Rio by East Berlin standards. And, the most amazing thing of all, there was jaywalking.

I had been in East Berlin three years before. And I had been standing on a corner of a perfectly empty Karl-Marx-Allee waiting for the light to change. All Germans are good about obeying traffic signals but pre-1989 East Germans were religious. If a bulb burned out they'd wait there until the state withered away and true communism arrived. So I was standing among about a dozen East Germans, meaning to follow the custom of the country, but my mind wandered and without thinking I stepped out into the street against the light. They all followed me. Then I realized I'd walked into the path of a speeding army truck. I froze in confusion. They froze in confusion. Finally I jumped back on the curb. And they did too, but not until I'd jumped first.

In 1986 I'd come through the border at Checkpoint Charlie, and getting in was a dreary and humiliating experience similar to visiting a brother-in-law in prison. There was much going through pairs of electrically locked doors and standing before counters fronted with bulletproof glass while young dolts in uniforms gave you the fish-eye. There were an inordinate number of "NO EXIT!" signs, and I remember thinking the exclamation points were a nice touch.

You had to exchange twenty-five perfectly good West German marks, worth about fifty cents apiece, for twenty-five perfectly useless

East German marks, worth nothing. I thought I'd see how fast I could blow my stack of East marks on the theory that the test of any society's strength and vigor is how quickly it Handi-Vacs your wallet.

I walked to Unter den Linden, old Berlin's Champs Elysées. The city was empty feeling, no construction noise, no music, no billboards or flashing lights. There were plenty of people around but they all seemed to be avoiding one another like patrons at a pornographic movie theater and, although it was a beautiful spring day, the East Berliners were moving with their shoulders hunched and heads turned down as though they were walking in the rain. The women were frumps but the men bore an odd resemblance to trendy New Yorkers. They had the same pallor and mixing-bowl haircuts. They wore the same funny, tight high-water pants with black clown shoes as big as rowboats and the same ugly 1950s geometric-patterned shirts buttoned to the neck. Except the East Berlin guys weren't kidding. This wasn't a style. These were their clothes.

Unter den Linden's six lanes served only a few deformed East German Wartburg sedans and some midget Trabant cars. The Trabants had two-cycle engines and made a sound like a coffee can full of steel washers and bees. They looked like they were made of plastic because they were. Other than that the traffic was mostly blimp-sized double-length articulated buses progressing down the vacant avenue at the speed of Dutch Elm disease.

The store windows were full of goods, however: a fifty-bottle pyramid of Rumanian berry liqueur, a hundred Russian nesting dolls, a whole enormous display devoted entirely to blue plastic toothbrushes with the bristles already falling out. The huge Centrum department store smelled as though the clothes were made from wet dogs. The knit dresses were already unraveling on their hangers. The sweaters were pilling on the shelves. The raincoats were made out of what looked like vinyl wallpaper. And there were thirty or forty people in line to buy anything, anything at all, that was for sale.

I went to a bar in the showplace Palace of the Republic. It took me thirty minutes to be waited on although there were two bartenders and only five other people in the place. The two bartenders were pretty busy washing out the bar's highball glass. I was amazed to see "Manhattan" listed on the drink menu and ordered it and should have known better. There was some kind of alcohol, but definitely not whiskey, in the thing and the sweet vermouth had been replaced with ersatz sloe gin.

Next, I stood in line for half an hour to see what Marxism could do to street-vendor pizza. It did not disappoint. The word *cottony* is sometimes used to describe bad pizza dough, but there was every reason to believe this pizza was really made of the stuff, or maybe a polyester blend. The slice—more accurately, lump—had no tomato whatsoever and was covered in a semiviscous imitation mozzarella, remarkably uncheeselike even for a coal-tar by-product. Then there was the sausage topping. One bite brought a flood of nostalgia. Nobody who's been through a fraternity initiation will ever forget this taste, this smell. It was dog food.

I went back to Checkpoint Charlie. You weren't allowed to take East German money out of the country. I don't know why. It's not like there was anything you could do with it in the west. The bills are too small for house-training puppies. But East Germany was so total in its totalitarianism that everything was banned which wasn't compulsory. Anyway, when I went through customs a dour official in his early twenties said, "Have you any currency of the German Democratic Republic?"

"Nope," I said. "I spent it all."

He looked skeptical, as well he might have. "Empty pockets, *bitte*," he ordered. I had twenty-one marks left over.

"Well, I'm coming back tomorrow," I said.

His expression changed for a moment to boyish amazement. "You *are?*" He resumed his governmental frown. "This once I will allow you to retain these currencies because you are coming back tomorrow," he said and rolled his eyes.

I did come back and this time couldn't find anything at all to spend money on. The only excitement available in East Berlin seemed to be opening the subway car doors and getting off the train before it came to a complete halt. But I couldn't figure out how to pay the subway fare so I couldn't even spend my money on this. I walked back toward Checkpoint Charlie with forty-six marks in my pocket. Then I did something my capitalist soul had never allowed me to do before in my life. I crumpled up money and threw it in a garbage can.

There was no question of throwing money away on my 1989 visit to East Berlin. The glimmering new Grand Hotel, standing on that very corner where the garbage can had been, accepted only hard currency. In return you got food you could swallow and Johnnie Walker Scotch at the bar (although something described as "cod liver in oil" still lurked on the restaurant menu).

There had been changes for the regular citizens of East Berlin as well. There were three or four times as many shops on the streets, some with pseudo-boutique names like "Medallion," "Panda" and "Joker." The stuff for sale was awful enough, but there was more of it. Thus at least half the law of supply and demand was being obeyed—if something's lousy, it's always available. The first line-up of shoppers I saw turned out to be waiting for an antique shop to open. The new Wartburg 353 models even had styling—not much styling and that borrowed from 1960s Saabs, but styling nonetheless.

However, the real change was the lack of fear, a palpable physical absence like letting go of your end of a piano. My note-taking—which in 1986 would have sent passers-by scuttling like roaches surprised in a kitchen—now went unremarked. American reporters were all over the place, of course. And in every hotel lobby and café you could hear East Germans griping loudly to the reporters while the reporters loudly explained how all this was feeling to the people of East Germany.

There were pictures everywhere of the new East German leader, Egon Krenz, just as there'd been pictures everywhere of the old East German leader, Erich Honecker. But these weren't the lifted chin, stalwart forward-looker vanguarding the masses photos. Egon—who resembles a demented nephew of Danny Thomas's—was shown spreading hugs around, tousling toddler mop-tops and doing the grip-and-grin at various humble functions. He was politicking, plain and simple. The Commies didn't quite have it right yet: they take office and *then* they run for it. But they're trying.

Personally I missed the old East Berlin. The only thing East Germany ever had going for it was a dramatic and sinister *film noir* atmosphere. When you passed through Checkpoint Charlie the movie footage seemed to switch to black and white. Steam rose from man-hole covers. Newspapers blew down wet, empty streets. You'd turn your trench coat collar up, hum a few bars of "Lili Marleen" and say to yourself, "This is me in East Berlin."

That's gone now and the place is revealed for what it's really been all along, just a screwed-up poor country with a dictatorship. The dictatorship part is understandable, but how the Commies managed to make a poor country out of a nation full of Germans is a mystery. The huge demonstrations that had shaken East Germany for the past several months had one characteristic which distinguished them from all other huge demonstrations in history—they never began until after work. I went to one of these at Humboldt University. The students were demanding economics courses. It was hard to reconcile this with my own memories of student protest. We were demanding free dope for life.

The students were also protesting the opening of the Wall. Not that they were against it. But they were furious that the East German government might think this was all it had to do. One picket sign showed a caricature of East Berlin's party boss, Gunther Schabowski, naked with a banana stuck in every orifice and a balloon reading, "Free at last!" No one made any attempt to break up the rally. Soldiers and police were there, but they were applauding the speakers.

Even though the guard dogs and the machine-gun nests were gone, the east side of the Berlin Wall was still pristine, smooth whitewashed pre-cast reinforced-concrete slabs a foot thick and ten feet high and separated from the rest of the city by thirty yards of police. On the west side, the Wall was in your face and covered with graffiti paint as thick as ravioli.

I went out Checkpoint Charlie—with nobody worrying over what I might do with my East German marks—and turned right on Zimmer Strasse, what Berliners call "Wall Street" because the Wall runs along the old curbstone, leaving only a sidewalk in front of the West Berlin buildings. There was a steely, rhythmic noise that, for a moment, I thought might be some new Kraftwerk-style Euro synthesizer music (Berliners are horribly up-to-date with that sort of thing). But it was the sound of hundreds of people going at the Wall with hammers, chisels, picks, sledges, screwdrivers and even pocket knives. The chipping and flaking had progressed in a week until long, mouse-gnawed-looking ellipses were appearing between the slabs with daylight and occasional glimpses of East German border guards visible on the other side. I saw thirty schoolchildren on a class excursion with their teacher, all beating the Wall in unison with rocks, sticks and anything that came to hand.

I talked to a man in his sixties who was going along the Wall with a rucksack and a geologist's hammer. He'd escaped from the East in 1980. He'd been in prison over there for his political opinions. He gestured at the layers of spray-painting, the hundreds of symbols, slogans and messages ranging from John Lennon quotes to "Fuck the IRA." "I want one piece of every color," he said.

A twenty-year-old West German named Heiko Lemke was attacking the Wall with a set of professional stonemason's tools. In two days he'd made a hole big enough to pass a house cat through, even though the police had twice confiscated his cold chisels—the West German police. During a one-minute breather Lemke said he was an engineering student, a supporter of the Christian Democratic Party, didn't want history to repeat itself and was going to come back to the Wall on the weekend with some serious equipment.

Two American teenagers, Neville Finnis and Daniel Sheire, from Berlin's English-language JFK high school were attempting to rip the top off one section of the Wall with their bare hands. The Wall is capped with six-foot-long two-hundred-pound half-pipes cast in ferro-concrete. These need to be lifted nearly a foot in the air before their edges clear the cement slab and they can be heaved to the ground. Neville and Daniel straddled the wall, in postures that would bring dollar signs to the eyes of any hernia surgeon, and lifted. When that didn't work, two more JFK students got up on the Wall and lifted Neville and Daniel while Neville and Daniel lifted the half-pipe. "Go for it! Go for it!" they yelled at each other. It was an American, rather than a scientific or methodical, approach. The half-pipe landed with a great thump. The political message was clear to all the JFK students. "Yeah!" shouted one. "Let's sell it!"

The East German border guards didn't interfere. Instead they came up to openings in the Wall and made V signs and posed for photographs. One of them even stuck his hand through and asked would somebody please give him a piece of the concrete to keep as a souvenir.

The hand of that border guard—that disembodied, palm-up, begging hand . . . I looked at that and I began to cry.

I really didn't understand before that moment, I didn't realize until just then—we won. The Free World won the Cold War. The fight against life-hating, soul-denying, slavish communism—which has shaped the world's politics this whole wretched century—was over.

The tears of victory ran down my face—and the snot of victory did too because it was a pretty cold day. I was blubbering like a lottery winner.

All the people who had been sent to gulags, who'd been crushed in the streets of Budapest, Prague and Warsaw, the soldiers who'd died in Korea and my friends and classmates who had been killed in Vietnam—it meant something now. All the treasure that we in America had poured into guns, planes, Star Wars and all the terrifying A-bombs we'd had to build and keep—it wasn't for nothing.

And I didn't get it until just then, when I saw that border guard's hand. And I think there are a lot of people who haven't gotten it yet. Our own President Bush seems to regard the events in Eastern Europe as some kind of odd dance craze or something. When I got back to the United States, I was looking through the magazines and newspapers and it seemed that all I saw were editorial writers pulling long faces about "Whither a United Germany" and "Whence America's Adjustments to the New Realities in Europe." Is that the kind of noise people were making in Times Square on V-E Day?

I say, Shut-up you egghead flap-gums. We've got the whole rest of history to sweat the small stuff. And those discredited peace creeps, they can zip their soup-coolers, too. They think Mikhail Gorbachev is a visionary? Yeah, he's a visionary. Like Hirohito was after Nagasaki. We won. And let's not let anybody forget it. We the people, the free and equal citizens of democracies, we living exemplars of the Rights of Man tore a new asshole in International Communism. Their wall is breached. Their gut-string is busted. The rot of their dead body politic fills the nostrils of the earth with a glorious stink. We cleaned the clock of Marxism. We mopped the floor with them. We ran the Reds through the wringer and hung them out to dry. The privileges of liberty and the sanctity of the individual went out and whipped butt.

And the best thing about our victory is the way we did it—not just with ICBMs and Green Berets and aid to the contras. Those things were important, but in the end we beat them with Levi 501 jeans. Seventy-two years of communist indoctrination and propaganda was drowned out by a three-ounce Sony Walkman. A huge totalitarian system with all its tanks and guns, gulag camps and secret police has been brought to its knees because nobody wants to wear Bulgarian shoes. They may have had the soldiers and the warheads and the fine-sounding ideology that suckered the college students and nitwit Third Worlders, but we had all the fun. Now they're lunch, and we're number one on the planet.

It made me want to do a little sack dance right there in the Cold

SPRINGTIME FOR GORBACHEV

Moscow, May 1988

Good evening and welcome to "International Family Feud!" Today's contestants are the Reagan family, Nancy and Ron, from Washington, America. Ron's a semi-retired President of the United States who enjoys naps and giving Stinger missiles to fanatical mujahedin. Nancy's a housewife with an interest in drugs. They'll be competing against the Gorbachev family of Moscow, Russia. Mike Gorbachev works as a male secretary for Russia's prestigious Communist Party. In his spare time he likes to have friends over for an evening of "Glasnost or Consequences." Mike's lovely wife, Raisa, enjoys making Nancy Reagan look like a shit.

Now, our first question, for one hundred points. How do you build a strong market-driven economy?

Bzzzzzzzzz!

Go for it, Mike!

"Um, well, you kill all the smart and pretty people in 1917 and scare the crap out of everybody else for about seventy years while building huge hydroelectric plants in places where there aren't any rivers. Then you let some people—as long as they aren't Jews or anything—start cooperative restaurants and let other people write crabby letters to *Izvestia* about how nothing works."

Blaaaaaaaaaaaaaaaaaaaaaat!

Wrong! Ron and Nancy? . . .

Give War a Chance

* * *

I'm making this up. This is not really how the game of international superpower diplomacy is played. The 1988 Moscow summit conference would've been *much* more interesting if they'd used a game-show format with audience participation, secret clues and valuable prizes at the end—such as an all-expense-paid potato harvest for the Soviets and a coherent foreign policy for us.

But they didn't do that, and the Moscow summit was pretty boring. In fact, it was a kind of harmonic convergence of monotony factors.

In the first place, this was the Soviet Union—a virtual museum of the drab, the irksome and the wearying.

In the second place, nothing dramatic happened. Gorbachev didn't tell everybody in the Eastern bloc to go to church on Sunday. Reagan didn't make a tearful confession that he was "just kidding" about SDI. All the world's nuclear submarines were not suddenly converted into underwater day-care centers for whales with working mothers. A few minor protocols were signed—things to do with exchanging high school students (anyone with an American high school student around the house knows we got a good deal on that, whatever they send us) and letting Soviet scientists come watch us test atomic bombs in Nevada (which we do underground, so the Soviets still aren't going to see anything).

Furthermore, this was a summit conference, and even when something dramatic does happen, summit conferences don't include enough high-speed car chases or bar-room punch-outs to make it in prime time. What you get is a couple of big squirts with their suit jackets buttoned standing around in the kind of government-owned fancy mansions that don't have a decent stereo system. They size each other up like dogs too dumb to know which end is interesting to sniff. Then they go to an Official Ceremony.

Official Ceremonies are a product of that terrifying human instinct for PTA meetings, Protestant church services, high school graduations and so forth. I can understand why mankind hasn't given up war. During a war you get to drive tanks through the sides of buildings and shoot foreigners—two things that are usually illegal during peacetime. But Official Ceremonies are another matter. Why, in God's name, after a million years of evolution, are we still torturing our fellow creatures with receiving lines, state dinners, speeches of welcome, addresses by dignitaries, tours of monuments, statements of mutual understanding, panels of experts and meetings with selected Soviet citizens? What if they gave a summit and nobody came?

And let's not forget the First Ladies. Were we sick of them or what? The world's two biggest catty clotheshorses are not doing the Equal Rights Amendment much good.

Get back in the kitchen, you two, and shut up.

At least the weather was good. Thanks to *perestroika* and the Supreme Soviet's complete restructuring of the Russian meteorological system, the USSR now has several months of breezy sunshine instead of year-round freezing cold and snow. Over five thousand summit-credentialed reporters were wandering around in that sun, and all of them (Russians included) were greeting every detectable change in the new Gorby-era Soviet life-style with unalloyed squeals of glee. "They have stone-washed jeans." "You can get New Coke!" "I saw a bowling alley!" Et cetera. *Moscow Spring* was the press-corps buzzword. In every Intourist hard-currency bar, you could hear reporters muttering, "I call it the 'Moscow Spring.'" "I'm going to work the 'Moscow Spring' angle in my lead." " 'Moscow Spring,' that's one way to look at it."

Moscow *has* changed. I was here in 1982, during the Brezhnev twilight, and things are better now. For instance, they've got litter. In 1982 there was nothing to litter *with*. People on the street don't dress like the cast in an amateur production of *Guys and Dolls* any more, and they've quit cutting their hair with tin snips. Only the little kids stare at foreigners. There are more cars. Rush hour in Moscow is now almost like 9:00 A.M. on a Sunday morning in Manhattan. The food is hugely improved. True, there was something called "julienne of meat" on my hotel dinner menu, but I'm pretty sure it was meat from a recognized domestic animal killed during recent history—and it *was* edible. I had several meals that were outright good, and not just in the privatized yuppienik cooperative restaurants. The state-owned Chew-and-Chokes had excellent caviar, good chicken and potted beef, passable smoked fish and several wines that didn't taste like pancake syrup.

There's a new, loose, laid-back attitude in Moscow. When people whisper, "Amerikanski? Change moneys?" they whisper it louder than they used to. Coming over to your hotel to meet for a drink is no longer a big secret mission for a Russian. People talk freely to strangers. In fact, once they've had that drink, you can't get them to shut up.

One young man sporting a radical flattop with a pigtail in the back staggered up to me on the street and said his favorite bands were Bauhaus, the Dead Kennedys and the Sex Pistols, but only the early Sex Pistols, when they were really good. Did I want to change moneys? He couldn't give me a very good rate, because he was saving to buy an electric guitar.

English has always been taught in Soviet schools, but students used to learn it the way Americans used to learn Latin. Russian kids would try to hold conversations with you in the English equivalent of *Gallia est omnis divisa in partes tres*. Nowadays the kids speak English pretty well. One rather shapely kid, who was leaning against a wall near Red Square at two o'clock in the morning, seemed particularly fluent. "How about you come over to my house and have a party?" she said.

The most extraordinary change in Moscow was Arbat Street, the USSR's first pedestrian mall. Of course, there's something a little sad about a pedestrian mall in a nation where few people own cars—the whole damn country's a pedestrian mall. But the Arbat has private vendors, street musicians, people reading poetry to the crowds, and kids hanging out and trying to break-dance to primitive East German boom boxes. And there are artists with palettes and easels selling the kind of modern art that Soviet art critics used to critique with bulldozers. Judging by the paintings I saw, the Soviets were right the first time. But even so, this whole boho scene would have been unthinkable in 1982, not to mention arrested and put in jail. The atmosphere at the Arbat verged on interesting.

I was impressed by my first day in Moscow. The air was cleaner; the prematurely postmodern Stalinesque architecture had had a coat of paint; the pervasive mushroom-cellar smell of bad drains and cheap disinfectant was gone. Sandwich stands and tents with Pepsi machines were set up on the no-longer-completely-dingy streets. There were consumer goods in shop windows; a few stabs had been made at Western-style window dressing, and every now and then Soviet television showed MTV videos. I even saw a power mower, something I'd never seen before in the Soviet Union. It looked like . . . I don't know if the Japanese made any kamikaze power mowers during World War II, but it looked like that. Anyway, it got the lawn mowed, something else I'd never seen before in the Soviet Union.

"Of course, you're here at a very special time," said Eleanor Pelton of ABC Radio, who's been stationed in Moscow for several years. And on my second day, I began to see her point. The consumer goods in the shop windows were mostly just that, in the shop windows. I wandered through the vast slime-green precincts of GUM—the world's largest department store with nothing in it. Prices were high, selection was minimal, and the quality stank. The average monthly wage in the Soviet Union is 195 rubles ($346). A man's topcoat that appeared to be made out of a rug mat cost 317 rubles ($563). Men's pants in the Goodwill Wino-Flair cut were 50 rubles ($88). A large Hasbro-toy-looking color TV went for 720 rubles ($1,279). And a stereo set with the same range and clarity of tone as a Chatty Cathy doll was priced at 390 rubles ($693).

At the counters where there was anything to buy, the lines put Disney World during Easter vacation to shame. I counted 150 women in one line. And they were serious about being in that line. Several policemen were keeping order. The women were waiting to buy horrible gray plastic-soled canvas sneakers on sale for 15 rubles ($27).

Give War a Chance

You don't just stand in line to buy something in the Soviet Union; you stand in line three times. You stand in one line to choose. You stand in another line to pay. And you stand in a third line to pick up your junky purchase. There is a premium put on busywork in the Soviet Union. You see, the Soviet Constitution guarantees everybody a job whether he or she wants it or likes it or does it or not. "Shop till you drop" is no joke at GUM.

The day President Reagan was scheduled to arrive, workmen were still slathering paint on downtown Moscow's building fronts. As I walked around, I noticed that the spruce and dapper buildings, smooth pavement and undusty streets coincided precisely with the area of the city the president was likely to see. Farther afield, Moscow looked like I remembered it looking in 1982—endless blocks of ugly, shabby "stack-a-prole" worker flats, many with nets of steel mesh around the cornices to catch pieces of crumbling masonry. Every object and machine was badly made, badly fitted, about to fall apart or jury-rigged back together. The Dinky Toy people had been brought out of retirement to manufacture the Moskovich and Lada cars. Overhead the electric wires looked like they'd been strung by kite-flying ten-year-olds. Underfoot was landscape gardening designed by paving contractors. And none of this was lightened by the slightest bit of local color, festivity or pep. If five thousand reporters had been sent to Dayton, Ohio, and Dayton looked like this, oh, the hollers of indignation and shouts for hardship pay you'd hear!

Now, at this point in the type of thing you're reading here, I believe it's customary for the broad-minded and fundamentally liberal author to pause and observe that—whatever criticisms may be made of Soviet systems or Soviet policies—the Soviet *people* are nevertheless a heck of a bunch. You couldn't prove it by me. Some are very nice, of course. But mostly the Russians walk around with sour expressions acting incredibly rude, shoving their way past you in a blur of facial warts, body odor and steel teeth. They are taciturn and morose when sober and terrifyingly friendly when drunk, which is quite a lot of the time. Ask a Russian clerk or waiter for anything, and it's an immediate grudge match. There's no such thing as Soviet courtesy or salesmanship, let alone service. The entire Soviet service economy is conducted in geological time.

Between mechanical incompetence and Soviet personnel attitude, it should be a real show if World War III ever *does* break out. There'll be missiles going all over the place. I pity the poor Eskimos when those CCCP MIRVs come across the pole. And Iceland will be a cinder.

Meanwhile, back at the summit, the Soviets had tried to create a version of the gigantic Max Newsroom media-cool press center they'd seen at the December summit in Washington in 1987. But the result was so . . . so *Soviet* (an adjective that speaks volumes after you've been in the country a few days). For one thing, until the summit, there were only eleven transatlantic phone lines running into Moscow. The Soviets had to let AT&T and ABC bring in grown-up electronics—miles of cables, stacks of satellite dishes and portable generating plants to run them. (It's worth nothing that once the summit was over and the capitalists had gone home, the Soviet Union still had a total of eleven transatlantic phone lines.) The credentials center looked like it had been set up for the Valparaiso, Indiana, hobby and craft show. Five or six semi-bilingual Russians were manning four folding tables and trying to give out credentials to thousands of reporters. The Soviets had lost most of the credential applications, which had been mailed months before. They kept trying to send credential-less reporters to the Soviet press headquarters to get new applications, except that this seemed to *be* the Soviet press headquarters. One very large and profusely sweating Russian in braces was running back and forth saying, "It is beyond my responsibility." Meanwhile, the other Russians kept repeating, "Wait! You must wait! You wait now! Just wait!"—the heraldic device of every Russian behind a desk or counter. Martin Walker, who has covered the Soviet Union for the *Guardian* since 1984, told David Remnick of the *Washington Post,* "What our visiting colleagues don't realize is that this may be the most organized operation in the history of the USSR."

As if the Russians weren't making enough trouble for themselves, President Reagan was also rattling their cage. He started teasing them through the bars even before he got there. In an interview with Soviet TV two days before the summit, Reagan told a Russian reporter, "You have a constitution; we have a constitution. The difference between our two constitutions is very simple. . . . Your constitution says these are the privileges, rights that the government provides for the people. Our constitution says we the people will allow the government to do the following things."

Speaking at Helsinki the night before his arrival and navigating deeper intellectual waters than is his wont (I detect the hand of a speechwriter), the prez quoted Czech writer Milan Kundera on the "totalitarian temptation"—"the age-old dream of a world where everybody would live in harmony, united by a single common will and faith, without secrets from one another." This Reagan defined as "the freedom of imposed perfection." "Such utopianism," he said, "has proven brutal and barren."

On Monday at Spaso House, the American ambassador's residence, Reagan met a group of Soviet dissidents and refuseniks who didn't regard Gorbachev as any kind of cuddly toy or view *perestroika* as the reunion of the Beatles or anything. And on Tuesday, Ron gave his Bill of Rights rap to the students at Moscow State, telling them that no matter how long a bird's tether is, it can always be pulled back into the cage.

Of course, there were the usual fuck-ups we've come to expect—even look forward to—from the Reagan administration. Ron presented Gorbachev with a videotape of the classic 1956 anti-war movie *Friendly Persuasion,* starring Gary Cooper. But the movie, it turned out, had been written by Michael Wilson, who'd been blacklisted for suspected communist activities. A group of American Indians were in Moscow protesting their plight, and Ronnie shrugged it off with a comment about there being lots of oil wells on Indian reservations—

P. J. O'Rourke

tell it to the Micmacs up in Maine. And one dissident at the Spaso House refusenik tea had, at least according to the Soviets, worked as a policeman for Nazi occupation forces.

Tass jumped right on that one, in a wire story dated the same night: "It was found out later that in 1942 Nikolai Rozhko had voluntarily joined the Nazi police, had participated in the killing of Soviet partisans, in arrests and tortures of civilians (maybe Jews, too?)." Subtle innuendo is apparently not on the course list yet at the Soviet State Institute of Yellow Journalism.

"Reagan is four or five years behind the times," Soviet officials kept saying about their human-rights situation—like so many Young Pioneers proclaiming, "We don't wet the bed *anymore.*"

"We don't like it when people from outside try to teach us how to live," said Soviet Foreign Ministry spokesman Gennadi Gerasimov.

The Big Gorb himself said that the Russians "will not accept any advice on how we run our affairs. We do not need anyone else's model. We do not need anyone else's values." Nah-nah-nah-nah-nah-nah.

You could see the Soviets had had their feelings hurt. They really are, in their own clumsy way, trying to open up their society and become full-fledged members of Western civilization. Although they're not completely clear yet about concepts like intellectual freedom and objective truth. "They canceled the history exam because of *glasnost,*" said a student during Nancy Reagan's visit to Moscow School Number 29. "History is changing."

That's something history doesn't do, but the present *is* undergoing a change. The improvements that Gorbachev, *glasnost, perestroika* and so forth have brought to the Soviet Union may not have turned the place into a gigantic fast-frozen Carmel, California, but they *are* improvements. It's just that the Soviets have got a long way to go before they've earned their pledge pins in the International Sorority of Halfway-Decent Nations.

Lots of countries are poor, and lots are dreary and oppressive. But the Soviet Union is a huge, healthy nation with more than twenty

23

million college graduates. It has all the land and mineral resources national avarice could imagine. And Russia has been part of—at least an idiot stepsister to—Western civilization for a thousand years. There's no alibi for the place.

THE PIECE OF IRELAND THAT PASSETH ALL UNDERSTANDING

Ulster, May 1988

"Acceptable level of violence"—the phrase was coined in 1973 by a British official trying to be British about Northern Ireland. "There's an acceptable level of violence," said the then Home Secretary, Reginald Maudling. It's like the air-quality index in an American city. During the week I spent in Ulster, that's what the violence level was, acceptable. Not excellent the way it was in 1972, 1916, 1798 or 1690 but fair to middling for a Connecticut-sized province with a population smaller than metropolitan Kansas City's.

On Sunday, the day before I arrived, two Protestant "paramilitaries" dropped into the Avenue Bar, a Catholic hangout in Belfast, and let fly with indiscriminate automatic-weapons fire, killing three tipplers and wounding six. This is called a "spray job." On Monday a Protestant reservist in the British army's Ulster Defense Regiment had a leg blown off by a bomb at his farm near Dungannon, and, in Catholic West Belfast, a young man was "kneecapped," that is, shot in a limb by the IRA as punishment for something or other. Tuesday the police found a Protestant arms cache in Whiteabby. Wednesday the home of a Catholic family in Dunmurry was attacked with what the newspapers called "a device." Thursday a bomb exploded in the middle of the Royal Ulster Agricultural Show, injuring four policemen and ten civilians, including two children. Friday there was another kneecapping in West Belfast and a British soldier was burned by preteens throwing Molotov cocktails. Saturday an army bomb-disposal expert and his explosives-sniffing dog were blasted to pieces in South Armagh and a part-time policeman was injured when his car was hit by three "drogue bombs," which are large, exploding versions of the parachute things every boy used to make out of tin soldiers and dad's hankies. And on Sunday, to begin the new week, a sniper attacked a Belfast police station, and two Londonderry Protestants were wounded by a car bomb (car bombs, incidentally, being an Irish invention).

You probably think Belfast looks like those photographs of Belfast you always see. Not at all. It's a charming port, one of the world's great deep-water harbors, cupped in rolling downs on the bight of Belfast Lough. Cave Hill rises to the north like Sugar Loaf Mountain above Ipanema beach, causing some to go so far as to call Belfast "an Hibernian Rio" (not that anybody really wants to see an Irish girl in a string bikini). The city is built in the best and earliest period of Victorian architecture with delicate brickwork on every humble warehouse and factory. Even the mill-hand tenement houses have Palladio's proportions in a miniature way and slate roofs you couldn't buy for money now.

The Belfast pictured in *Time* magazine, the rubble-and-barbed-wire, litter-and-graffiti Belfast, is, in fact, a patch of highly photogenic impoverishment no more than a mile long and half a mile wide. It's as though *Architectural Digest* came to "do" a house and only took pictures of the teenager's bedroom. The rubble is from slum clearance, not bombs (though which is worse may be argued by critics of the modern welfare state). And the barbed wire is on top of the "Peace Wall," a kind of sociological toddler gate erected by the British to keep the ragamuffin Protestant homicidal maniacs of Shankhill Road away from the tatterdemalion Catholic murderers in Falls Road two blocks over. The graffiti and litter are real.

People who live in this heck's half acre have been worked over by social scientists until there's hardly one of them who's not a footnote on somebody's master's thesis. And they're so thoroughly journalized that urchins in the street ask, "Will you be needing a sound bite?" and criticize your choice of shutter speeds.

Photographer Tony Suau and I had hired a Belfast driver, whom I'll call Dick Cullen—an experienced wheelman for the Grub Street crowd. Cullen took us straight from the airport to the heart of the Falls Road Catholic ghetto without even being asked. Here was one filthy low-income high-rise complex, the notorious Divis Flats, built in the sixties before city planners discovered that you can't stack poor people who drink. But Divis was on its way to being demolished and the rest of the area was filled with small, new "townhouses" and "garden apartments"—some jerry-built and fairly depressing, some faced with brick and verging on pleasant.

As in all the world's poor places, there were plenty of idle young men with tattoos and beer. (Unemployment in the district is about 125%, if you accept the locals' figures.) These neighborhood toughs greeted Tony and me with friendly waves and lengthy chats about political economy, international law, theoretical analysis of Irish history since the Battle of the Boyne and how they couldn't talk to us at all until we'd checked in with the Sinn Fein, the reasonably legal, political arm of the IRA.

"You Irish have got a lot to learn about slums," I told Cullen when we got back in the car. "Where's your incoherent rage? Where's your homeless living in Hefty bags? Where's your crack vials, your gang colors, your six-foot hairy-legged transvestites with knives? Slum, *hah*. I could take you down streets in New York where you'd be mugged in broad daylight three times in a block and that's the good part of town."

"Well, you wouldn't want to leave your car unlocked around here," said Cullen, a bit on the defensive, "not with expensive camera equipment laying on the seat."

"I hope you've at least got some heroin addicts?"

"Well, no," said Cullen. "The IRA shoots them."

The rest of Belfast consists of tidy lower-middle-class neighborhoods, tidy middle-class neighborhoods, a few rich neighborhoods—

also very tidy—and tidy commercial and industrial zones. The local economy is suffering a mild upswing. A nascent trendiness is spreading south from the old town center, along the "Golden Mile" of Dublin Road—here a hanging plant, there a bare brick wall and here and there a restaurant with a foreign word in its name. (Though you still get potatoes with every meal. Even the Chinese joint had boiled, baked and fried potatoes on the menu.) The people of Northern Ireland, however, have escaped a fate of suburban tedium and petite bourgeois anomie.

"MURDER" it says in black block letters in the upper corner of the *Belfast News* front page, where "weather" or "Today's Chuckle" would be in an American paper:

> MURDER
> If you know anything about terrorist activities—threats, murders or explosives—please speak *now* to the CONFIDENTIAL TELEPHONE . . .

Take a walk down the most humdrum residential street and there will come, thundering like the juggernaut of Vishnu, a huge British Sacreen personnel carrier with soldiers bobbing in and out of its hatches, leveling their weapons on all and sundry.

And the boring and commonplace downtown shopping district is enclosed by an exciting spiked fence. Armed guards watch your every move as you shop.

Tony Suau and I were hanging around Divis Flats one afternoon, looking for photos of woe and injustice. The day was warm and clear. Kids were playing soccer in the parking lots and women were sunning their babies and having their tea all over the lawns. The scene was entirely too cheery for journalism. We were just about to give it up and go have a drink when an army patrol in head-to-toe jungle camouflage materialized from behind a trash dumpster. They moved in combat formation through the picnickers, Enfields at the ready, crouching low. One soldier walked backward, sweeping his rifle from side to side, keeping the soccer team covered while the squad's point man picked his way between perambulators.

The patrol reached safety under cover of a swing set and dropped into prone firing positions. The soldiers were sighting through their rifle scopes at anything suspicious—which, in this case, happened to be Tony and me. We also seemed to be the only people who could see these guys. The Irish didn't even ignore the Brits, they looked and talked straight through them. Perhaps jungle camo works better than you'd think it would in a Belfast slum, a place where the best protective coloration would be a stiff drink to get the right wobble in your walk.

Anyway, there we were, standing in a balmy greensward midst tableaux of domestic felicity, staring down the gun barrels of a guerrilla-warfare unit which looked like it got lost on the way back from the 1948 Malay States Emergency and which was maybe invisible, too. Finally a child of eighteen months or so wandered over and tried to give his ball to a soldier. The soldier gently turned the kid around, gave him a pat and sent him back to his mother, who never glanced up from her knitting. It was a perfect "photo op," but Tony, who's been strafed in Ethiopia, besieged in Afghanistan and nearly shot to pieces in Sri Lanka, Angola and Haiti, was too rattled to snap a single frame.

Northern Ireland's countryside has also been rescued from banality. The worst John Greenleaf Whittier poem couldn't conjure a landscape so tiresomely pretty, so unrelentingly restful to the eyes. And the deeper you go into the Catholic counties, the more soporific the scenery becomes, until you arrive in South Armagh, close by the Irish Republic's border, in the most narcoleptically bucolic spot on the face of the earth. This is "Bandit Country." There are places around here where the British army cannot move by land at all, and the soldiers have to be helicoptered in and out as though it were Khe Sanh.

The chopper pad at Bessbrook military base is the busiest in the world. It sits behind corrugated metal walls in the middle of a perfect eighteenth-century town like an oil rig in a gallery of the Louvre. The local sheep and people have grown oblivious to the din.

Elsewhere in South Armagh, the cow pastures are decorated with extraordinary British observation towers—gangling, soaring contraptions of guy wire and pipe that look like building scaffolds crossbred with the Martian war machines of H. G. Wells.

The town of Crossmaglen, where the demolition expert and his dog had been blown up, is as cute as anything on a train layout. The people are cheerful and garrulous. There's a sweet town square lined with chip shops and pubs. And smack in the middle of Main Street is a huge edifice of black steel and gray cement, forty feet high, with a dinosaur spine of radio masts out the top and sides, covered in lappings and layers of anti-bomb mesh. This is the police station in Mayberry, IRA.

Tony and I were only a few miles from Crossmaglen when the bomb went off. We rushed to the scene though there was nothing to see, just some dirt and branches scattered across a lane. The jungle fighters were there again, pointing their guns at us from a hedgerow. Their camouflage still didn't work. Ireland is so lush and trim, you'd swear it was plotted out in fairways by Robert Trent Jones. The only uniform that would blend with this war-torn landscape would be orange pants, a purple sweater, white tassled shoes and a five iron.

Tony and I also visited the Avenue Bar, where Protestant gunmen had shot Catholics for no reason. It took us a few days to get up the nerve. The same bar had been bombed in 1976 and again in 1983. How friendly could the regulars be? And would the place be open at all?

Of course it was. The Friday after the killings, the Avenue Bar was jammed. There was a guard at the door, but when he saw Tony's cameras he all but pulled us inside. "Sure, you're American reporters, you are," said somebody, thrusting pints of beer into our hands before we'd had a chance to try the subtle conversational gambits we'd composed to break the ice with the hostile and suspicious Avenue patrons. "An O'Rourke, you say?" And I got to hear the entire history of my clan.

It seems we were kings in the olden days. But who wasn't? It must have been interesting, the Ireland of Zero A.D.: "I'm the king—from this rock down to the creek and from that cow to the tree. And this is my wife, the Queen, and our dog, Prince." And it must have been every bit as peaceful as it is today, with a million or two kings on one island.

Would anybody be willing to talk about the horrible crime that took place last Sunday? No, no, they all said, it was too dreadful to speak about, "the way the Protestant animals came in the front door just there, looking as normal as day and one pulls out an AK-47 from beneath his long coat and shoots up this corner here where Damien Devlin and Paul McBride died, and then he shoots down the length of the bar this way, killing poor Stephen McGaghan and bullets going right into the women's loo—if there'd been anyone in there, they'd have died certain."

Most of the sixty or eighty people in the bar on Friday had been among the twenty customers there at the time of the slaughter. "I was here," said one, patting his seat. "I thought I was dead. I said a Hail Mary and jumped over the back of the booth."

The barmaid was urged out from behind the taps to hold the lead that had been dug out of the walls, her hand still shaking from terror. The customers stood Tony on a chair, to get the proper dramatic photo angle on the flattened slugs, and they held lamps to make sure his exposure was right. Two or three dozen people retold the story of the massacre. Some things are too awful for words, they agreed.

"This murder was, oh, a terrible, low and disgusting thing." "The work of crazy-minded men." "A foul deed, senseless and cowardly, too." "Only the Protestants do things like that." "The IRA would never." "No." "They're selective, they are." "And the three lads mown down, not political at all, innocent as lambs." "Not a political thought in their heads." "The Avenue isn't a political place." "No, indeed." "Protestants are welcome here." "They are." A dozen hands pointed to pictures framed on the walls—Protestant Orange Lodge members holding fêtes at the Avenue Bar. "Could have been anyone killed." "Why, mothers and babies had been in here earlier that very day."

The evening news came on the bar's TV with a report of the bomb at the Royal Ulster Agricultural Show. "Now *that's* selective, you see." "Only a seven-and-a-half-pound bomb." "In a police-recruiting booth." "People should know to stay away from there." "Yes." "That's certain."

"If I was arrested and in a police station, I'd be proud to die in an IRA bomb," announced one young man drinking two beers at once.

Tony and I stayed at the Avenue Bar until we were nearly too stewed to walk. No one would let us buy a drink. It took a full half hour of handshakes and back slaps for us to get out the door. It was one of the most pleasant evenings I've spent in years.

The best thing about the violence in Northern Ireland is that it's all so ancient and honorable. And I'm proud to say it began in the household of my own relative Tighernan O'Rourke, Prince of Breffni. In 1152 Tighernan's comely wife Dervorgilla ran off with Diaruid MacMurrough, King of Leinster. Cousin O'Rourke raised such a stink (and army) that MacMurrough had to call King Henry II of England for help. The Brits arrived, somewhat tardily, in 1169 and proceeded to commit the unforgivable sin of having long bows and chain mail. For the next 819 years (and counting) the English stole land, crushed rebellions, exploited the populace, persecuted Catholics, dragged a bunch of Scottish settlers into Ulster, crushed more rebellions, held potato famines, hanged patriots, stamped out the language, taxed everybody's pig, crushed more rebellions yet and generally behaved in a manner much different than the Irish would have if it had been the Irish who invaded England and the shoe was on the other foot (assuming the Irish could afford shoes).

At any rate, the Irish are in the same terrific position as the Shi'ites in Lebanon, the peasants in El Salvador, the blacks in America, the Jews in Palestine, the Palestinians in Israel (and everybody everywhere, if you read your history)—enough barbarism has been visited on the Irish to excuse all barbarities by the Irish barbarians.

Not that the Irish seemed like barbarians to *me*. The Sinn Fein office on lower Falls Road was the very picture of the sixties "Movement" crash pads where I spent my own uncivilized years. The walls were decorated with leftist slogans, and two Birkenstock-shod women with the kind of dirty hair that serious political thought seems to cause were designing a poster and discussing how to avoid using "wives" or "girlfriends" or other nouns that might offend feminists. They settled on the phrase "partners of political prisoners."

The Sinn Fein spokesman, whom I'll call Tom, looked like an art teacher. He was a small, sweatered man of about thirty-five with wire-rim glasses and a friendly air. He had, however, been interned by the British for four years and sent to British prison for another four and there was a flak jacket in the kneehole of his desk.

"Isn't there something," I ventured, "that you could try besides violence?"

"There's *no* other course of action—no other *possible course*," said Tom, as though he were Churchill and England were Nazi Germany and I were an American pacifist fool (a group of similes that rings true enough to any real Irish patriot). "We're completely isolated," said Tom. "We have no allies. The leftists in Britain don't care. There's no other liberation situation like ours left in Europe except perhaps the Basque ETA."

"Tony Suau, here, actually *is* a Basque," I said. But Tom kept on. It was obviously more interesting to be alone in noble resistance, bloody but unbowed, ever beaten but ne'er defeated, etc.

"Even if you do become part of the Republic of Ireland, the IRA is just as illegal down there," I said.

" 'The real war begins when the Brits pull out,' as they say," said Tom with a smile. "I don't want the country unified under the system it has now in the Republic. I wouldn't expect the Shankhill Road people to accept that either." By which I gather he meant that not only does Ireland get to have British fighting Irish and Irish fighting Irish but a class war, too. Tom then gave me a load of socialist cant.

What seemed to bother him most about private property was Englishmen owning exclusive fly-fishing rights on Irish trout streams. "I'm a keen fisherman myself," he said.

I don't mean to give the impression that it's only the Catholic "nationalist" or "republican" Irish who are perfectly justified in their maiming and slaughter. The Protestant "orange" or "loyalist" Irish have plenty of excuses themselves. They're patriots after all. "We'll fight anybody to stay British, even the British," they like to say. What could be more patriotic than that? And they've been in Ulster since the 1600s and have nowhere else to go. It's not like our New York City gentrification where the poor can move out and get new homes under bridges and in the bus station. And the Protestants are very frightened of popery, which might seep into their houses through cracks beneath the doors and suddenly quadruple their number of dirty, unemployable children.

I talked to Sammy Wilson, former Lord Mayor of Belfast and a figure in the Democratic Unionist Party, a hard-line "Prod" political faction led by nuthatch Ian Paisley. Sammy, thirty-four, also looked like a teacher which, in fact, he is, although he used to be a policeman; just like Tom, at Sinn Fein, used to be a policeman's opposite number. And just like Tom, Sammy was forthright and gregarious. He and Tom didn't disagree about anything you'd kill anybody over unless you really wanted to, and, if you're Irish, you do.

According to my notes:

SAMMY: . . . admitted there was prejudice against Catholics in Northern Ireland but said it was less than it had been.

TOM: "The bigotry isn't as hard as it was."

SAMMY: . . . complained that the people of Northern Ireland were ruled directly from London and needed a bill of rights.

TOM: "The Brits can't afford a bill of rights; the whole origin of this statelet was not democratic."

SAMMY: "I would have no objection to Catholics bearing their fair share in the burden of policing Northern Ireland."

TOM: . . . said there were Protestants in the IRA.

SAMMY: "Loyalists and republicans could both argue that police and army are directed toward them."

But agreement is something the Irish can always overcome.

And what about the Brits? This is legally part of their country. Shouldn't they have as much right as anyone to kill, cripple and imprison the population here? I had lunch with Brian Mawhinney, the Thatcher government's Northern Ireland Under Secretary of State for Education. He was every bit as amiable as Sammy and Tom and laid on a fine spread with three wines.

Mawhinney explained how folding your tent and pulling a sneak is not the done thing in the nation-state game. He expressed bewilderment about why Americans are so proud of their own civil war and so indignant about Ireland's. Simple British withdrawal from Northern Ireland would be, he said, equivalent to a unilateral expulsion of Hawaii without consulting the Hawaiians (though anyone who's been to Waikiki lately might consider it). Mawhinney didn't want me to think he was letting principle run away with itself. If the Brits just left there'd be "a lot of blood," he said. I might have replied, "What's this you've got now?" But that would have been rude with my mouth full. Besides, Mawhinney and his press secretary, Andy Wood, both said that working in Northern Ireland was "incredibly interesting" and "never dull," and I think more people should have jobs they enjoy.

Of course there are some spoilsports and wet blankets who think enough's enough and say things like "let's get on with our lives." I talked to one businessman, a Catholic from the "hard" neighborhoods who'd made his millions in computers and thought the whole "troubles" thing was a crock. He pointed out that you could never unite the North with the rest of Ireland because the Irish Republic couldn't afford the welfare system that keeps the gunmen's families fed while the "boyos" are out shooting and bombing each other. He thought unemployment was the whole cause of the fighting. Well, he admitted, *almost* the whole cause. He had a plan. He wanted to send the entire population of Northern Ireland overseas, five thousand at a time, so the Irish could see how normal people lead quiet, harmonious, industrious lives—New York on St. Patrick's Day, for example, he suggested. "I've been there five or six times, now. It's a helluva thing."

A student leader at a Belfast peace rally had a similar plan. He, too, was from West Belfast and admitted he'd gotten a kick from the riots when he was a boy. "But the kids in Northern Ireland," he said, "should be sent out to see the world, expand their horizons, understand that the world does not revolve around shooting on Shankhill Road to achieve some mystical, magical end." The peace march had attracted all of forty people. "Maybe a good natural disaster would solve this problem," said the student leader.

And the women who'd lost their sons and lovers in the Avenue Bar shootings didn't look like they were deriving any thrill from the brilliant Irish struggle and its age-old glorious history.

I went to Damien Devlin's funeral. His mother had already had another son killed, shot by the IRA for "hooliganism." She looked as good as dead as she followed the coffin from the church to the cemetery and watched her second boy be buried in the same grave as the first.

Six hours later, after another of the Avenue Bar funerals, I went back to the cemetery with Stephen McGaghan's body. Damien Devlin's girlfriend was still there, alone on the other side of the graveyard, sitting, head in hands, among the flower arrangements.

People walked out of both these funerals because the priests denounced paramilitary violence.

*   *   *

Tony and I spent our last day in Northern Ireland with the police, who are much like the police anywhere in the world—apprehending shoplifters, tracing stolen VCRs, quieting domestic tiffs—except they perform these duties wearing flak vests, carrying submachine guns and riding in armored cars.

"It's not such a bad job," said the police sergeant as we rode in the cramped olive-drab interior of a "pig"—an eight-man vehicle specially designed for duty in Northern Ireland, with bomb skirts, run-flat tires and a device for clearing paint bombs off the bullet-proof, mesh-covered windshield. "It's basically a law-abiding community," said the sergeant, peering out a gun port. "We have the highest detection rate in the U.K." A stone bounced off the armor-plate roof.

The sergeant gave us the official version of the "security situation." It's the same info you get at army briefings or from the government in London—hardly anybody's involved in the violence. "It's three percent of the population, one and a half percent on each side, that carry this thing on," the sergeant said. The authorities always tell you there are only a few hundred actual Protestant and Catholic gunmen. Though these few somehow manage to keep 10,000 regular army soldiers, 6,500 members of the Ulster Defense Regiment, 8,000 police officers and 4,500 members of the police reserve pretty busy. "You're dealing with smart fellows here," said the sergeant. The authorities also say it's nothing more than gangsterism when you get right down to it. "Go into a republican bar," said the sergeant, "and you'll see Protestant gunmen. They divide up territories. They're doing business. You go into some of these fellows' homes, and there are three or four color TVs—I've only got one. You're ankle-deep in carpet. Drinks cabinet over there. Three- or four-bedroom bungalows with beautiful views." He sighed. "It's the wee fellows who pay. Always the wee fellows take the risks. They pay . . ."

"With their lives," I almost said.

". . . higher car insurance," said the sergeant.

It seems the paramilitaries steal a lot of cars to use in their "actions."

Give War a Chance

We got out of the pig to have a smoke in a Protestant neighborhood near the Peace Wall. All around us were little pin-neat houses with weedless, butch-cut rug-sized lawns and ceramic bunnies in the marigold beds. "We're not usually attacked in the loyalist neighborhoods," said the sergeant. "We're more likely to get tea over here." But the first cop killed in the current round of Northern Ireland troubles was shot, in 1969, in the Shankhill Road, one block away.

"Come on," I said to the sergeant, "there's got to be more to this than an organized-crime spree or, for that matter, than a debate over governance or hurt feeling about what King Billy did four hundred years ago."

"Oh, it's not hard to give a poor man a cause," said the sergeant. "Why, you read about it in poems and plays and books, and it almost convinces *me*."

"You don't see any end to it?"

He looked slightly puzzled. "This is an acceptable level of violence," he said.

DEMOCRACY
IN ITS DIAPERS

Paraguay, April 1989

Asunción, Paraguay, is farther from New York than Moscow. Not that it matters how far away a thing is if you don't know where it's at. My friends couldn't quite place Paraguay. Most of them thought Paraguay was where Uruguay is. Others thought it was between Colombia and Peru. And one young lady—a college graduate—had it confused with Papua New Guinea. Paraguay is the difference between a B and a B− on a geography exam, or would be if people took geography anymore, which they don't. United States diplomats privately refer to Paraguay as "the Tibet of South America." (Though the mystical religion of Paraguay has never caught on with New Age types because there's no such thing as Tantric Catholicism.) Paraguay is nowhere and it's famous for nothing.

Or almost nothing. Paraguay has been a popular hiding place for Nazi war criminals such as Josef Mengele because when a Nazi war criminal hides in Paraguay everybody goes looking for him in Uruguay and Papua New Guinea. And Paraguay used to have this classic of a tinpot dictator, General Alfredo Stroessner, who'd been *El Sleazo Caudillo* since 1954. They don't make them like the Stroess anymore. Stroessner was so old and nasty that if Latin America were a soap opera—and some argue it is—you could cast him as the cold, disciplinarian dad that young, sensitive, caring Augusto Pinochet rebels against. Stroessner was all wizened and drooly and spent his days reviewing troops, sitting in the stands in a uniform copied off the cover of *Sgt. Pepper's Lonely Hearts Club Band* and wearing one of those great big general hats with two pounds of brass macaroni on the brim which would fall down over his eyes while he snoozed to the lulling sound of goose steps.

In Latin America—as in any good soap opera—the worse a situation is, the longer it lasts. So it came as a surprise and a shock to everyone when Man-Mummy Stroessner got a *coup* in the *état* from his own army chief of staff, the porky, affable and corrupt General Andrés Rodríguez.

General Rodríguez promptly called for elections. Elections are a fad in the developing world for the same reason portable tape decks are a fad in the inner city. Elections and tape decks both make a lot of noise. They both attract attention. And having an election, like having a tape deck, is crucial to achieving job skills and social justice.

Suddenly Paraguay was news. Page 8, one-paragraph, wire-service-filler-item-news, but news. Dozens, okay, one dozen American reporters flew to Asunción. And U.S. diplomats began privately referring to Paraguay as "the *former* Tibet of South America."

I was not prepared to love Paraguay. I was not prepared to do anything but upchuck and die after the eight-hour night flight from Miami on an Air Paraguay DC-8 older than most second wives that flew through the center of five Dr. Frankenstein-your-lab-is-on-the-phone lightning storms and aboard which I was served a dinner of roast softball in oleo. But as we shuddered down out of the atmosphere dawn cut loose with that annoying beauty which I never get to see except when I'm sick to my stomach from some life disruption. Mists soft and transparent as excuses flapped across pastures the color of crap-table felt. Out on the tarmac the air was cool, moist and floral—God's Wash'n Dri. The Paraguayan customs inspection was a most informal formality. The taxi cab, an Alfa-Romeo sedan, was old and dented but rubbed to a shine. And the taxi driver was the only taxi driver on earth able to drive from an international airport to a downtown hotel without opening his yap.

There was nothing Latin American about the ride into Asunción, no litter, no shanty towns, no remains of horrendous bus wrecks. Traffic stayed in its lane and obeyed the posted speed limit—phenomena unusual enough to trigger a police investigation in most places south of the Rio Grande. Every street was lined with palms and frangipanis and pink-blossoming bottle trees. Every street was also lined with children going cheerfully, even willingly, to school. Each face was scrubbed, each head combed just so. Uniform blouses were as white and stiff as typing paper. The little boys wore shorts. Bigger boys wore ties with all-thumb four-in-hand knots. Teenage girls moved with the first wiggles of self-consciousness inside their modest frocks. I felt a completely unprofessional sense of cheery peace descending upon me. This is *tranquilo,* a very Paraguayan state of mind. The hotel was good. The breakfast was better. I poured myself a small restorative from the mini-bar and slept until siesta. Then I got up and took a nap.

Journalists aren't supposed to praise things. It's a violation of work rules almost as serious as buying drinks with our own money or absolving the CIA of something. Not only that, but if a journalist shows a facility for praise he's liable to be offered a job in public relations or advertising and the next thing you know he's got a big office, a huge salary and is living in a fine home with a lovely wife and swell kids—another career blown to hell. So I'm wrestling with the angel of reportage here, fully aware that good news is no news, but I can't help myself. Even a person with the soul of a foreign correspondent has to like something sometime, and I like Paraguay.

Asunción is a city with about the same population as Austin, Texas. It is built on unassuming hills overlooking a New York Harbor–sized backwater of the River Paraguay. This is the third largest river in the western hemisphere and even here, one thousand miles from its mouth on the Atlantic, its waters are so broad and calm that Paraguay hardly seems to be a landlocked country. You'd think you were in some balmy coast, Florida maybe. Paraguay's climate is almost identical to Florida's but more comfortable since nobody has to wear a giant mouse costume to make a living.

Zoning is not a concept hereabouts, so Asunción is a pleasant jumble of buildings—office towers next to mansions next to little shops next to big hotels. Some of the architecture is the Río de la Plata Argentine type, a distant cousin of the Taco Bell school. And the newer buildings are that kind of modernistic which is looking so old-fashioned these days. But most of Asunción was built around the turn of the century in what's called the "academic style," where elements of the classical, baroque and beaux-arts were gathered higgledy-piggledy and set down hodgepodge in painted stucco instead of carved stone. It's a kind of imitation European facade I've only seen in one other place—Russia. The design influences are French and Italian but the effect is subtropical Leningrad, a very relaxed subtropical Leningrad.

Asunción is *so* relaxed that there are no traffic lights or stop signs at the downtown intersections. Cars just noodle up to the corners and wave one another by. I accidentally ran a road block by the Presidential Palace and the soldiers shrugged. The whole city closes, firmly and without exception, at noon. People go out and have a few drinks and a big lunch. Then they go home, make love, doze, take a shower, change clothes and return to work—refreshed to the point of exhaustion—at three. Stores and offices stay open until seven. Or six. Four-thirty, anyway.

Paraguay is a poor country. Twice as poor as Mexico, if you believe in statistics. Yet the people are tall and sleek. You don't see goiters or toothless mouths or milk-white eyeballs. The old women in the market stalls are well turned out. The shoeshine boys are clean and kempt. Asunción has so few beggars that they're known by name. There are slums. One of the worst is a squatter settlement on the mud flats below the cathedral. But the hovels have small yards and flowers and trees, and there's a clipped and chalk-lined soccer field in the midst of them. The cars on the streets are mostly old, but they're interesting old cars like my airport taxi, the kind you used to see in

American college towns—Volkswagen Beetles with Baja Bug front ends, comical 2CV Citroens, out-of-tune 914 Porsches with Bondo on the fenders and plumply dignified little Mercedes sedans from the 1950s. I was told that a lot of these cars were stolen in Brazil. If so, it's a tasteful and understated kind of car theft.

Another of Paraguay's happy surprises was seeing the U.S. State Department going about its business there without a foot in its mouth or a thumb up its butt. This is because Paraguay is not a vital nation. Therefore the State Department is allowed to send a first-rate ambassador to Paraguay. Vital nations get political-appointment-type ambassadors—Arizona condominium developers who think the earth is flat but who are uniquely qualified to be ambassadors to vital nations because of the statesmanlike wisdom they exhibited in donating a jillion dollars to the Willie Horton Appreciation Day PAC in 1988. Actually, this is about what most vital nations—such as France, Israel and Japan—deserve. Anyway, the American ambassador to Paraguay, Timothy Towell, is not that type. He is educated, amusing, well-mannered and a career diplomat who even—and I'll bet this shocked the natives—savvies the lingo.

Ambassador Towell invited the American press to the embassy residence for a briefing and little sandwiches with the crusts cut off. Timothy Towell is a fine human, and the invitation proved his beautiful wife, Dane Towell, is another. Imagine having journalists in your own home and not even covering the furniture with plastic sheets first.

I'm afraid we weren't exactly the media's A team, either. None of us had the kind of wit, vision and heartfelt empathy for the underdog which characterizes, for instance, a Jane Pauley. The more important journalists were off reporting on more important elections, in Panama, Argentina, Bolivia and other countries that Americans know the whereabouts of or, anyway, get their dope from. We in the Asunción press corps called Paraguay "The Land That Time Forgot—also *Life* and *Newsweek*." And this was one more nice thing about Paraguay, no important journalists. The clatter of rented helicopters, the yammer of electronic up-links, the hiss of inflating egos—it's impossible to get a decent siesta when important journalists are around.

I'm a particularly *un*important journalist. I can't even remember the "Four W's" or whether four is the number of W's there are supposed to be. Which? Whatchamajigger? Whoa? What the fuck? It's something like that. So I was confused by the embassy briefing. Ambassador Towell kept going on and off the record. That is, sometimes when he said something he was "Ambassador Towell." And sometimes when he said something he was "a highly placed diplomatic source." True, it does make you feel mature and privileged to be spoken to off the record, like when you were a kid and your dad took you into a bar with him and on the way home he said, "I don't think your mother has to know about this." On the other hand it's a big responsibility trying to make sure the attractive and hospitable Towells don't wind up in the U.S. embassy on the Ross Ice Shelf. Thus it was Ambassador Towell who said, "I genuinely like this country," and a highly placed diplomatic source who called it "the former Tibet of South America."

The gist of the briefing was that the coup had been fun. Paraguay's Presidential Palace, its Defense Department and the home of Stroessner's mistress (where the old goat was finally run to ground) are all within a few blocks of the American embassy. The diplomats got to stay up all night and use the embassy's emergency bunker and all its communications bells and whistles while mortar shells flew overhead. Maybe this doesn't sound like entertainment to you, but you have to understand that Asunción is a dull place.

"When Rodríguez came to power we assumed we were just getting a new general for an old one," said a highly placed diplomatic source. "Then Rodríguez did things that he said he was going to do." The ambassador shrugged. His staff shrugged. The members of the press all shrugged.

Rodríguez has canceled the country's perennial state of emergency, eliminated censorship, legalized opposition parties, released political prisoners and welcomed exiled dissidents home. He has ordered prison torture cells destroyed, begun dismantling state economic controls and even launched a couple of corruption investigations (though not of himself). It's part of a worldwide trend in unaccountable and irrational dictator behavior.

Gorbachev, Jaruzelski, Roh Tae Woo, Pinochet—they're all acting nutty, and there have been outbreaks of freedom and democracy in such unlikely places as Estonia, Namibia, Hungary and the New York City mayoral race. Did somebody dip the International Monetary Fund debt notices in XTC? Don't tell me the CIA has finally done its job and infiltrated all these governments and is making them be good. "Are diplomats supposed to be optimistic or cynical?" asked a highly placed diplomatic source.

That night I went out to a *parrillada,* a commercial version of that exotic Paraguayan custom known as a backyard cookout. I had a big piece of steak and a big glass of whiskey and more steak and more whiskey and a salad made out of a quarter head of iceberg lettuce—my kind of cuisine. Then I had an excellent cup of coffee, a cognac about the same vintage as that DC-8 and a big, smelly Cuban cigar. All told, it cost me eight dollars.

I walked back to the hotel with an American who'd been coming to Paraguay for a decade. At ten P.M. the downtown streets were mostly dark and wholly deserted. "Don't worry," said the American, "it's safe to walk around at night. There's virtually no street crime. It has to be one of the last really safe places left in the world." He paused as an ugly thought crossed his mind. "I wonder if that will survive democracy, huh?"

There were some things about Paraguay which *did* make ugly thoughts cross your mind: a Nazi helmet for sale in a downtown antique store, ominously large embassies from naughty nations such as South Africa and Nationalist China, reports in the newly legal opposition press of "secret graves" where Stroessner opponents were said to be numerous and a sign in Spanish advertising "Von Stroheim's Tae Kwan Do Parlor"—the last an apparent effort to bring together a little bit of the worst in all the world's cultures. Also, for a country with only four and a half million people, a country that's been out of the Realpolitik loop for more than three centuries, Paraguay has a lot of war memorials, way too many.

Paraguay is a pleasant place all right, but not for the right reasons. It's not like the United States. It wasn't hard work, good luck and vigorous immigrant stock that made Paraguay nice. Paraguayan *tranquilo* is the product of a horrible and ridiculous history.

The conquistadors ignored Paraguay. It didn't have any gold. Wealth was to be gotten in farming, but the colonial Spanish were rarely tempted by manual labor. Madrid let missionaries do whatever they wanted with the place. In 1609 the Jesuits began gathering up the nomadic Indians, the Guaraní, and putting them into *reductions*. These were theocratic agricultural communes of about three thousand people where the Indians could be drilled in the use of Christian sacraments and the moldboard plow. Eventually some hundred thousand Guaranís were "reduced." The Spanish Jesuits, who wanted the Indians' souls for God, were quite brave about fighting off the Brazilian *banderiantes* who wanted the Indians' bodies for slavery. For this reason, and because the Jesuits didn't kill Guaranís or rape their women very often, the *reductions* of Paraguay became famous examples of utopia and the subject of a Robert De Niro movie, *The Mission*. Voltaire, Jesuit-hater though he was, called the *reductions* "the triumph of humanity, expiating the cruelties of the first conquerors" and set part of *Candide* in Paraguay. Robert Southey, one of England's less talented poet laureates, wrote an immense poem about this alleged paradise:

> For in history's mournful map, the eye
> On Paraguay, as on a sunny spot,
> May rest complacent: to humanity,
> There, and there only, hath a peaceful lot
> Been granted, by Ambition troubled not . . .
> Etc., etc., etc., etc.

The *reductions* preserved Guaraní culture. Today ninety percent of Paraguayans speak the Guaraní language. But at what cost, nobody ever bothered to ask the Guaranís. Perhaps the *reductions* were as pleasant as the collective farms we've seen in this century in the Ukraine and China. Anyway, when the Jesuits were kicked out of the New World in 1766, the Guaranís skedaddled and the *reductions* collapsed. This is generally called a tragedy in Paraguayan history, but it's hard to say where tragedies leave off and benefits begin in Paraguay.

The nation achieved independence in 1811 without firing a shot at the Spanish. There's some doubt if Spain even noticed. Paraguay was promptly taken over by a lunatic (and national hero) named Dr. José Gaspar Rodriguez Francia. Dr. Francia—elected *El Supremo* for life in 1814—forced the Spanish upper class to intermarry with the *mestizos*. He forbade newspapers, fiestas and foreign trade. The clergy was suppressed. No one was allowed to emigrate. Immigrants were arrested and put to forced labor. Francia leveled Asunción and laid new avenues in a formal grid for fear conspirators might lurk in twisty back streets. He dressed all in black except for a scarlet cape and was fanatically honest with the national treasury—possibly the reason he was never known to smile. *El Supremo* died in 1840. More than a quarter century of his loathsome rule left Paraguay culturally homogeneous, economically self-sufficient, well-defended and possessed of a large budget surplus.

The next leader, Carlos Antonio López, freed political prisoners, granted citizenship to Indians, encouraged education and foreign investment, built one of South America's first railroads and is not nearly as well thought of today as Dr. Francia.

Carlos López's son, Marshal Francisco Solano López, was another hero. *El Mariscal* is revered for destroying the nation. He was trying to play Argentina off against its traditional rival, Brazil, and he somehow managed to get into a war with Brazil and Argentina both and Uruguay besides. The War of the Triple Alliance lasted from 1865 to 1870. When it was done there was hardly a Paraguay left. Fifty-five thousand square miles had been conquered and annexed and the rest of the country was occupied, razed, starved, burned and pillaged. More than half the population was dead, including *El Mariscal* and eighty percent of the adult males. To this day one of the nicest things about Paraguay is that there's no overcrowding.

Paraguayans are very proud of the War of the Triple Alliance. "We fought desperately because we loved our land insanely," as one war veteran too aptly put it.

It took Paraguay more than sixty years to recover. As soon as it did, it got into another amazingly bloody conflict you've never heard of—the Chaco War. This was fought with Bolivia from 1932 through 1935. One hundred thousand soldiers were killed battling over non-existent oil deposits in the Chaco, an immense region of grassland and thornbush populated mostly by dead soldiers.

Paraguay spent the following nineteen years recovering again while having ten presidents and the odd civil war and helping make Latin America the world's governance laughingstock. Then Stroessner arrived, bringing tyranny with shelf life; and for thirty-five years Paraguay had *tranquilo* (unless, of course, you were some kind of Commie or agrarian reformer or civil libertarian big-mouth, in which case you became permanently tranquil).

I was getting pretty tranquil myself. Paraguay was making me so mellow and content that I could feel my social conscience dribbling out my ears and I.Q. points flaking off my head like dandruff. Before long I had the brain of a tourist. I even caught myself getting interested in church architecture.

Paraguayan church architecture is no-nonsense stuff. The churches look like horse barns with verandas. But, inside, they're real retina-thrashers. The eighteenth-century church in the town of Yaguarón contains two thousand square feet of crazed whittling, a masterpiece of Paraguayan baroque. It's as ridiculously detailed as anything from the Europe of that era but with fun Guaraní Indian touches such as drug-trip color combinations and altar chairs with armrests that turn into snakes. I took a close look at some of the carved portraits of saints, and I think the Guaranís were pulling the padres' legs vis-à-vis conversion to Christianity.

Nearby in the town of Capiatá a modern woodcarver had created a one-man museum of Guaraní mythology. The front rooms of a large Spanish colonial house were filled with life-sized, that is, living-dead-sized Guaraní bugaboos such as the Plata Yryguy, a headless dog; the Curupi, a smug, plump fellow with his penis wrapped three times around his waist; the Kaaguy Pori, which has a big tentacle for a body, another tentacle for a leg, a bunch of tentacles for arms and tentacles growing out of its nose; and the Ao-Ao, which is too terrible to discuss. How convenient for the Guaranís that they had a mythology all ready to describe the conquering Spaniards and the subsequent history of Paraguay.

Paraguay is the size of California, so I didn't tourize it all. But I put five hundred miles on the rental car and was unable to find an ugly place except the Asunción Zoo. It was a very casual and dirty zoo where most of the cages were made of chain-link fence and fastened closed with twisted bits of wire. The hippo was chewing determinedly on its chain links and seemed three-quarters of the way to an escape. I don't know much about hippos. Are they one of those animals, like alligators, that look slow but *Wild Kingdom* always tells us can run faster than a horse? A lot of other cages had birds in them. There were cages full of chickens, ducks and pigeons as though the zookeepers just caged up whatever was handy. The bear cage smelled disgusting, and the bear looked dead. The puma cage smelled worse. The female puma was sleeping something off and the male puma was trying to get romantic but didn't seem to know what part of him he was supposed to stick in what part of her, romantically speaking. One small cage in a corner had a large ugly bird in it labeled "Yryvu" with a small placard underneath reading *"Alimentación: animales putrefactos."* And how.

Give War a Chance

If it weren't for *tranquilo* I could probably tell you what the Asunción Zoo says about Paraguayan society and the Paraguayan political system. But, as it was, it was just a dirty zoo.

In truth, I can't even tell you what *Paraguay* says about Paraguayan society and the Paraguayan political system. I was doing for journalism about what the puma was doing for his mate. I did look up Martin Bormann in the phone book, but I guess he had an unlisted phone number. These Nazi war criminals are getting so old anyway, what would you do with them? Shorten one leg on their walker? Put a frog in their colostomy bag? Stick a playing card in their wheelchair spokes so they make a lot of noise and are easier for the Mossad to find?

I did finally go to a campaign event, in spite of myself. I got stuck in traffic in front of one.

A speech was being given by the principal opposition leader, Domingo Laino, presidential candidate of the Authentic Radical Liberal Party. This as opposed to the Fake Conventional Stingy Party, which, I guess, is what Rodríguez represents. Laino, a youthful-ish fifty-three, bewhiskered and just slightly thick around the middle, looked like a former college activist, which is what he is. Rodríguez supporters call him "the detestable beard." Stroessner used to throw him in jail a lot, so he can't be all bad. On the other hand, Stroessner never killed him, so maybe he's not *that* good.

Having covered the U.S. presidential campaigns all through 1988, I was profoundly relieved to have absolutely no idea what the issues were in this election. The usual choice in Latin America is oppression combined with economically disastrous corruption causing a left-wing insurgency versus incompetence combined with economically disastrous social programs causing a right-wing coup. Laino has a Ph.D. in economics, so he probably favors incompetence.

He's an impassioned and highly indignant orator, whatever his platform. The rally had begun at 2:00 P.M. I happened by at four and the Beard was still going strong. Whenever he said anything particularly indignant, the crowd would respond with the Jesse Jackson "The People United / Will Never Be Defeated" chant. That was about all I could make out with my bar-floor Spanish. I stood below the podium trying to imagine what was being said with such vigor.

MY OPPONENT WEARS UNDERPANTS WITH LITTLE BUNNIES ON THEM!
HIS DAUGHTERS KISS BOYS THEY ARE NOT ENGAGED TO!
HE PUTS SINK WASHERS INTO THE POOR BOX AT CHRISTMAS AND HAS GIVEN INSULTING AND RIDICULOUS NAMES TO HIS DOGS!
VOTE FOR ME, I WILL TIE THE POINTS OF HIS SHIRT COLLAR TOGETHER UNDER HIS NOSE!
I WILL WIGGLE MY BEHIND AT HIS HOUSE!
I WILL GO ON THE RADIO AND SAY HIS NAME IN A MOCKING TONE OF VOICE!

This was a huge improvement on listening to political speeches and understanding them.

Well, fair's fair, so I went to a Rodríguez rally, too. Colorado is the real name of Rodríguez's party and the Colorados have functioned for the past forty-two years pretty much the way Italy's Fascist party used to. All public employees and military men are required to belong and dues are withheld from their paychecks. And there's an election law, cribbed from one written by Mussolini in 1923, that automatically gives a two-thirds congressional majority to the party that steals the most votes.

The Laino speech had been given in a public park and attracted five or six thousand people. They were a seemly, middle-class bunch who walked away at the end talking enthusiastically among themselves like tennis fans after a well-played match. "What a prepositional phrase he has!" "Those adjectives—incredibly precise!"

The Rodríguez stumper was more for the José six-pack crowd. It was held in the municipal soccer stadium with the police and the army cordoning off surrounding streets and scores of charter buses bringing in the party faithful. There were packs of food vendors and yards of banners and bushels of fireworks and two *polca* bands (not to be confused with polka bands, which are more melodious entirely). However, the turnout was not extraordinary, only about twice the Laino draw.

Rodríguez spoke from the top of the stands, where he was almost obscured by his overfed coterie. They looked like sausages in suits, cooking in the TV lights and about to split their polyester-blend skins. All I could see of the big man himself was a slice of plump forehead. Though, if a forehead can smile, his was doing it. Rodríguez has been all smiles ever since the coup.

The speech itself was a dull, pleasant thing. I kept hearing the words *"democracia"* and *"patria"* and *"necesario."* I suppose Rodríguez was saying, "Democracy is necessary for the country and the country is necessarily for democracy and with country and democracy together we can build the democracy that's necessary for the country," with the soldiers and the police providing the unspoken subtext, "Vote for me and goons won't come to your house and hit you in the head with a board."

Whenever Rodríguez said anything particularly pleasant the stadium crowd would break into the same "People United" chant that the Laino supporters used. Despite this evidence of double-barreled Jesse Jackson influence, no anti-Americanism was heard from either party. Maybe that's a testimony to Ambassador Towell's diplomatic evenhandedness. Or maybe that shows how completely out-of-it Paraguay really is.

The stadium infield was filled with the Colorado Party's most fervid supporters getting more fervid all the time on sugar-cane rum. They were operating noisemakers and compressed air sirens and were snake-dancing and waving huge Paraguayan flags, and sometimes they were just cutting loose and running in all directions like zanies. Hundreds of Colorado Party trademark red neckerchiefs made the scene look like a scout jamboree gone amuck.

I went out on the field and was quickly accosted by a group of

P. J. O'Rourke

Rodríguez supporters so fervid they could barely walk. Laino propo-
nents had been thrilled by the sight of press credentials. Liberals have
a quaint and touching faith that truth is on their side and an even
quainter faith that journalists are on the side of truth. Not these
stewed conservatives. There were five of them at the violently amiable
stage of inebriation. They spoke a kind of collective English where
one of them could pronounce a few words and a second understood
a few words and a third explained to the first pair what they'd said
and heard. A fourth began a performance in mime concerning the
depth of his devotion to the pudgy general, falling at last to his knees
and praying in the direction of Avoirdupois André. The five of them
pushed me around for a bit, reading my credentials aloud and saying
"Rolling Stone," that is, "Roy-ee-guh Stow-nay" over and over.
After which the prayerful fellow insisted I write down his official title
in some sublocal Colorado Party organization. (It is the beauty of
well-designed fascism that it gives every piss-ant an ant hill to piss
from.) Then the fifth and largest and homeliest of the group grabbed
my notebook and pen and scribbled laboriously for ten minutes. I had
this screed translated later and it turned out to be something that
could have come from the opposition press editorial pages. It was a
demand for "absolute democracy" and for an end to mandatory
party membership and for academic and religious freedom. And
it came complete with my bully's signature and his government-
identity-card number.

The prayerful guy took off his red neckerchief and shook it in my
face. "Colorado—no comunista! Colorado—no comunista!" he
yelled, meaning that he wore red not because he was a Communist
but because he was a member of the Colorado party. (Colorado, of
course, means "red" in Spanish, not "overpriced ski resorts and
dingbats who live in Boulder and teach feminist dance therapy.") The
five of them helped one another tie the material around my head
Rambo-style, except most of it wound up hanging down in front of
my face so I couldn't see anything. Then they all pumped my hand
and shouted adiós.

Not everybody at the Colorado rally was quite this enthusiastic.

I noticed later, in the stadium men's room, that somebody had used a red neckerchief to wipe his ass.

I spent election day itself in a little town called Tobatí, fifty miles east of Asunción. This was the first even slightly honest election in the history of Paraguay, and there was some confusion about the mechanics of voting. No one under the age of sixty had ever voted for anyone but Stroessner. I watched a peasant girl arrive at one of the polling places. She was checked off on the voter registration list and had her index finger dipped in ink so she couldn't vote again until she'd washed really well. She went into the *puerta obscura,* as the Paraguayans quite appropriately call a voting booth, came back out and asked the election officials something—who to vote for, I think. They made a little speech about *democracia.* The peasant girl went inside again and returned with a Colorado ballot and a quizzical expression, "would this be good?" The election officials waved their arms and turned their heads away. This was supposed to be a *secret* ballot. One of the officials covered his eyes and held up an envelope. The girl came out of the booth the third time with envelope and ballot folded and refolded like a love note passed in a high school class. She and the officials together couldn't get this wad through the slot in the ballot-box lid.

Rodríguez won the election, by the way.

I guess it's like love and marriage, political freedom being so poetic and noble when people are trying to achieve it and so boring and silly in practice. Well, something poetic and noble—and thoroughly awful—will happen soon in Paraguay if the past is anything to go by. In the meanwhile—*tranquilo.*

RETURN OF THE
DEATH OF COMMUNISM

Nicaragua, February 1990

On the morning of the 26th, the day after Violeta Chamorro's victory over Danny Ortega, I walked into the Inter-Continental hotel in Managua and Bianca Jagger was sitting alone in the lobby. Bianca had been ubiquitous during the election campaign: There was Bianca looking smart in an unconstructed linen jacket and yellow socks to match, Bianca looking serious with press pass and camera, Bianca looking thoughtful listening to Jimmy Carter, Bianca looking concerned conferring with Senator Christopher Dodd, Bianca looking committed in simple tennis shoes and neatly mussed hair, Bianca looking important wearing sunglasses after dark. But this morning Bianca looked . . . her age. Here we had a not very bright, fortyish, discarded rock-star wife, trapped in the lonely hell of the formerly cute—one bummed-out show-biz lefty.

I was feeling great myself, ready to turn somersaults over the Ortega defeat, full of good cheer and pleased with all the world. But then the forlorn, sagging little shape of Bianca caught my eye and, all of a sudden, I felt EVEN BETTER.

I hadn't come to Nicaragua prepared for such joy. Like most readers of papers and watchers of newscasts, I thought the Sandinistas were supposed to win this one. I'm a member of the working press; you'd think I'd know better than to listen to journalists. But there's a little bit of the pigeon in every good confidence man. I even believed the February 21st ABC-*Washington Post* poll that had Ortega leading Chamorro by sixteen percentage points. That is—I blush to admit this—I accepted the results of an opinion poll taken in a country where it was illegal to hold certain opinions. You can imagine the poll-taking process: "Hello, Mr. Peasant, I'm an inquisitive and frightening stranger. God knows who I work for. Would you care to ostensibly support the dictatorship which controls every facet of your existence, or shall we put you down as in favor of the UNO opposition and just tear up your ration card right here and now?"

Furthermore, when I arrived in Nicaragua I found an Ortega political machine that was positively Bushian in its relentless drumming on the issue-free upbeat. Danny's smiling (I presume they used a photo retoucher) face and Danny's heartthrob-of-the-poli-sci-department mustache were everywhere to be seen. As was Danny—pestering babies, attempting dance steps, wearing Ed Begley, Jr., the-dog-was-sick-on-the-carpet shirts and tossing free baseballs into crowds of squealing totalitarianism fans. The Sandinistas' black and red, Doberman-mouth party colors were painted anyplace paint could stick. Sandinista songs played from every radio. The Danny for President slogan *todo sera mejor* (meaning "everything will be better" and not, as I momentarily thought, "major dried toads") was as perfect an all-purpose campaign promise as I have ever heard. There were Sandinista music videos with singing and dancing that could send Paula Abdul back to wagging pom-poms for the L.A. Lakers. And there were Sandinista ad campaigns tailored to every segment of the electorate. A billboard for city youth (the voting age is sixteen in Nicaragua) showed a moonstruck couple in Ortega T-shirts walking hand-in-hand toward a voting booth beneath the headline "When you do it for the first time, do it for love." Banners for the countryside showed a fierce portrait of Ortega with the motto *Daniel Es Mi Gallo,* "Daniel Is My Fighting Cock." (These can now be profitably recycled by the Kentucky Fried Chicken franchise outlets soon to open in Nicaragua.)

P. J. O'Rourke

I confess I believed the Sandys had all the corners nailed down, and I spent the last couple of days before the election committing that original sin of journalism, "writing the lead on the way to the ball-park." What was I going to say about a loathsome Sandinista victory? I supposed I'd have to natter on about the unfair advantages of using state resources for party ends, about how Sandinista control of the transit system prevented UNO supporters from attending rallies, how Sandinista domination of the army forced soldiers to vote for Ortega and how Sandinista bureaucracy kept $3.3 million of U.S. campaign aid from getting to UNO while Danny spent three million donated by overseas pinks and millions and millions more from the Nicaraguan treasury, etc.

But this seemed like weak-tea, crybaby stuff. No, I thought, I'll have to go shoveling in the manure pile of political science, trying to uncover the appeal that Marxism and other infantile world views still hold for people. One nice thing about being a conservative, at least I wouldn't feel betrayed by the masses. Democracy is only one of human liberty's safeguards and not always the most effective one. Back in the U.S. we've got a House of Representatives full of bed-wetting liberals to prove it.

THE DOG IS DEAD BUT THE TAIL STILL WAGS

That was what I planned to call this piece. (It's still a good title—I'll save it for my review of Christopher Hitchens's next book.)

Thus I was in a grim frame of mind when I went to the press conference held by that most ex- of America's ex-presidents, Jimmy Carter. The press conference was at the Sandinista's imposing media complex, one of the few buildings in Managua that won't fall down if you piss against the side of it. This propaganda palace was built with money donated by patsy Swedes, named after their bumped-off prime minister, Olof Palme, and hence called, by the small contingent of conservatives present, the "Good Socialist Press Center."

Carter was the head of one of the three principal international election-monitoring groups which were fluttering around Nicaragua pronouncing everything they saw fair and equitable. There was the U.N. ("the turkeys"), the OAS ("the chickens") and Carter's group, the Council of Freely Elected Heads of Government ("the geese").

What Carter thought he was doing, besides proving there are worse things than Marines that the U.S. can send to Nicaragua, I don't know. But there he was, the man who gave the store away in the first place, still grinning like a raccoon eating fish guts out of a wire brush and still talking in that prissy, nose-first, goober-grabber accent, except this time in Spanish: " . . . new-WAY-vuh Knicker-RAH-wuh deh-muh-crat-TICK-uh . . . "

Carter oozed moral equivalence. "There have been serious problems in the campaign process on both sides," said Carter. "We have to give credit to the Nicaraguan people for establishing an excellent electoral process," said Carter. "If the election is certified as honest and fair, the United States should lift sanctions," said Carter. It's a shame Jimmy was too young to be an international observer at Germany's elections in 1932. "We have to give credit to the German people for establishing an excellent electoral process." Maybe he could have given Hitler some help rearming.

The "press" at the press conference was a dirty and confused bunch, even by press corps standards. Inspection of credentials showed most of them to be correspondents for the Xeroxed newsletter of the Berkeley High-Colonic Liberation Front or television reporters from the Ann Arbor Reincarnation for Peace Coalition's public-access cable program. When a genuine newsman asked Carter about a report of UNO poll-watchers being arrested, the backpack journalists hissed.

A number of celebrity fellow travelers were in Nicaragua for the vote-off—Jackson Browne, Jimmy Cliff, the Sandinistas' Washington lawyer Paul (where's-the-Smith-Act-when-we-need-it) Reichler and Ed Asner, who didn't look like he'd missed any meals due to the injustice of the capitalist economic system. But the real show was these *sandalistas,* prosperous, educated lefties from the United States who've flocked to Nicaragua for a decade to . . . well, to *help.* Although it's something of a puzzle why rebellious middle-class

Americans went to Nicaragua to help Sandinistas wreck Central America, instead of, say, going to South Africa to help Boers chase schoolchildren with whips, or to Uganda to help Idi Amin eat people.

Some say the *sandalistas* are just young and dumb. But those folks are only half right. At first glance the Birkenstock Bolshies seem young. They wear "youth" clothes and have adolescent body language—constantly distributing hugs and touches and squirming with emotion rather than sitting still in thought. But, looking closely at the uniform ponytails and earrings (many of the women wear them too), I noticed the tresses that were still long in back were oft-times gone on top, and the lady *sandalistas,* their underarm hair was streaked with gray.

A number of college-age kids were present, too—earnest and homely and not at all the type who would have been lefties in my day of high-fashion revolt. In 1968 these kids would have been in the ham radio club or Future Stenographers of America.

The Ortega-snugglers were dressed as though they were going to a Weather Underground Days of Rage costume party. They were all in jean skirts and drawstring pants, clogs, folk-art jewelry and tie-dyed tank tops—fashions fully twenty years out of style. I wonder what my hip friends and I in the summer of love would have thought about people wearing zoot suit jackets and reat pleat pants with key chains dangling to the ground.

The Carter press conference was on Saturday morning, the day before the election. That afternoon I attended a less complacent press conference given by the Center for Democracy at the Inter-Continental Hotel. The same bunch of backpack journalists were here, too, hissing even before anybody asked a question. Some of these life-style leftovers had gone so far as to don the red and black Sandinista neckerchief, which, like the neckerchief of Paraguay's fascist Colorado Party, is an item of apparel identical to that worn by the Boy Scouts of America. In Nicaragua the effect was of a scout troop gone deeply, seriously wrong, growing older and older but never graduating to Explorer and earning merit badges in "Lenin," "marijuana" and "poor hygiene."

I hadn't been keeping up to speed on Nicaraguan nonsense and had no idea why the lefties were heckling the Center for Democracy. The Center is one of those painstakingly bipartisan, painfully fair organizations that I usually heckle myself. CFD was the first election-monitoring group invited to Nicaragua. It was invited by both sides and had been observing the election campaign since the spring of last year. But now the CFD's credentials were downgraded so that its observers couldn't enter polling places, and more than fifty CFD observers had been denied Nicaraguan visas at the last minute.

The trouble was, the Center for Democracy had gotten caught telling the truth. CFD observers were at a UNO rally in the town of Masatepe on December 10, 1989, and they saw a Sandinista mob set upon Chamorro supporters with machetes. The mob killed one person and chopped the arms off a couple of others while the Sandinista police stood around like potted palms. Now, it's all right for observer groups to observe such things, that's what they're there for. But if the Sandinistas had wanted truth-telling groups, that's what they would have asked for. The OAS observers at the Masatepe rally obligingly waffled and claimed "both sides" were to blame. But the CFD delegation—which included such dyed-in-the-hair-shirt liberals as Bob Beckel—was outraged by the Sandinista attack and said so.

Thus the press conference questions directed to Center for Democracy president Allen Weinstein weren't questions at all but diatribes capped with little rhetorical inquisitions such as, "How are you going to overcome your bias?" and, "Don't you think it's idiosyncratic that yours is the only observer group complaining about credential problems?" after which half the press conference attendees would clap. One particularly impassioned and bearded fellow named Carlos, a professor at Glendale College in California, where he teaches "Chicano Studies," explained how the fact that the CFD was an observer group in the first place and came to Nicaragua at all proved its members had no respect for Nicaraguan sovereignty.

*   *   *

I'd gone to Nicaragua with the head of the National Forum Foundation, Jim Denton. Forum has been sponsoring interns from newly de-communized Eastern Europe, bringing them to the United States so that they can see how democratic institutions work and can learn to avoid making terrible mistakes like electing Jimmy Carter. Denton took two of these interns, Slawek Gorecki from Poland and Martin Weiss from Czechoslovakia, to Managua. Jim and I thought the *sandalistas* were funny. Martin and Slawek did not. They were sickened and enraged that citizens of a free nation would go somewhere to promote dictatorship. Even more than disgusted, they were mystified. Trying to explain American lefties to Martin and Slawek was like—simile fails me—trying to explain American lefties to two reasonable and intelligent people who'd never seen any.

Martin and Slawek—and Jim and I too, for that matter—preferred meeting with Commandante Raphael Solis, President of the Sandinista National Assembly. Here was a comprehensible scum bag, somebody who was making a buck off the evil he espoused.

Solis was master of the world-weary idealist act—lots of rueful smiles and care-laden brow rubs. His manners were gracious and welcoming, his grin warm and genuine. He was the kind of Commie who'd never ship anyone to a concentration camp in a boxcar; he'd send them in a taxi.

Solis said he was confident of an Ortega victory and of a large majority in the new National Assembly. But was he? With the improved sensitivity and increased intelligence that hindsight brings, I detect some loyal-opposition bullpen warm-up from Solis. He claimed he was looking forward to national reconciliation and hoped the UNO parties would play a part in it. He dismissed the statement by Interior Minister (and head of the secret police) Tomas Borge that the Sandinistas were "prepared to lose the election but not to lose power."

"That is," said Solis with the aplomb of a born politician,

"campaign rhetoric." He touted a *"perestroika* atmosphere" in Nicaragua, predicted "foreign-policy compromises" and, in response to needling from Slawek he said, "As to the changes in Eastern Europe, I haven't heard any criticism from the Sandinista leadership. We think these changes are positive, democratic." And he went on to claim that Nicaragua would be making the same changes soon and, also, had made them already.

At sunrise on election morning we headed around Lake Managua and north into the mountains, visiting polling places in Sebaco and Matagalpa and little villages in between. Then we drove further north to Jinotega in what had been contra territory. Everywhere we went it was the same: awful roads through beautiful scenery to lousy towns. The whole country is cracked, shattered, dirty, worn-out. Everything dates from the Somoza era or before. Ten years of revolution have produced nothing but the Olof Palme Press Center. Even the lamest People's Republic cosmetic touches were missing. Sandinista graffiti is the only fresh paint in Nicaragua. The nation looks—and smells—like that paradigm of socialism, a public restroom.

The voting was done in dingy schoolrooms with all the window glass broken or missing and bare wires running across the ceiling to fifteen-watt light bulbs. Every voter had the ballot-marking process explained to him personally so that the election went forward at the speed of mammal evolution. People were waiting in line by the hundreds to vote.

Each polling place was run by a brisk, snippy, managing Sandinista woman of middle age, the kind of woman who, in a free society, is known as "my first wife." Denton, Martin, Slawek and I didn't have the proper credentials to enter polling places, but we did anyway and, for the most part, got away with it—though at the price of being treated like ex-husbands.

The U.N., the OAS and the Carter group were all going around doing about the same thing we were in the way of checking for vote fraud. That is, they popped their heads in and made sure there was no Sandinista with a pistol in a toddler's ear saying, "Vote for Danny or the rug monkey gets it." We didn't see any cheating like that, and the U.N., the OAS and the Carter group said they didn't either.

We did see a truckload of soldiers being hauled around to vote. "Who are you for?" we yelled. *"Cinco! Cinco!"* they shouted, holding up five fingers to indicate they were voting for the fifth line on the ballot, the Sandinistas. "Uno," said one little fellow in the back, and they all giggled and made as if to pummel him.

In the village of San Ramón we saw some horseplay. The men and women had decided to get in separate lines. Then the line of men shoved the line of women off the school porch and into the rain. The women confided to us that the men were going to vote for Ortega.

And we saw former Democratic presidential hopeful Bruce Babbitt standing around at one polling place, looking clueless. Jim Denton said, "That's Bruce Babbitt," but for the life of me I couldn't remember who Bruce Babbitt was. I guess this tells us all we need to know about Bruce's political future.

The only Nicaraguan we heard complain was a guy who wasn't allowed to vote because he was drunk. "He admits that he's drunk," the Sandinista policeman told us. "Everybody makes mistakes," the drunk told us. And we told the policeman, "They let Teddy Kennedy vote in the Senate."

When we came back through Sebaco late in the afternoon, some of the same people who'd been standing in line to vote at seven that morning were still waiting. "We've been in line since four in the morning, since three in the morning, since two in the morning," one person told us with cheerful rural vagueness about time. "And if it is necessary we will stay here until . . . *ten!*" said another man, naming the latest hour of the evening he could think of offhand.

Of course people don't stand in line for twelve hours in drizzly weather at the ass end of nowhere to vote for the status quo. So there were three hints I'd been given that Ortega might lose. But there's no getting through to the highly perceptive. It wasn't until another journalist told me the Sandinistas were in trouble that I believed it.

We'd gone back to the Olof Palme center to wait for returns. Around 11:00 P.M. a network television newsman with (don't be shocked) left-wing connections came by looking agitated. "P.J., I was just over at Sandy headquarters and something's gone seriously wrong," he said, meaning the opposite. "All of Ortega's people are really upset. The early returns show them getting . . ." Getting what the billboard said when you do for the first time, you should do for love.

The UNO people had heard the same buzz and were in a mood of contained but swollen hope. Chamorro's coalition was holding its election-night party at a restaurant in one of Managua's few remaining middle-class enclaves. The crowd was a model of bourgeois propriety. Occasionally someone would stand on a chair and say, "*Viva UNO*" in a loud voice, but that was about it. The place was all clean shirts, hearty handshakes, polite honorifics and, "How's your brother in Miami?" It was difficult to picture these decent, hard-working, prosperous, common-sensical people overthrowing a government. Sometimes it's hard to remember that bourgeois propriety is the real revolutionary force these days. All over the world we're bringing down dictatorships—or at least forcing them to go condo.

The Sandinista "victory party" was, on the other hand, a massive street disco populated by kids who in the U.S. would have been selling crack, getting the name of their favorite heavy metal band tattooed on their butts or planning a drive-by shooting. These are the last people on earth that *sandalista* types would consort with back home. But all sorts of big, homely dirty-haired American girls in stained T-shirts and dweeby little chicken-necked American boys in ripped jeans were fraternizing the hell out of the lumpen Nicaraguans (who were dressed in their Sunday best, by the way).

There was no evidence of Danny difficulties at the street dance, really no trace of politics except the general air of thuggishness that hangs over all "mass" political movements. Lots of beer and cane liquor was being consumed and much smooching in the shadows was being done and fistfights and lunch-blowings were beginning to dot the crowd. After half an hour of walking around with our hands over our wallet pockets, we decided our little group of *wing-tipistas* belonged back at the Chamorro party or—even better by the standards of the bourgeois propriety revolution now afoot—asleep in our beds.

I awoke to the sound of lugubrious Spanish on the television. It was Danny Boy giving his concession speech, old Landslide Daniel. I understand Jimmy Carter had tracked Danny down in the middle of the night and told him—loser-to-loser—the jig was up. The Sandinistas had done everything they could to ensure the validity of this election in the eyes of the world. Now they had to eat what they had cooked. Quite a bit of "crow in red sauce" was served around the globe in 1989 and '90.

Danny's speech was a long one. There are no brief excuses for communism. And it was punctuated with more pauses for dramatic effect than a high school production of *Macbeth*. Lined up behind Daniel was most of the Sandinista *nomenklatura*, pouting and sniffling and generally looking like dear Uncle Bill had died and left his fortune to the cat. At the end of Danny's speech, he and his pals raised their fists in the air and warbled the Sandinista battle anthem, the one with the last line about Yankees being "the enemies of all humankind," singing us farewell in the manner of the Mickey Mouse Club, except this crowd couldn't carry a tune on a shovel. The TV cameras pulled back to show the Olof Palme press corps singing along through their tears.

Me, I was singing myself, making up little tunes and dancing and capering around:

> *Benjamin Linder was blown to a flinder,*
> *Dennis Wilson run o'er by a train,*
> *Now it's hasta luego to Danny Ortega,*
> *And United Fruit's come back again!*

Give War a Chance

I rushed out to gloat. I especially wanted to gloat over the Americans—the ripe-suck liberals and MasterCard Marxists—see them backing and filling and blowing smoke out their pants cuffs. At the Inter-Continental, across the lobby from Bianca, Paul Reichler was excusing the Nicaraguan people to the news media, saying they had "voted with their stomach." The poor misguided fools. I suppose they should have voted with their ——hole, Paul Reichler. A few yards away that human rum-blossom Senator Chris Dodd was telling reporters the election "wasn't a victory for UNO. The Nicaraguan people just wanted change." Yes, yes. And the 1988 presidential race wasn't a victory for Republicans either. The American people just wanted Michael Dukakis ground into a heap and sold as fiber supplement.

Driving through the streets of Managua, seeing American hippy-dips all fiddle-faced and dejected, it was hard to resist the temptation to yell things out the car window. "Get a job!" Or, "What's the matter with your legs, toots, don't you know 'Fur is dead'?" In fact I couldn't resist it. My favorite thing to do was just make a little pistol motion with my hand and shout, "Nicolae Ceausescu!!!"

I headed for the Olof Palme center to rank on the backpack journalists. Oh, it was almost too sweet for telling, how they bellyached and sourpussed and went around in sulks. Carlos, the professor of "Chicano Studies," tried to look on the sunny side. "We can't abandon the people of Nicaragua," he said with a straight face, and, "The struggle will continue. People will be even more committed." But in the end, Carlos was reduced to racism in his attempt to explain why the polls said Danny would win but the voters said otherwise. "It's the Latino culture," said Carlos. "People love to say one thing and do another."

The younger *sandalistas* looked like they'd just seen Lee Atwater open for the Grateful Dead. They weren't angry, really, just deeply, deeply disappointed. Here they'd blown their semester break and Mom was going to have a cow when she got the VISA bill for the plane ticket, and then the Nicaraguan people went and let them down like this. But the old *sandalistas*, the New Left geezers, they looked like they'd gone to hell in a bong. It's into the trash can with this sixties litter, and you could see they knew it. They looked like Abbie Hoffman was looking the last couple years of his life, as though every night when they go to sleep a BMW chases them through their dreams.

And in that BMW, or hoping to be there soon, were all the regular Nicaraguans down at the Eastern Market.

Were they surprised that UNO won? They laughed. "We expected victory, especially the mothers," said a mother.

"All the mothers are happy," said another mom.

"We hope Violeta fulfills her promises," said the proprietress of a shoe store. "Or we'll get rid of her too," she added in the tone of an experienced democrat.

"If Ortega doesn't give in, the people will rise up," said a cobbler. "We have *other countries* that will help us." And he nodded toward the Congressional Press Gallery I.D. I was wearing around my neck.

"What about the polls?" I asked. "Why were they so wrong?"

"People were afraid," said a man in a barbershop.

"The same old experts who always come here came here and gave us the same old results they always give," said the barber.

Another customer began yelling, "All we had to eat was old lard and the kind of sugar they feed to cattle!"

And that set off a passing drunk who may have been confused about geopolitics—or maybe not—but, anyway, had the right attitude. "Tomorrow, Japan!" he shouted.

RETURN OF THE DEATH OF COMMUNISM, PART III—THE SAGA CONTINUES

Kiev and Tibilisi, September 1991

"*Do they remember the good times? 'Yes, under Stalin in the early 1950s. There was enough food and there was order.' What do they want for their grandchildren? 'Lots of food and order.'*"

—NATALYA KRAMINOVA, INTERVIEWING RUSSIAN VILLAGERS FOR THE *MOSCOW NEWS*, SEPTEMBER 22, 1991

It's impossible to get decent Chinese takeout in China, Cuban cigars are rationed in Cuba, and that's all you need to know about communism. But communism is illegal in the USSR or the Soviet Union or the Union of Sovereign So-and-So Republics or whatever they're calling themselves, so when you order Chicken Kiev in Kiev . . . "Chicken is finish," said the large, mopey waiter, making two fists and banging his forearms together in the national signal for "we're out of it or we're closed or anyway the hell with you."

I never did get to place an order. "Is beefsteak," the waiter explained when he'd returned from the hour-long hourly break which is the customary right of all Soviet food-service employees. A plate full of something and cabbage was deposited in front of me. It was, in fact, beef, though not the steak kind. It tasted all right, but this was Monday. I would get "beefsteak" for lunch every day that week. I would order veal, pork, fish and something I couldn't pronounce, and

I would get beefsteak. Monday's beef was, as I said, fine. Tuesday's was middling. Wednesday's wasn't very good. Thursday's was pretty bad. And Friday's was the color of gunmetal and smelled. That was when I realized that all my beefsteaks had been cut from the same large and increasingly elderly piece of meat.

Marina, my Intourist guide, said this was the best restaurant in Kiev. At the table next to mine another smaller, more dandruffy waiter was chatting up a customer's date. The little waiter filled her wineglass, managing to dribble some of the wine on himself. Then he grabbed the skirt of the tablecloth and wiped his hands. Over by the kitchen door the restaurant's busboy was drinking the dregs out of mineral-water bottles. In the kitchen itself three or four people were conducting a loud quarrel punctuated with thrown pans. And a total of seven restaurant employees were operating the cash register. They passed my lunch tab around among themselves for almost half an hour before I was allowed to pay the bill, which amounted to 16 rubles, 53¢.

But you couldn't blame communism. Communism was illegal. And communism was extra-specially double-illegal in Kiev—Kiev being the free and democratic capital of the entirely and completely, you-bet independent republic of the Ukraine. On September 15th, the day I arrived, there was a huge rally downtown where thousands of citizens cheered as members of the Ukraine Parliament officially declared the Ukraine independent. "This is the fourth time they have officially declared this," said Marina. So I guess independence in these parts works the same way the restaurants do. Anyway, the Ukraine was independent, and the only reason it didn't have borders and money and an army and a post office was that the people in charge of those things were waiting for somebody to add up their lunch checks.

You could tell for sure that there was no more communism in the Ukraine because all the giant statues of Communists had been hit in the face with paint bombs. Every bronze, concrete and marble Communist had a big white paint splash across the kisser, making the Ukraine look like a country that acquired its national heros in a custard-pie fight. In the main square a particularly huge statue of Lenin—which, besides paint-bomb disfigurement, had KILLER and FASCIST graffitied on its base—was being torn down (or would have been if anyone could have found the crane operator). All the avenues, plazas and thoroughfares commemorating Bolshevism were getting "Oak Street"–type monikers. And the most popular piece of wearing apparel was a stone-washed denim shirt with a label over the breast pocket reading "U.S. Army."

Private enterprise had appeared in Kiev, at least a larval stage of it. Street vendors didn't exactly hawk their wares but they did sit behind tables and impassively offer for purchase books, flowers and clothes. Almost every neighborhood had a private market selling food—good food. There were big, fat potatoes in Coppertone skins; turnips the size of artillery shells; beets with a *grand cru* tint; noble, leonine heads of cabbage; pot cheese with curds in folds as white as tuxedo shirts; and melons as big and fresh as diaper-commercial babies. The meat counters were impressive, too, though not some-place you'd take k. d. lang on a date. Massive chunks of animals were being heaved around and chopped to pieces. Tongues, brains, hooves, feet and personal, private parts decorated the cutting boards. The tile floor was sloppy with blood puddles. But the meat was good-looking if you could bear to look: pink-champagne-colored pork, beef red like valentines and crocheted with savory fat, good teeth in the sheep skulls and clear eyes staring from the future-soup-stock cow heads.

They were fabulous markets. They'd do any nation proud. Except for one little problem—no customers. Some people were wandering around but it was the kind of wandering that Americans do in Porsche showrooms. Prices in the private markets were high. Meat was selling for 25 rubles a kilo. That's 38¢ a pound, but the average Ukrainian makes 250 rubles a month. So 38¢ a pound is like going to the Safeway and getting 16 ounces of London broil for a hundred bucks. But it wasn't poverty alone that made the private markets such dysfunctional and unbustling places. Prices weren't just high, they were bizarre. For one thing, they were all the same. Each babushkaed grandmother selling lentils was selling lentils for the same price as every other grandmother—no premium for quality, no discount for quantity and no haggling.

I asked Marina about the beef. I said, "Isn't beef cheaper this time of year? I mean, if you don't slaughter cattle in the fall, then you have to feed them in the barn all winter, and, especially in a country with a grain shortage, I'd expect lots of people would be bringing cattle to market right now, increasing supply and driving down prices."

"No," said Marina.

"Now pigs, on the other hand," I said, "are raised on slops, and people are going to be tossing out food scraps year 'round, so the price of pork would tend to remain constant."

"Meat," said Marina, "sells for twenty-five rubles a kilo."

"Beef and pork, they both sell for the same price?"

"Meat," said Marina, "sells for twenty-five rubles a kilo."

"Fresh spring lamb?"

"Twenty-five rubles a kilo."

"Stringy old mutton?"

"Twenty-five rubles a kilo. Meat," said Marina, "sells for twenty-five rubles a kilo."

There was another way to buy food in Kiev, at the state food stores with their long, scuffling lines at the head of which was nothing, just about nothing at all. There was bread, sometimes, that you could use as a medicine ball or a boat anchor. There were ten or a dozen five-gallon jars full of murky liquid with a few unidentifiable pickled things resting in the bottoms and other jars of the same kind which contained plain water. The sausages, when there were any to see, were a shock and a horror, looking like nothing but discarded sex toys. The produce was appalling. The potatoes resembled gray prunes and no other vegetable was distinguishable from compost.

But the prices were right. The state store's carrots—which could have passed as criminal evidence, wizened remains of a kidnap victim's severed fingers maybe—cost 50 kopecks. And a kopeck is three-thousandths of a penny. The carrots in the private markets cost six times as much. Thus the Soviet economy is undermined by a kind of reverse black market from an anti-matter universe, a black market where it is legal to buy things you don't want too cheaply.

Every aspect of material life in the Soviet Union works this way. If you stand in line long enough the state provides goods and services. The services are out of service and the goods are no good, but food, clothing, shelter and medical care are—just barely—available. And they are hilariously inexpensive. The babushkas in the private markets don't really have to sell you anything. They're there to make money, not a living. If you don't buy the food, well, then . . . fist/fist, forearm/forearm . . . they'll take it home and eat it themselves, and you can stand in line for mummified carrots.

Marina, eyeing a selection of lard in a broken dairy cooler at the state food store, said, "The two most difficult things in the Soviet Union are getting enough food and losing weight."

An American's first reaction to the Soviet Union is to roll up his sleeves. There is so much to be done. Of course, that's true in any poor country, but in the Soviet Union there is the what with which to do it. Give an American a couple of gallons of paint, some Murphy's oil soap, a mop and a can of Lysol spray disinfectant and the private food markets would look like Balducci's. The beefsteak restaurant could be fixed in an afternoon, just turn anybody's grandmother loose in there with a Fannie Farmer cookbook, a copy of *Emily Post's Etiquette* and a .38 revolver. Something could even be done with the lurching, squealing, backfiring, oil-dribbling Volga sedan in which I was being driven around town. Two cans of Bondo and it's a 1956 Studebaker President—a real collector's item on the classic-car market.

Not that the Soviets are incapable of helping themselves. Marina described how her friends take local goods to Poland to sell them for hard currency (it says something that Soviets consider the zloty a hard currency) then fly to Turkey because that's the cheapest Western country (it says more that Soviets consider Turkey a Western country). In Turkey they buy clothes and dry goods and bring these back and sell them for a sizable profit in consignment stores. But Marina was embarrassed by this. "We hate to be seen trading," she said. "It makes us feel almost like Negroes."

Out in the country north of Kiev the topsoil was turned up in lustrous brunet furrows and smelled so rich it seemed like you wouldn't need to grow food, you could just cook soup from the loam itself (the beefsteak restaurant tried this). The peasant houses were big and well-proportioned, made of clay-tile bricks with hipped roofs of tin sheeting. Doors and windows were deep-set in elaborately carved wooden frames. On the second story of most houses was a large glassed-in porch, the Ukrainian equivalent of a Florida room, a Siberia salon perhaps. The homes all had generous yards surrounded by Tom Sawyer board fences, many with the palings painted alternately blue and yellow, the Ukrainian national colors. These quaint but substantial homes could be sold by the thousands as vacation getaways for two-income urban professional families if only the Ukraine could be made trendy. And who knows? Fashion is an odd thing. Collective farming may replace skiing or tennis as the thing to do. Hollywood executives could start driving wheat combines to work. And Ralph Lauren might bring out a Potato Digger line of leisure clothes. This would be a great relief to the Ukrainian peasants, who would then be able to move somewhere—anywhere—besides these handsome villages surrounded by the best farm land in the world.

Because there was nothing in those villages. There were no stores except the state food stores and no food in these. Out in the fields men and women were using the kind of wooden farm implements which decorate walls in the United States. There were no roads, just mud spaces impassable for half the year. "At least the highway to Kiev is well-paved," I said to Marina. She laughed. The highway was paved because this was the highway to the dachas belonging to high officials in the Ukrainian Communist Party. (Not that they're high officials in the Ukrainian Communist Party anymore, now they're high officials in the National Government of the Ukraine.) The peasant's houses all had wells outside, with cranks and buckets and little roofs over them.

I thought they were lawn ornaments. They were the only source of water. The wells were shallow and there were no sewers, only cesspits even shallower than the wells. If any of these had really been wishing wells, what the peasants would have wished for was clean water. And it was all so easily put right—one day with a drilling rig and a pick-up truck full of cheap pipe would do it. Even Soweto has indoor plumbing. A septic tank is nothing but a concrete box, and, to judge by Soviet architecture, the locals were plenty capable of making one. The Dnieper river was only a few miles away. A couple cartloads of riverbed gravel, some shovel work and a tractor or an ox or the kids pulling a log drag would make for weatherproof roads.

"We need some economist to give us a plan," said Marina.

"You had that already," I said.

We drove about fifty miles north on the dacha highway to the edge of the "closed zone" around Chernobyl. The zone has a radius of just eighteen miles. Right outside, food crops were still growing, dairy cows were still grazing and people were still living—sick, maybe, but still living. The irradiated ground did not glow or make drive-in–movie noises. No giant mutant predators or revivified lizard monsters stalked across it. I would have felt better if I'd seen one. A cicada the size of Space Mountain would have gotten somebody's attention, even in the Soviet Union. But radiation doesn't have very immediate or clearly visible effects, so nothing very immediate or clearly visible was being done about it. The border of the closed zone was one strand of barbed wire. There was a checkpoint on the road with a sign reading, "Citizen, attention. You enter a place of special regime." Another sign warned visitors not to hunt, fish, swim, camp, pick mushrooms or drink water.

Three atomic reactors (one of which has since caught fire) were still operating at Chernobyl. A busload of men and women coming home from work stopped on the other side of the checkpoint. None wore protective clothing. The bus was given a cursory check with a Geiger counter. The workers passed in one door of a little shed and

out another faster than passengers go through an airport metal detec-
tor. They looked depressed, but, then again, everybody in the Soviet
Union looked depressed.

"Do you want to interview them?" said Marina.

"I want to know why they're still working there."

"For pay," said Marina. And I couldn't think of anything else to
ask.

On our way back we stopped to look at a hydroelectric dam
with rusty sluice gates and unkempt high-tension wires. It was imme-
diately upriver from the city. Thirty-three feet of water loomed above
downtown Kiev—a Super-Soaker of Damocles held in place by the
same quality of materials and engineering that went into the Chernobyl reactors.

Marina was pessimistic about the dam. "One day—woosh." Marina
was pessimistic about everything. She explained how it was now legal
for Soviet citizens to buy Western goods in the special hard-currency
shops but still illegal for them to own hard currency. "We visit these
stores like you would visit a museum," she said. (She meant Porsche
dealership.) Nothing had happened with land reform. "It's like
knocking on a door that isn't there," said Marina. And, although all
the property of the Communist Party had been confiscated, it had
been confiscated by the state that was created by this Party. "So,
what," I said, "does that mean?" Marina shrugged.

Marina's grandfather had been a government official in the
Ukraine when Stalin was in power, and, like many government offi-
cials then, he'd been sent to a prison camp. He got out only because
Stalin died. Nonetheless Marina grew up with a certain faith in the
Soviet system. Then when she was in high school in the 1970s she
heard Alexander Solzhenitsyn's *Gulag Archipelago* being read on
Radio Liberty broadcasts from the West. "This upset me terribly,"
she said. In 1979 she was allowed, as an Intourist guide, to travel to
Western Europe. She spent the first hard currency she ever possessed
on Solzhenitsyn books, which she could only find in English. She hid

them carefully in her luggage because she knew that if they were found, she wouldn't be traveling to Western Europe again.

Marina read these books aloud to her family. They sat every night around the kitchen table with Marina translating, a Russian-English dictionary by her side for words she didn't recognize. "Too many intellectuals were killed, imprisoned," said Marina. "No one wants to be an intellectual here. In America you call somebody a fool, we call them an intellectual."

Tibilisi

There was no shortage of foolish intellectuals in the Republic of Georgia. And they all had guns.

Georgia is, of course, claiming independence from the Soviet Union. The whole Soviet Union is claiming independence from the Soviet Union. And all the independent places have places claiming independence from them. Something called South Ossetia is trying to secede from Georgia. I'll bet South Ossetia starts having trouble with South-Central Ossetia soon. And what was once the second most powerful nation in the world is becoming a collection of countries with names like "The Republic of Me and You and I'm Not Sure About Me."

But that's not why the intellectuals had guns in Georgia. They weren't rebelling against somebody else's government. They were rebelling against their own.

Last May Georgia held its first free elections since the Neolithic Age and elected one Zvaid K. Gamsakhurdia president. Gamsakhurdia (pronounced sort of like "Gram's accordion" but not really) is a distinguished-looking, hammy-acting university professor and a prominent Georgian nationalist. He helped found the local Helsinki Watch civil-liberties monitoring group, was convicted by the Brezhnev government of monitoring civil liberties and was sent to jail for it. Gamsakhurdia was quite the local hero and was elected by an 87 percent margin.

Once in office, however, Gamsakhurdia began acting like a butt-head. He closed newspapers, arrested opposition leaders, fired everybody in the government who didn't agree with him, spent $460,000 on bullet-proof Mercedes limousines, forbade Georgians to sell meat, vegetables or building materials anywhere except Georgia, blocked business privatization and land-reform programs and accused the United States of conspiring with Moscow to prevent Georgia from becoming independent.

So Georgians began to demonstrate. Thousands of them marched up and down Rustaveli Prospect, Tibilisi's main street. The anti-Gamsakhurdia protesters occupied their own opposition-party headquarters, but that seemed inadequate, somehow, so they took over the National Congress Building and swore to stay there until . . . I'm not sure until what. The government responded, not by attacking the protesters but by calling on protesters of its own to protest in favor of itself. Gamsakhurdia went on national television and asked people from all the little towns and villages of Georgia to come to the capital and protect him. And come they did, in scores of flag-decked buses. Thousands more Georgians marched up and down Rustaveli Prospect. Police used the village buses to build barricades around the National Government Building, down the street from the National Congress Building, and the pro-Gamsakhurdia protesters swore to stay there until whatever, too.

Actually, the government did attack the opposition a little bit. On September 2nd, Georgian Special Security Forces (which may not have been very special because up until September 2nd Georgia hadn't had any Special Security Forces) shot at some demonstrators. But, despite a lot of impassioned rhetoric, no one managed to die until September 21st, when a thirty-five-year-old cardiologist set himself on fire in front of the National Opera Building, on Rustaveli between the National Congress Building and the National Government Building, leaving a note saying, "If Georgia needs blood to settle the conflict then take mine." Although, up until then, Georgia hadn't.

Meanwhile Georgia's National Guard—which is commanded by a sculptor and looks about as professional as a group of middle-aged duck hunters—split into two groups professing neutrality. One group was neutral and prepared to defend the nation against opposition lawlessness, and one group was neutral and prepared to defend the nation against government oppression.

The anti-Gamsakhurdia protesters and the part of the National Guard that was neutrally on their side then took over the national television station, but, since this is a very bureaucratic society, they stormed the offices of the television station's bureaucracy, leaving the government with the actual broadcast facilities.

If none of this makes sense it's because—believe me, I was there—none of this makes sense.

Georgia was less perfectly depressing than the Ukraine. The food was better. The weather was cute. The Caucasus Mountains are—I don't think I'm saying this just because I'm Caucasian—really beautiful. Tibilisi, the capital of Georgia, squats prettily in the Kura River valley about 160 miles inland from the Black Sea at what was once the extreme southeast corner of Hellenic civilization. Medea, of Golden Fleece fame, was from Georgia. After Medea got divorced by her Argonaut husband, Jason, she murdered Jason's second wife, tore her own sons limb from limb and ran off to Athens in a chariot pulled by dragons. I'm told that this, except for the dragons, is not untypical Georgian behavior. Stalin was from Georgia, too.

Anyway, Tibilisi is sort of charming and old. There are little, crimped streets overhung with New Orleans–style balconies, some Constantinople Jr. churches, lots of midget stucco houses with grape vines tangling their patios and only a large—rather than an infinite—number of horrible communist cement apartment houses. The city has been destroyed forty times in Georgia's quarrelsome fifteen-hundred-year history, but not lately. In 1801 the last king of Georgia—named, as you might have guessed, George—turned the whole country over to Russia. If Stalin, Medea and the protesters on Rustaveli Prospect are anything to go by, who can blame him?

There were huge demonstrations the night I arrived. I wasn't scheduled to meet my Intourist guide until the next morning. I don't

speak a word of Georgian and the only word of Russian I speak—
tovarish, "comrade"—is a word you don't say anymore. So I didn't
have any idea who was demonstrating against what. I knew the
opposition was made up of intellectual urban elites, and I knew the
pro-government people were peasants and factory workers, but everybody dresses so badly in the Soviet Union that it was impossible
to tell which was which. All of them, including some members of the
National Guard, were wearing those stone-washed denim shirts with
"U.S. Army" on the pocket.

Sometimes the two sides marched around ignoring each other
and sometimes the two sides argued with each other and sometimes
I couldn't tell for sure if there really were two sides. I gave up and
went to my hotel, where I found the restaurant closed because—as
best I understood—"it was dinner time."

This hotel was just off Rustaveli, around the corner from the
occupied National Congress Building (though I didn't know that was
what it was). I left the door to my balcony open so I could hear if
whoever started fighting with whomever else. Which, at three in the
morning, they did, but I slept through it.

When I woke up everybody was really mad. Barricades and
sitters-in had been forcibly removed from the Congress Building. My
Intourist guide, Nina, and I drove to the TV station, where Nina went
looking for people for me to interview. She produced a large, bearded
fellow still blood-splattered from being whacked on the head early
that morning. "I will never move from here! I will defend democracy!
I want the world to know!" he said, although what he wanted the
world to know I had a hard time getting him to tell me. Not that I
understood when he finally did. According to my notes, pro-Gamsakhurdia protesters approached the barricades at the Congress Building
in a friendly manner so that the bearded man thought they were
coming for a reconciliation. But then they attacked the barricades
with a crane. Three A.M. seems an odd time to be reconciled and a
crane an unlikely item to bring on the errand, but never mind.
"Stones were thrown." The bearded man got hit by one "the size of
a cabbage." Pro-Gamsakhurdia protesters further attacked him,

pushing him into a building, but then, when these attackers saw that he was covered in blood, they helped him out of the building and tried to get him to an ambulance. However, he was attacked by other pro-Gamsakhurdia protesters, but the pro-Gamsakhurdia protesters who'd attacked him first attacked the attackers, drove them back and got him medical treatment after all. "I really felt the support of those people who attacked us," said the bearded man.

Several thousand people were gathered at the TV station, most of them infected with that happy sense of purpose people have when they are standing up for a principle they haven't really been knocked down for yet. People who direct mob scenes in movies have obviously never seen a mob. Movie mobs are decided and purposeful and achieve instant internal government by means of one guy who stands on a chair and yells, "hanging's too good for 'em." Then off the mob goes to lynch Sidney Poitier. Real mobs just mill around acting point-lessly upset while being addressed by a series of half-important people speaking into P.A. systems that turn all human speech into car-theft-alarm noises. Nobody knew what was going on, which made every-body talk loudly about what was happening, and it was embarrassing if you talked too loudly because then everyone in the mob would come cluster around you hoping to hear some bewilderment more illuminating than their own.

Nina took me to talk with the leaders of the TV-station protest. This was one of five or six political interviews that I did while I was in the Soviet Union—with Ukrainian Nationalists, Ukrainian non-Nationalists, a member of the Ukrainian Parliament, anti-Gamsak-hurdian Georgians, pro-Gamsakhurdian Georgians and some people I don't know who they were.

I can tell you what they all had to say, if you like, I mean if you're having trouble getting to sleep or something. I would ask them what their group advocated, and they would say, "Democracy must be defended." I would ask, "How do you propose to do this?" They would say, "There must be a structure of democracy in our society." I would ask, "What are your specific proposals?" They would say,

"We must build democratic institutions." I would ask, "By what means?" They would say, "Building democratic institutions is necessary so that there is a structure of democracy in our society at all levels." And by this time I'd be yelling, "BUT WHAT ARE YOU GOING TO DO??!!" And they would say, "Democracy must be defended."

The Soviets were firmly rooted in the abstract, had both their feet planted on the air. It was impossible to get them to understand that government isn't a philosophical concept, it's a utility, a service industry—a way to get roads built and have Iraqis killed. Talking politics to Soviets gave me the same dull headache that I'd had, back in college, reading *Anna Karenina*. There was Tolstoi gibbering for pages about the Russian peasant's spiritual relationship to yackitty-yackitty-yack and me going, "Leo, why'd she fuck the guy?"

By the time I got done with the interview at the TV station, I was surrounded by two or three hundred pushing, crowding eavesdroppers. The men and boys were armed. I thought civilians didn't have guns in the Soviet Union, but I was wrong. There are liberals who have nightmares about the NRA, and those nightmares look like this crowd. Every kind of firearm imaginable was being waved around with brainless gusto. There were ancient shotguns and decrepit hunting rifles, rusty burp guns from World War II and broom-handle Mauser pistols that looked like they'd been buried in the yard since the revolution. There were scatterguns and target rifles and air pistols and hundreds of AK-47s. I saw a twelve-year-old carrying one of these. He was guarding the place where the mob had parked its cars. (Remember, this was a mob of urban elites.) I'm actually a member of the NRA and it was still a nightmare. The Second Amendment says the people have a right to "keep and bear arms" not a right to wildly swing, waggle in your face, mispoint, stare down the barrel of and accidentally discharge the things. (Somebody did do that, fortunately into a flower bed.)

"Just what," I said to Nina, "is going on here? What are you people trying to accomplish? What gives?"

Nina, who was very pro-anti-Gamsakhurdia, repeated all the

complaints against the man. "But," she said, "in reality the problem is our president is not acting rationally. He behaves in a hysterical manner. He is crazy."

"Crazy?" I said. "Is that all? Nina, in the United States we elect crazy presidents all the time. You people really *don't* understand democracy, do you?"

The pro-Gamsakhurdia protesters, gathered in their own mob in front of the National Government Building, had fewer guns but seemed more dangerous—that is, more likely to beat you up instead of talk you to death.

The peasants and factory workers who supported the government were angry rather than indignant. And they'd come a long way for the purpose of being angry. On close inspection they were easy enough to distinguish from the urban elites. The pro-Gamsakhurdia protesters were older, thicker-limbed and fewer-toothed. Their clothes were the same but smellier. They were sleeping on their buses or the street and being fed free bread and pieces of dense, salty goat cheese. A movie theater had been requisitioned so they could use the rest rooms as wash stalls.

The Gamsakhurdia supporters looked satisfied enough with their accommodations. The lines for food and toilets were shorter than most lines in the Soviet Union. I watched one magnificent old man snoring on the neoclassical portico of the Government Building. He was dressed in a wrinkled suit with World War II campaign ribbons on the jacket pocket. He had shoulders as wide as a wing-back chair, hands like Kool-Aid pitchers and his huge head of white hair was pillowed on a four-foot cudgel.

These were the same kind of poor, benighted slobs who supported Noriega in Panama, Pinochet in Chile, Marcos in the Philippines and Nixon during Watergate. They were mindlessly patriotic and full of ignorance and prejudices. The people at the TV station were much more like us. They really cared about human rights and social justice and even ecology, too. They were hip. They were smart. And they were wrong. The president had been duly elected. He hadn't done anything terribly unconstitutional. In fact, by the standards of the Soviet Union, he hadn't done anything worth mentioning. When, at the TV station, I'd interviewed Nodar Notadze, leader of the anti-Gamsakhurdia opposition in the Georgian Parliament, Notadze had said, "There is no legal ground to demand his resignation. But there is moral ground." The anti-Gamaskhurdia protesters were so smart, so hip and so much like us that you just knew, as soon as freedom and democratic government really were established in Georgia, they'd be voting for Jerry Brown.

Not that the anti-Gamsakhurdia protesters were as wimpy as Jerry Brown voters yet. Wednesday morning, September 25th, at 3 A.M. again, they tried to destroy the Tibilisi electric-power system, killing three pro-Gamsakhurdia National Guardsmen and getting two of themselves killed in the attack.

I could hear it happening—the unmistakable "Buddha-Buddha" of AK-47 fire. I got out of bed and went rushing around the empty streets of Tibilisi looking for some sign of panic or alarm. Then I tried to call the other foreign reporters in the city, but the phone in my hotel room had a large label reading:

You are being served by Kvazy-Electronic telephone station "KVANT."
—Do not lift the receiver while it rings!
—Do not delay dialing!
—Do not depress the lever on the phone!

And so forth. I gave up.

It wasn't until ten in the morning that I found the site of the shooting. It was on a suburban side street, an unprepossessing structure with bullet holes and lots of shattered glass. A very rattled night manager named Jemal Bibileishvili was still behind his desk. "I do not understand what they wanted," he said. "We do not control anything here."

It turned out the anti-Gamsakhurdia protesters had attacked the office of the electric company's maintenance dispatcher. "There is nothing here but a telephone," said the night manager. I asked him if he could think of any possible reason for the protesters to attack this particular building. "No," he said, "only, when power goes out, this is the place everyone comes to protest."

There's a joke people tell in the Soviet Union: Mitterrand, Bush and Gorbachev have a meeting with God. Mitterrand says, "My country faces many difficult problems—lagging exports, Muslim minorities, European unification. How long will it be before France's problems are solved?" God says, "Fifteen years." Mitterrand begins to cry. "I'm an old man," says Mitterrand. "I'll be dead by then. I'll never see France's problems solved." Then Bush says, "My country faces many difficult problems—recession, crime, racial prejudice. How long will it be before America's problems are solved?" God says, "Ten years." Bush begins to cry. "I'm an old man," says Bush. "I'll be out of office by then. I won't get any credit for solving America's problems." Then Gorbachev says, "My country faces many, many difficult problems. How long will it be before the Soviet Union's problems are solved?" *God begins to cry.*

SECOND

THOUGHTS

A SERIOUS PROBLEM

"Is it serious?" we ask the doctor. "I'm not kidding," we tell the child. "What's so funny?" says the voice of authority from classroom to army camp to editorial page of the *New York Times*. The threat of solemnity haunts our lives. Little profit and less pleasure accrue from most somber occasions. The smiles of people emerging from courtrooms, church services and even wedding ceremonies are usually smiles of relief. Life is weighty, important, grave, critical, momentous, etc. Not for nothing does *Roget's Thesaurus* say, "*Antonyms*—See DRUNKENNESS, FRIVOLITY, PLAYFULNESS, UNIMPORTANCE." Yes, indeed, let's see them right away.

But though wise men spend their days trying to stay out of serious trouble, there are other people who frankly wallow in sobriety. They look serious, think about serious things, pick serious topics and speak about them seriously. These are the dinner partners who discuss famine over oysters, the house guests who lecture infirm great-aunts on the importance of aerobic exercise, the journalists who author articles titled "Whither Gambia" (a kind of writing known in the trade as MEGO: "My Eyes Glaze Over"). Why do they do it?

My guess is self-loathing. Self-loathing is one of those odd, illogical leaps of human intuition that is almost always correct. "Serious" people are dense and know it. But, they think, if they can be grave enough about Yugoslavia their gravity will make up for the fact that—like most people—they don't know what's going on there, and—like all people—they don't know what to do about it. Seriousness is stupidity sent to college.

Serious topics also make unimportant people feel as important as what they're discussing. Of course, it's necessary to make sure everyone understands how important the topic is. Hemingway was just a tourist watching Spaniards tease farm animals. But if he could make cattle-pestering a grand and tragic thing in the eyes of the public, he'd become grand and tragic too, because he'd been there while somebody did it.

Truly serious topics give this kind of bore a rare conversational advantage. There isn't any decent way to shut him up. Nobody wants to be caught saying, "Who cares if seventy thousand people drowned in Bangladesh?"

Seriousness is also the great excuse for sin. These days anything can be forgiven if the person was sincere about his actions. "I did what I thought was best at the time" is the modern equivalent of a perfect act of contrition. Personally, I'd be more inclined to absolve George Bush if he'd let Saddam Hussein live from pure good nature. But "I was acting in what I felt to be the best interests of the nation" seems to be more what the public wants to hear.

Seriousness lends force to bad arguments. If a person is earnest enough about what he says, he must have *some* point. There's a movement in some of our school systems to give creationists equal time in science class. Man was plopped down on earth the week before last, is one rib short on the left, and because silly people are serious about this so are we.

Seriousness is also the only practical tone to take when lying. The phrase "to lie with a straight face" is prolix. All lies are told with a straight face. It's truth that's said with a dismissive giggle.

Real seriousness is involuntary. If you're held at gunpoint or run over by a bus, you'll be serious about it. If you're a decent person, you'll also have some serious feelings when you see someone else threatened or squashed. In fact, if you're a decent person faced with the world's catastrophes, horrors and pleas for help, you'll do the right thing whether you're serious or not.

Sir Thomas More jested with his head on the block. "My neck is very short," he warned the executioner. "Take heed, therefore, thou strike not awry, for saving of thine honesty." The Persian king Xerxes was astonished when his scouts told him the Spartans holding the pass at Thermopylae were combing their hair and changing into clean clothes for the battle. Gallantry is the proper tone for those who are worth being taken seriously. With one exception—serious looks and serious voice are absolutely necessary when calling the dog.

SECOND THOUGHTS
ABOUT THE 1960s

What I Believed in the Sixties

Everything. You name it and I believed it. I believed love was all you need. I believed you should be here now. I believed drugs could make everyone a better person. I believed I could hitchhike to California with thirty-five cents and people would be glad to feed me. I believed Mao was cute. I believed private property was wrong. I believed my girlfriend was a witch. I believed my parents were Nazi space monsters. I believed the university was putting saltpeter in the cafeteria food. I believed stones had souls. I believed the NLF were the good guys in Vietnam. I believed Lyndon Johnson was plotting to murder all the Negroes. I believed Yoko One was an artist. I believed Bob Dylan was a musician. I believed I would live forever or until twenty-one, whichever came first. I believed the world was about to end. I believed the Age of Aquarius was about to happen. I believed the *I Ching* said to cut classes and take over the dean's office. I believed wearing my hair long would end poverty and injustice. I believed there was a great throbbing web of psychic mucus and we were all part of it somehow. I managed to believe Gandhi and H. Rap Brown at the same time. With the exception of anything my mom and dad said, I believed everything.

P. J. O'Rourke

What Caused Me to Have Second Thoughts

One distinct incident sent me scuttling back to Brooks Brothers. From 1969 to 1971 I was a member of a "collective" running an "underground" newspaper in Baltimore. The newspaper was called, of all things, *Harry*. When *Harry* was founded, nobody could think what to name the thing so some girl's two-year-old son was asked. His grandfather was Harry and he was calling everything Harry just then so he said, "Harry," and *Harry* was what the paper was called. It was the spirit of the age.

Harry was filled with the usual hippie blather, yea drugs and revolution, boo war and corporate profits. But it was an easy-going publication and not without a sense of humor. The want-ads section was headlined "Free Harry Classifieds Help Hep Cats and Kittens Fight Dippy Capitalist Exploitation." And once when the office was raided by the cops (they were looking for marijuana, I might add, not sedition), *Harry* published a page-one photo of the mess left by the police search. The caption read, "Harry office after bust by pigs." Next to it was an identical photo captioned, "Harry office before bust by pigs."

Our "collective" was more interested in listening to Captain Beefheart records and testing that new invention, the water bed, than in overthrowing the state. And some of the more radical types in Baltimore regarded us as lightweights or worse. Thus, one night in the summer of 1970, the *Harry* collective was invaded by some twenty-five blithering Maoists armed with large sticks. They called themselves, and I'm not making this up, the "Balto Cong." They claimed they were liberating the paper in the name of "the people." In vain we tried to tell them that the only thing the people were going to get by liberating *Harry* was ten thousand dollars in debts and a mouse-infested row house with overdue rent.

There were about eight *Harry* staffers in the office that evening. The Balto Cong held us prisoner all night and subjected each of us to individual "consciousness-raising" sessions. You'd be hauled off to

another room where ten or a dozen of these nutcakes would sit in a
circle and scream that you were a revisionist running dog imperialist
paper tiger whatchama-thing. I don't know about the rest of the staff,
but I conceded as quick as I could to every word they said.

Finally, about 6:00 A.M., we mollified the Balto Cong by agreeing
to set up a "people's committee" to run the paper. It would be made
up of their group and our staff. We would all meet that night on
neutral turf at the Free Clinic. The Balto Cong left in triumph. My
airhead girlfriend had been converted to Maoism during her consciousness-raising session. And she left with them.

While the Balto Cong went home to take throat pastilles and
make new sticks or whatever, we rolled into action. There were, in
those days, about a hundred burned-out "street people" who de-
pended on peddling *Harry* for their livelihood. We rallied all of these,
including several members of a friendly motorcycle gang, and explained to them how little sales appeal *Harry* would have if it were
filled with quotations from Ho Chi Minh instead of free-love person-
als. They saw our point. Then we phoned the Balto Cong crash pad
and told them we were ready for the meeting. "But," we said, "is the
Free Clinic large enough to hold us all?" "What do you mean?" they
said. "Well," we said, "we're bringing about a hundred of our staff
members and there's, what, twenty-five of you, so . . ." They said,
um, they'd get back to us.

We were by no means sure the Balto Cong threat had abated.
Therefore the staff photographer, whom I'll call Bob, and I were set
to guard the *Harry* household. Bob and I were the only two people
on the staff who owned guns. Bob was an ex-Marine and something
of a flop as a hippie. He could never get the hair and the clothes right
and preferred beer to pot. But he was very enthusiastic about hippie
girls. Bob still had his service automatic. I had a little .22-caliber
pistol that I'd bought in a fit of wild self-dramatization during the '68
riots. "You never know when the heavy shit is going to come down,"
I had been fond of saying. Although I'd pictured it "coming down"
more from the Richard Nixon than the Balto Cong direction. Anyway, Bob and I stood guard. We stood anxious guard every night for

two weeks, which seemed an immense length of time back in 1970. Of course we began to get slack, not to say stoned, and forgot things like locking the front door. And through that front door, at the end of two weeks, came a half dozen hulking Balto Cong. Bob and I were at the back of the first-floor office. Bob had his pistol in the waistband of his ill-fitting bell-bottoms. He went to fast draw and, instead, knocked the thing down the front of his pants. My pistol was in the top drawer of a desk. I reached in and grabbed it, but I was so nervous that I got my thigh in front of the desk drawer and couldn't get my hand with the pistol in it out. I yanked like mad but I was stuck. I was faced with a terrible dilemma. I could either let go of the pistol and pull my hand out of the drawer or I could keep hold of the pistol and leave my hand stuck in there. It never occurred to me to move my leg.

The invading Balto Cong were faced with one man fishing madly in his crotch and another apparently being eaten by a desk. It stopped them cold. As they stood perplexed I was struck by an inspiration. It was a wooden desk. I would simply fire through it. I flipped the safety off the .22, pointed the barrel at the Balto Cong and was just curling my finger around the trigger when the Maoists parted and there, in the line of fire, stood my airhead ex-girlfriend. "I've come to get my ironing board and my Hermann Hesse novels," she said, and led her companions upstairs to our former bedroom.

"It's a trap!" said Bob, extracting his gun from the bottom of a pants leg. When the Balto Cong and the ex-girlfriend came back downstairs they faced two exceedingly wide-eyed guys crouching like leopards behind an impromptu barricade of overturned book cases. They sped for the exit.

It turned out later that Bob was an undercover cop. He'd infiltrated the *Harry* collective shortly after the first issue. All his photos had been developed at the police laboratory. We'd wondered why every time we got busted for marijuana the case was dropped. Bob would always go to the District Attorney's office and convince them a trial would "blow his cover." It was important for him to remain undetected so he could keep his eye on . . . well, on a lot of hippie girls. Bob was in no rush to get back to the Grand Theft Auto detail.

Give War a Chance

I eventually read some of the reports Bob filed with the police department. They were made up of "—— is involved in the *Harry* 'scene' primarily as a means of upsetting his parents who are socially prominent," and other such. Today, Bob is an insurance investigator in Baltimore. He's still friends with the old *Harry* staff. And, of the whole bunch of us, I believe there's only one who's far enough to the left to even be called a Democrat.

What I Believe Now

Nothing. Well, nothing much. I mean, I believe things that can be proven by reason and by experiment, and, believe you me, I want to see the logic and the lab equipment. I believe that Western civilization, after some disgusting glitches, has become almost civilized. I believe it is our first duty to protect that civilization. I believe it is our second duty to improve it. I believe it is our third duty to extend it if we can. But let's be careful about that last point. Not everybody is ready to be civilized. I wasn't in 1969.

Is There Anything to Be Gained by Re-Examining All This Nonsense?

I like to think of my behavior in the sixties as a "learning experience." Then again, I like to think of anything stupid I've done as a "learning experience." It makes me feel less stupid. However, I actually did learn one thing in the 1960s (besides how to make a hash pipe out of an empty toilet-paper roll and some aluminum foil). I learned the awful power of make-believe.

There is a deep-seated and frighteningly strong human need to make believe things are different than they are—that salamanders live forever, we all secretly have three legs and there's an enormous conspiracy somewhere which controls our every thought and deed, etc. And it's not just ignorant heathen, trying to brighten their squalid days, who think up such things. Figments of the imagination can be equally persuasive right here in clean, reasonable, education-chocked middle America. People are greedy. Life is never so full it shouldn't be fuller. What more can Shirley MacLaine, for instance, want from existence? She's already been rewarded far beyond her abilities or worth. But nothing will do until she's also been King Tut and Marie of Romania. It was this kind of hoggish appetite for epistemological romance that sent my spoiled and petulant generation on a journey to Oz, a journey from which some of us are only now straggling back, in intellectual tatters.

Many people think fantastical ideas are limited to the likes of harmonic convergences, quartz crystals that ward off cancer or, at worst, harebrained theories about who killed JFK. Unfortunately, this is not the case, especially not in this century. Two of the most fecund areas for cheap fiction are politics and economics. Which brings me to Marxism.

Marxism is a perfect example of the chimeras that fueled the sixties. And it was probably the most potent one. Albeit, much of this Marxism would have been unrecognizable to Marx. It was Marxism watered down, Marxism spiked with LSD and Marxism adulterated with mystical food coloring. But it was Marxism nonetheless because the wildest hippie and the sternest member of the Politburo shared the same daydream, the daydream that underlies all Marxism: *that a thing might somehow be worth other than what people will give for it.* This just is not true. And any system that bases itself on such a will-o'-the-wisp is bound to fail. Communes don't work. Cuba doesn't either.

Now this might not seem like much to have learned. You may think I could have gleaned more from a half dozen years spent ruining chromosomes, morals and any chance of ever getting elected to political office. After all, the hippies are gone and—if current events are any indication—the Communists are going. But there is a part of the world where politico-economic fish stories are still greeted with gape-jawed credulity. It's a part of the world that pretty much includes everybody except us, the Japanese, some Europeans and a few of the most cynical Russians. You can call it the Third World, the Under-developed World or just the Part of the World That's Completely Screwed.

Over the past eight years, working as a foreign correspondent, I've spent a lot of time in the part of the world that's completely screwed. It's always seemed a comfortable and familiar-feeling place to me. The reason is, Third World countries are undergoing national adolescences very similar to the personal adolescence I underwent in the sixties. Woodstock Nation isn't dead; it's just become poor, brown, distant and filled with chaos and starvation.

Marxism has tremendous appeal in the Third World for exactly the same reason it had tremendous appeal to me in college. It gives you something to believe in when what surrounds you seems unbelievable. It gives you someone to blame besides yourself. It's theoretically tidy. And, best of all, it's fully imaginary so it can never be disproved.

The Third World attitude toward the United States is also easy to understand if you think of it in terms of adolescence. The citizens of the Third World are in a teenage muddle about us—full of envy, imitation, anger and blind puppy love. I have been held at gunpoint by a Shi'ite youth in West Beirut who told me in one breath that America was "pig Satan devil" and that he planned to go to dental school in Dearborn as soon as he got his green card. In Ulundi, in Zululand, I talked to a young man who, as usual, blamed apartheid on the United States. However, he had just visited the U.S. with a church group and also told me, "Everything is so wonderful there. The race relations are so good. And everyone is rich." Just what part of America had he visited, I asked. "The South Side of Chicago," he said.

We are a beautiful twenty-year-old woman and they are a wildly infatuated thirteen-year-old boy. They think of us every moment of the day and we take no notice of them whatsoever. If they can't have a chance to love us, a chance to pester us will do—by becoming "Communists," for example. Anything for attention.

Isn't this very like the relationship we "dropouts" of the sixties had to the "straight" society of our parents? Weren't we citizens of our own Underdeveloped World, the world of American teenage pop culture?

So what are we supposed to do about all this? How do we keep the disaffected youth of the West out of mental Disney World? How do we keep the poor denizens of Africa, Asia and Latin America from embracing a myth that will make their lives even worse than they are already? How do we keep everyone from falling under the spell of some even more vile and barbaric phantom such as religious fundamentalism? We have to offer an alternative to nonsense, an alternative that is just as engaging but actually means something.

Maybe we should start by remembering that we already live in a highly idealistic, totally revolutionary society. And that our revolution is based on reality, not buncombe. Furthermore, it works. Look at America, Western Europe and Japan. It works like all hell. We have to remember it was the American Revolution, not the Bolshevik, that set the world on fire. Maybe we should start acting like we believe in that American Revolution again. This means turning our face against not only the Saddams, Qaddafis, Castros and Dengs of the world, but also against most of the U.S. House of Representatives and half the Senate.

The President and his advisors will not have to sit up late working on a speech to fire the public in this cause. There's a perfectly suitable text already in print:

> We hold these truths to be self-evident; that all men are created equal; that they are endowed by their Creator with certain unalienable Rights; that among these are Life, Liberty and the pursuit of Happiness; that to secure these rights, Governments are instituted among Men, deriving their just powers from the consent of the governed. . . .

And that is a much wilder idea than anything which occurred to me during the 1960s.

FIDDLING WHILE
AFRICA STARVES

When the "We Are the World" video first slithered into public view, I was sitting around with a friend who himself happens to be in show business. The thing gave him the willies. Me too. But neither of us could figure exactly why. "Whenever you see people that pleased with themselves on a stage," said my friend, "you know you're in for a bad show." And the USA for Africa performers did have that self-satisfied look of toddlers on a pot. But in this world of behemoth evils, such a minor lapse of taste shouldn't have upset us. We changed the channel.

Half a year later, in the middle of the Live Aid broadcast, my friend called me. "Turn on your television," he said. "This is horrible. They're in a frenzy."

"Well," I said, "at least it's a frenzy of charity."

"Oh, no," he said, "it could be *anything*. Next time it might be 'Kill the Jews.'"

A mob, even an eleemosynary mob, is an ugly thing to see. No good ever came of mass emotion. The audience that's easily moved to tears is as easily moved to sadistic dementia. People are not thinking under such circumstances. And poor, dreadful Africa is something which surely needs thought.

The Band Aid, Live Aid, USA for Africa concerts and records (and videos, posters, T-shirts, lunch buckets, thermos bottles, bath toys, etc.) are supposed to illuminate the plight of the Africans. Note the insights provided by these lyrics:

> *We are the world* [solipsism], *we are the*
>   *children* [average age near forty]
> *We are the ones to make a brighter day* [unproven]
> *So let's start giving* [logical inference
>   supplied without argument]
> *There's a choice we're making* [true as far
>   as it goes]
> *We're saving our own lives* [absurd]
> *It's true we'll make a better day* [see line 2 above]
> *Just you and me* [statistically unlikely]

That's three palpable untruths, two dubious assertions, nine uses of a first-person pronoun, not a single reference to trouble or anybody in it and no facts. The verse contains, literally, neither rhyme nor reason.

And these musical riots of philanthropy address themselves to the wrong problems. There is, of course, a shortage of food among Africans, but that doesn't mean there's a shortage of food *in* Africa. "A huge backlog of emergency grain has built up at the Red Sea port of Assab," says the *Christian Science Monitor*. "Food sits rotting in Ethiopia," reads a headline in the *St. Louis Post-Dispatch*. And according to hunger maven William Shawcross, 200,000 tons of food aid delivered to Ethiopia is being held in storage by the country's government.

There's also, of course, a lack of transport for that food. But that's not the real problem either. The authorities in Addis Ababa have plenty of trucks for their military operations against the Eritrean rebels, and much of the rest of Ethiopia's haulage is being used for forcibly resettling people instead of feeding them. Western governments are reluctant to send more trucks, for fear they'll be used the same way. And similar behavior can be seen in the rest of miserable Africa.

Give War a Chance

The African relief fad serves to distract attention from the real issues. There is famine in Ethiopia, Chad, Sudan and areas of Mozambique. All these countries are involved in pointless civil wars. There are pockets of famine in Mauritania, Niger and Mali—the result of desertification caused mostly by idiot agricultural policies. African famine is not a visitation of fate. It is largely man-made, and the men who made it are largely Africans.

Enormous irrigation projects have been put onto lands that cannot support them and into cultures that cannot use them. Feeble-witted nationalism puts borders in the way of nomadic peoples who used to pick up and move when things got dry. Rural poverty drives populations to African cities where governments keep food prices artificially low, thus increasing rural poverty. Bumbling and corrupt central planning stymies farm production. And the hideous regimes use hunger as a weapon to suppress rebellion. People are not just starving. They are *being* starved.

"Socialist" ideals infest Africa like malaria or dengue fever. African leaders, lost in the frippery of centrist thinking, fail to deal with market forces or any other natural phenomena. Leave it to a Marxist to see the world as the world is not. It's not unusual for African intellectuals to receive their education at such august bodies of learning as Patrice Lumumba U. in Moscow. That is, they are trained by a nation which intentionally starved millions of its citizens in order to collectivize farming.

Death is the result of bad politics. And the Aid concerts are examples of the bad logic that leads to bad politics. It's probably not going too far to say that Africa's problems have been produced by the same kind of dim, ignorant thinking found among American pop artists. "If we take, say, six months and not spend any money on nuclear weapons, and just spend it on food, I think we could make a big dent," says Waylon Jennings in the USA for Africa publicity packet. In fact, a small nuclear weapon placed directly under Haile Mariam Mengistu and his pals would probably make a more beneficial dent than a whole U.S. defense budget worth of canned goods.

Anyway, money is not going to solve the problem. Yet the

concert nonsense is all put strictly in terms of cash. Perhaps it is the only thing the idiot famous understand.

Getting people to give vast amounts of money when there's no firm idea what that money will do is like throwing maidens down a well. It's an appeal to magic. And the results are likely to be as stupid and disappointing as the results of magic usually are.

But, say some, Live Aid sets a good example for today's selfish youth, reminding them to be socially concerned. Nonsense. The circus atmosphere of the Live Aid concerts makes the world's problems seem easy and fun to solve and implies that the solutions are naturally uncontroversial. As an example of charity, Live Aid couldn't be worse. Charity entails sacrifice. Yet the Live Aid performers are sacrificing nothing. Indeed, they're gaining public adulation and a thoroughly unmerited good opinion of themselves. Plus it's free advertising. These LPs, performances and multiform by-products have nothing in common with charity. Instead they levy a sort of regressive alms tax on the befuddled millions. The performers donate their time, which is wholly worthless. Big corporations donate their services, which are worth little enough. Then the poor audience pledges all the contributions and buys all the trash with money it can ill afford. The worst nineteenth-century robber barons wouldn't have had the cheek to put forward such a bunco scheme. They may have given away tainted money, but at least they didn't ask you to give away yours.

One more thing, the music's lousy. If we must save the world with a song, what's the matter with the Metropolitan Opera Company?

Rock and roll's dopey crusade against African hunger has, I posit, added to the stock of human misery. And not just audibly. Any religious person—whether he worships at a pile of gazelle bones or in the Cathedral of St. Paul—will tell you egotism is the source of sin. The lust for power that destroys the benighted Ethiope has the same fountainhead as the lust for fame that propels the lousy pop band. "Not every one that saith unto me, Lord, Lord, shall enter into the kingdom of heaven." Let alone everyone that saith sha la la la la and doobie doobie do.

THE TWO-THOUSAND-YEAR-OLD U.S. MIDDLE EAST POLICY EXPERT

Since we as a nation insist on interfering in the Middle East, it behooves us to do some background reading. One all too appropriate book is *The Jewish War,* written nearly two millennia ago by Flavius Josephus.

Josephus gives a contemporary account of the great Jewish rebellion against Rome. The insurrection began in 66 A.D. and lasted seven years. The Middle East described by Josephus is perfectly familiar—a politically fractionalized land populated with a jumble of ethnic and religious groups. There are Jews, Arabs, Egyptians, Syrians, Greeks, Italians, and (presumably) a smattering of Christians. Each detests the others. Extreme political and theological views prevail. Terrorism and assassination are commonplace. Alliances are momentary. Grudges, perennial. And neither colonial subjugation nor local autonomy suffices to keep the peace.

The political events are familiar, too. Rome first intervened in the region as a peace-keeper, brokering a dispute between Seleucid Mesopotamia and Ptolemaic Egypt. Later the Middle East appeared vital to Rome because Roman trade routes passed through the region and because of the Parthian threat to the empire's eastern frontier. The Romans were lured into deeper military and political involvement, and this triggered continual insurrections.

The rebellion of 66 A.D., however, did not begin as a war of national liberation. It began as communal rioting in the seaport town of Caesarea—Greeks versus Jews over an empty lot next to a synagogue. This inspired sympathetic rioting in Jerusalem, and a ham-fisted Roman attempt to quell the disturbances worsened them instead. The result was one of those great wallows of siege, massacre, treachery, persecution, revenge, plunder, and self-destruction to which the Middle East is so often host.

Before the revolt was fairly under way, quarreling had broken out between radical and moderate factions in Jerusalem. Meanwhile, local government troops withdrew from the fray, leaving a greatly outnumbered Roman garrison trapped in the Palace of Herod. The Romans surrendered to the mob on a guarantee of safe conduct—and were murdered as soon as they laid down their weapons.

The rising in Jerusalem set off a reaction among the non-Jewish inhabitants of the region, who indulged themselves in wild pogroms, with killings taking place as far away as Damascus and Alexandria.

Roman military forces were not sufficient to quash the rebellion. Jewish forces were not sufficient to defeat the Romans in open combat. Guerrilla warfare ensued, with predictable consequences to the populace.

The Romans were notable for vigorous foreign-policy responses. The Emperor Nero sent Vespasian and three legions to pacify Judea.

Using a great deal of slaughter and some tactics, Vespasian drove the rebels back to the environs of Jerusalem. He was prevented from ending the war, however, by political confusion at home. Nero was ousted and three worthless and short-lived emperors followed within the year.

The Jews made use of this breathing space by engaging in urban warfare with themselves and by committing all conceivable and some inconceivable atrocities upon their coreligionists.

Vespasian himself was finally proclaimed emperor by the Roman army, and the war was resumed under the direction of his son Titus.

Give War a Chance

After a prolonged and disgusting siege, Jerusalem was taken. And after another prolonged and even more disgusting siege, Masada, the last rebel stronghold, fell.

The Temple was destroyed, the Jewish upper classes were dispersed, and a Roman army was permanently stationed in Judea. Even then the peace did not hold, and rebellion would break out anew in the reign of Hadrian.

Normally the patterns of history are reassuring. To hear of tsarist Russia pressing for warm-water ports or eighteenth-century England fighting hegemony on the continent or Ming China clashing with Japan over the fate of Korea is to feel a continuity, a comprehensibility, in human affairs. But in *The Jewish War* the shock of recognition is just a shock. Here, sixty generations ago, is nearly the same cast of characters engaged in exactly the same obsessive, vicious, and fatal behavior for the same terrifying reasons on the same cursed, reeking, ugly chunk of land.

Who fails to learn history is doomed to repeat it. But we seemed doomed to repeat this history anyway. And what can we possibly learn from hearing that the man who was to become the most temperate and decent of Roman emperors entered the rebellious city of Gabara and "put to the sword all but small children . . . showing mercy to neither young nor old through hatred of the nation . . ."? What can we learn by reading how the partisans in besieged Jerusalem tortured the plump in order to find hidden stores of food? And what can we learn from the defenders of Masada, who murdered their wives and children and chose suicide over a final battle so the Romans would be "dumbfounded by our death and awed by our courage"?

Yet *The Jewish War* fascinates. We are spellbound by the ineluctability of events. This is history taking the tragic form exactly as described by Aristotle in *Poetics*: ". . . with incidents arousing pity and terror, wherewith to accomplish its catharsis of such emotions."

And there is an even more compelling aspect to the book in the narrator himself. Josephus must be the most unabashedly contemptible character ever to have left an accurate self-portrait in print.

Born Joseph ben Matthais, scion of a well-connected Jewish family, he played an important role in the rebellion from its beginning. He was appointed general of the rebel armies in Galilee, making no protest though he claims he "saw the inevitable end awaiting the Jews, and knew that their one safety lay in a change of heart." He goes on to say, "He himself, he felt sure, would be pardoned if he went over to the Romans."

During the first year of the war Josephus was surrounded by Vespasian's forces in the hill town of Jotapata. Josephus tried to sneak away, but the townsfolk prevented him. Jotapata was stormed, and when the defenses collapsed Josephus took a few remaining soldiers and hid in a cave. After a while he suggested that he surrender himself. His men threatened to kill him if he tried. He then suggested suicide with everyone drawing lots and killing each other in turn. Josephus manipulated the lottery, left himself as the last to die, and surrendered anyway.

He gained favor with his captor by making a shrewd and flattering prophecy that Vespasian would be emperor. When this indeed happened, Josephus was freed with honors. He became an active, if timid, member of Titus's staff. (At one point Titus tried to send Josephus to parlay with a group of wavering rebels. "But Josephus refused to go himself, since the petitioners meant no good. . . .")

During the siege of Jerusalem, "Josephus circled the wall, striving to keep out of range but within hearing. . . ." He yelled Roman propaganda at the battlements that were protecting, among other things, Josephus's wife and mother. " 'It might well be reasonable,' " he quotes himself as hollering, " 'to disdain meaner masters, but not the lords of the whole world. What corner of earth has escaped the Romans, unless heat or cold made it of no value to them? From every side fortune has passed on to them, and God, who handed domination over from nation to nation around the world, abode now in

Italy.' " That can hardly have been an effective tack. And the message was, Josephus admits, "received by the defenders with howls of derision or execration, sometimes with showers of stones."

These and many other treasons, peculations, and self-seekings Josephus recounts with enthusiasm. He is broad-minded in his shamelessness. He lards every description of Rome and Romans with fawning praise. Then he extols the rebels for their courage and claims himself to be a champion of the Jews. It's worth noting that after the war he retired to an apartment in the Imperial Palace and spent the rest of his life writing best-sellers about his experiences.

Reason dictates we should hate this man. But it's hard to get angry at Josephus. What, after all, did he do? A few soldiers were tricked into suicide. Some demoralizing claptrap was shouted at a beleaguered army. A wife was distressed. (She survived, incidently, and Josephus divorced her for a Roman heiress.) And sundry other crimes were committed, all of which pale by comparison to what the good men did. For it was the loyal, the idealistic and the brave who did the real damage. The devout and patriotic leaders of Jerusalem sacrificed tens of thousands of lives to the cause of freedom. Vespasian and Titus sacrificed tens of thousands more to the cause of civil order. Even Agrippa II, the Roman client king of Judea who did all he could to prevent the war, ended by supervising the destruction of half a dozen of his cities and the sale of their inhabitants into slavery. How much better for everyone if all the principal figures of the region had been slithering filth like Josephus.

The Jewish War is a moral oxymoron. It doesn't help us understand the Middle East or know what to do there. But it does lend a fullness and a depth to our incomprehension. And it provides us with a vast crowd of historical company in our impotence and confusion.

STUDYING FOR
OUR DRUG TEST

Commercial airline pilots smoke marijuana in the cockpit all the time. They giggle and get silly and make P.A. announcements like, "If you look out the left side you'll see a big wing." Then they gobble up the tourist-class desserts and collide with Piper Cubs. All the high school seniors in America are hooked on crack. They run through band practice tearing the uniforms off majorettes with their teeth. After school they mug their moms and drive the nation's violent crime rate through the roof. Many U.S. submarine captains take PCP, which is why they go into murderous frenzies, release Polaris missiles and start accidental atomic wars so often.

This is the impression I get from newspapers, magazines and the network news. President Reagan and his missis must have gotten the same impression. They went on television together in September 1986, looking worried and a bit peeved. "Drugs are menacing our society," said the President. "They're threatening our values and undercutting our institutions. They're killing our children."

"Drugs take away the dream from every child's heart and replace it with a nightmare," said the First Lady, and she pointed out that "drug criminals are ingenious. They work every day at plotting ways to take our children away from us."

But, said the President, "people who are terrorizing America will find themselves facing the greatest force for good in the world." Then he invoked God, country and U.S. war dead and promised us all drug-free schools and workplaces. Because, you see, there is a solution to the American drug catastrophe, and the President announced it the very next day—drug tests.

On Monday, September 15, 1986, President Reagan signed an executive order requiring drug tests for all U.S. government employees in "sensitive" positions. This includes federal law-enforcement officers, presidential appointees and people who handle classified information. It also includes everyone whose job is related to national security or public health and the safety or protection of life and property plus anyone in a position requiring a "high degree of trust and confidence." Broadly speaking, it means the janitor at the Yosemite National Park comfort station and all the rest of the federal government's 2.8 million civilian employees. Many state and municipal workers can expect to be tested, too. And over twenty-five percent of U.S. corporations already have employee drug-test programs, with more to come. Soon everyone will be tested for drugs except Mother Teresa (and we can catch her at Customs and Immigration).

What a good idea. Poof! The national cancer of drug abuse will disappear faster than the family farm. All we have to do is whizz in a dish, tinkle in a cup, take a leak in a test tube and generally piddle ourselves dry, and we will never have any accidental atomic wars started by narco-crazed sub commanders again.

Of course, we don't have any accidental atomic wars started by narco-crazed sub commanders now. But never mind, lots of other horrible stuff is caused by drugs. Drugs are tearing our society apart and destroying everything we hold dear. Aren't they? If drugs weren't causing monstrous and terrifying calamities there wouldn't be all this prate and gabble in the media. Would there? I called the Federal Aviation Administration's Office of Aviation Safety and put it to them square. "How many fatal accidents on major airlines have involved drug use by flight crews, air-traffic controllers or other responsible personnel?" I asked FAA spokesman Fred Farrar.

"None."

"That's it," I said. "Just 'none'?"

"Yes," said Farrar. "The answer is none."

I called the FBI and asked for statistics from their *United States Uniform Crime Reports*. It turns out the nation's violent crime rate is not through the roof. There was a slight rise, 3.1%, from 1984 to 1985. But, overall, violent crime has dropped 6.4% in the past five years, the first sustained decrease since the Second World War.*

Then I called the Public Health Service's Institute on Drug Abuse. They had just completed a major survey on illegal drugs. "Is drug use up?" I asked.

"It's basically stable," said Press Officer Lucy Walker with, I think, a hint of regret in her voice. According to the figures Ms. Walker gave me, 22% of young people ages eighteen to twenty-five use marijuana, down from 27% in 1982. Cocaine use is up from 7% to 8% in the same period. And hallucinogens are holding steady at 2%. Among the general population, the trends are about the same. If drugs are tearing our society apart and destroying everything we hold dear, they are taking their time about it.

Now, nobody wants to be quoted as saying drugs are cute or a swell thing to give babies. Drugs are bad. Anybody who's watched *1941* on a videocassette knows this. Drugs have caused a lot of people to do a lot of stupid things, such as hock their kid's Apple II, recite Rod McKuen poetry and stab Nancy Spungen. And drugs have given several of my friends one-way backstage passes to the hereafter. But let's get this thing in perspective. In 1986, 563 people died from cocaine overdoses, 3,170 expired from gallstones, and more than 43,000 kicked just tooling around on the highway. Drugs are a problem. We shouldn't stop worrying about the problem. But maybe we should start worrying about the solution.

Drug tests are justifiable in certain circumstances. As part of a drug-rehabilitation program, for example, they make very good sense. And DEA agents should take drug tests. People who've been set

---

*Here the author spoke too soon. Violent crime is through the roof after all. But it's hard to see how drug testing would fix that. It's very difficult to get a urine sample from a crack-addled teenager when he's in the middle of shooting a 7-Eleven clerk.

to guard the henhouse shouldn't develop a taste for chicken. We the general public have a right, as helpless cowards, to ask that drug tests be given to those who hold our lives in their hands. Marine Corps drill instructors, IRS auditors and U.S. Presidents should all be given drug tests if we think they're acting loopy. Most IRS auditors do act loopy, and all recent Presidents have.

But the current fad for wide-scale drug tests doesn't have much to do with justifiable circumstances. Note that the drug test hubbub began with testing professional athletes. We don't depend on these guys for anything except covering the Superbowl point spread, and there's some doubt about whether they do that better with or without drugs. True, children look up to professional athletes. But children are short and look up to everything.

Also note that there's one drug nobody's saying much about. This is the big drug—tonsil polish, idiot oil, vitamin XXX. When it comes to getting sideways we are not a buzzed nation. We are not a zoned nation. We are Drunk Country. An estimated 14 million Americans are alcoholics or problem drinkers, me for one. Alcoholism costs us around $116 billion a year in lost work, medical expenses, car wrecks and removal of stubborn carpet stains. Booze is responsible for something like 95,000 deaths per annum and who knows how many dumb marriages.

There are simple, cheap and accurate tests for alcohol use. However, nearly half of American adults drink, and that's a lot of voters. So alcohol testing is done sparingly, with probable cause, under highly justifiable circumstances—usually when you're on your way home from a toga party. Nobody is trying to make alcohol tests a regular feature of work or school, let alone government employment. How many congressmen would care to be tested after 6:00 P.M.? A bird can't fly on one wing. A cat can't walk on three legs. Freshen that up for you, Senator?

Anyway, no drug, not even alcohol, causes the fundamental ills of society. If we're looking for the source of our troubles, we shouldn't test people for drugs, we should test them for stupidity, ignorance, greed and love of power. And we have these tests, too. But

I.Q. scores are kept strictly secret. Releasing I.Q. scores would cause Congress more embarrassment than a boxcar of Breathalyzers. And no one is ever sent to Daytop Center because he flunked civics. P.E. is substituted instead. And, if you get a positive result on life's tests for greed and power lust, you don't lose your job, you get rich and elected.

So it's much better to test for drugs. What the hell, they're illegal, so all we're going to catch is criminals anyway. And drugs make a great patsy. Why blame crime and poverty on something complicated and difficult to fix like the disintegration of family structure or Phil Donahue? Blame them on drugs.

Actually, using drugs as a scapegoat shows we're making social progress. It's a big improvement over "The Freemasons are poisoning the wells." But the logic is just as bad. And this bad logic is probably inescapable. Drugs are just too good as a political issue. Drug abuse is one of those home-and-mother oratorical points that let politicians bray without fear of offending any powerful lobbying groups, unless they're running for President of Colombia. Nobody except Timothy Leary and me at about four in the morning is going to say a word in defense of illegal drugs.

And drug tests are an ideal way to use the drug issue. Widespread drug tests make it look like our national leaders are "doing something about the problem." To be "doing something about the problem" is a fundamental American trait and by and large a good one. But, in our love of problem-solving, we sometimes forget to ask what the problem is or even whether it's a problem. And once we start doing something, we often lose sight of whether that something is the thing to do. I give you Vietnam, just for instance.

Drug abuse *is* a problem. But the real solutions—education, rehabilitation and medical research—are difficult, complex and uncertain of success. In other words, the real solutions are like reality itself. And reality has never been anything politicians could stand much of. Besides, some of the solutions to the drug problem are politically suicidal. One of the most terrible proven side effects of illegal drug use is jail. Jail will screw up your life worse than a whole

Glad bag full of daffy dust. But with drug hysteria in the air, no politico is going to advocate legalization of even the lamest grade of Oaxacan ditch weed. And drug education, to be effective, would be controversial, too. It would have to speak the truth. We can't tell monsters-under-the-bed stories if we want children to believe us about dope. We can't tell them that they'll turn into hydrocephalic unwed welfare mothers if they get downwind from one whiff of crack. Children are dumb enough to try drugs, but they aren't dumb enough to listen to this.

Drug tests are no solution whatsoever. They're just a method of avoiding the problem, and not a harmless method either. Drug tests are inaccurate. The Federal Center for Disease Control studied thirteen drug-testing laboratories from 1972 to 1981. They found that only one out of eleven of these laboratories could test accurately for cocaine. And the Center for Disease Control considered eighty percent accuracy acceptable. Common urine-analysis tests for marijuana can show false-positive results from painkillers such as Advil and Nuprin. Contac will trigger false positives for amphetamines. And tonic water can make it look like you're shooting smack. Even the most sophisticated gas-chromatography and mass-spectrometry tests are only accurate in the ninety-five percent range. This means one out of twenty people tested could end up driving a school bus on LSD or going to jail because he sipped a G&T last week.

A person who got a false-positive result on a drug test and held one of those ill-defined "sensitive" jobs would face . . . I hardly have the stomach to write about it. At best he would, like Hamilton Jordan in the Carter administration, emerge from a bureaucratic tag-team match and ugly court fight with his reputation indelibly smeared. No doubt some government agency will be established to prevent such miscarriages of justice. Government agencies being what they are, this should make things much worse.

And drug tests are expensive. The most accurate kind cost $100 each, which gives new meaning to the words "piddling sum." Between $200 and $300 million a year is already being spent on drug testing. The military alone spent $47.6 million last year. And the *New*

P. J. O'Rourke

York Times estimates that if annual drug tests were to be given to the whole work force, the cost would be several billion dollars. Surely there is something that we need several billion dollars worth of more than we need several billion dollars worth of falsely accused citizens and scot-free hopheads.

But even if drug tests were free and one-hundred percent accurate they would still be unconstitutional. There is going to be a lot of legal rhubarb over this. And I don't know what the Supreme Court is finally going to decide. But I take the same attitude toward the Constitution that Reformation Protestants took toward the Bible: anyone can read it and witness the truth thereof. Amendment 4 is perfectly straightforward:

> The right of the people to be secure in their persons, houses, papers, and effects, against unreasonable searches and seizures, shall not be violated, and no warrants shall issue, but upon probable cause, supported by an oath or affirmation, and particularly describing the place to be searched, and the persons or things to be seized.

It's hard to see how scattershot drug testing could be legal under the Fourth Amendment, no matter how particularly the government describes the way you take a leak.

And the Fifth Amendment is also clear: "No person . . . shall be compelled in any criminal case to be a witness against himself." If using the contents of your bladder isn't making you a witness against yourself, then I suggest that crapping on a Supreme Court justice isn't assault and battery.

Furthermore, the president of Beth Israel hospital in New York has been quoted as saying that during drug tests, someone "must watch each person urinate into a bottle. If that is not done, it's a sham." I haven't gone through the Constitution with a fine comb, but I'm sure our Founding Fathers wouldn't have let this nation get off the ground without putting something in there about the natural rights of man to go to the bathroom alone.

Give War a Chance

Drug tests are illegal, expensive, inaccurate and stupid, and those are their comforting aspects. More frightening is what widespread drug tests would do to our country. They would create a national atmosphere of distrust, resentment and demoralization. We all remember how we felt when dad sniffed our breath for beer after we came home on Saturday night. We all remember how we acted when mom went through our dresser drawers looking for cigarettes. And we remember what we wanted to do when our parents peeked through the rec-room door to see if we'd arrived at second base with our dates. Does any country in its right mind want an entire population feeling this way about its government? We will have a nationwide outbreak of adolescent tantrums, sulks and screaming matches, but it will be the Mom-and-Pop elected officials who may find themselves grounded without TV forever.

And it will be worse if the nation doesn't blow up. We will have allowed the government to make an unprecedented and probably irreversible intrusion into our private lives. This is the first step toward totalitarianism. Of course it won't be the bread-line and barbed-wire totalitarianism the North Koreans have. It will be an all-American, clean-cut, safety-first, goody-two-shoes totalitarianism where everybody takes care of his health, keeps his lawn nice and never ever does anything naughty or dirty or fun. And there won't be any troublesome, offbeat creative people left to screw it up either. Try giving drug tests to the great men of arts and letters. There goes Coleridge, Poe, Freud, William James, Rimbaud, Aldous Huxley, and the whole cast of *National Lampoon's Animal House*.

I can think of only one good thing about drug tests. All important government officials will have to take them, and we get to watch. We get to stand and stare while the powers that be go potty. This is a democracy and we're all equal before the law. If they don't trust us, why should we trust them? I think this will be a salutary experience. The high and the mighty will be humbled in the public eye, always a good thing. And—when it comes to certain members of Congress and the administration—we the people will have it confirmed once and for all that they are lacking two specific bits of anatomy.

AN ARGUMENT IN FAVOR OF AUTOMOBILES VS. PEDESTRIANS

We often hear automobiles criticized. Safety experts say they are dangerous. Ecologists tell us they pollute the air. Economists claim cars are responsible for U.S. trade deficits and high energy costs. Social scientists blame them for the deterioration of our inner cities. And aesthetes damn them for roadside blight. But even if all these accusations are true, the automobile is still an improvement on its principal alternative, the pedestrian.

Pedestrians are easily damaged. Try this test: Hit a pedestrian with a car. Now have the pedestrian hit the car back. Then roll a pedestrian and a car through four inches of slush and road salt at sixty miles an hour. Take a coin-operated spray gun and hose off their undersides. Which is in better shape? Also, most automobiles have 5 MPH bumpers. But a pedestrian cannot be run into a wall at even 3 MPH (approximate walking speed) without getting a bloody nose. And pedestrians are notoriously expensive to repair.

Automobiles are cleaner than pedestrians. Even diesel exhaust smells better than a dirty human. Pedestrians wiggle and squeal when you try to scrub them, and they are hard to wax. A dented and rusty automobile is still more attractive than the average pedestrian. Strip a car of its paint. Strip a person of his clothes. Which looks worse in broad daylight?

Cars last a hundred thousand miles or so. Just try to take anybody that far on foot.

Pedestrians are slow, require complex maintenance procedures and have bewildering fuel requirements.

There are no quality-control or safety standards for pedestrians. And if the anti-abortion lobby gets its way, we won't even be able to recall them.

Most of the time you can predict what an automobile will do. And if you lose control of an automobile you can jump out of it. But pedestrians are completely unpredictable. And when you're a pedestrian it's difficult to jump out of yourself.

Not only are automobiles better than people in most respects but people behave better when they are in automobiles than they do when they are on foot. A great big crowd of people in automobiles is a traffic jam. It's unpleasant, yes—horns honk, tempers flare, etc. But a great big crowd of people *out* of automobiles is a mob. And that's worse. No traffic jam ever stormed the Winter Palace, cheered a lynching or voted Adolf Hitler into power.

Most good things can be experienced in a car—eating, sleeping, sex, listening to Handel's *Water Music*. But the experience of evil is severely limited. Think how much less evil Central America would have experienced if, for example, all the Sandinistas had been in cars. They would have been stuck in the jungle, axle-deep in mud, and would never have been able to enslave peasants, kill contras or get any Russian weapons into El Salvador.

It's hard for people to mug you from inside an automobile, and virtually impossible for them to rob your apartment without getting out of the car.

People on foot are more likely not only to steal, but to litter. The normal business suit has no convenient place, such as the backseat floor, to toss candy wrappers, old newspapers and empty beer cans.

When people are in a car driving down the road it's hard to hear them lie, complain, argue and spread malicious gossip—especially if you're in your own car headed the other way.

Consider how much better the United Nations Assembly would

be if all the delegates were speeding around the Assembly floor in old junkers having a figure-eight race and smashing into each other. It would be more interesting for everybody, and the intellectual quality of debate would be greatly improved. The same goes double for Congress.

True, some trouble, such as drive-by shootings and fatal crashes, can be caused in an automobile. But often it's just a pedestrian who gets killed. And though drunk drivers are a menace, drunk parents are a worse one. They do more damage to society stumbling around the house than anybody ever did in a head-on collision.

All children should be given a car as soon as they are old enough to wash it and vacuum the seats. Owning and caring for an automobile builds good citizenship. Children can learn a great deal by watching their automobile and following its example. Automobiles are democratic. A Plymouth Belvedere is more than a match for a Lamborghini in a six-car pile-up. Automobiles are egalitarian, as anybody who's ever drag raced a Bentley in an old Mustang knows.

Automobiles are strangers to sexism. You can't possibly say that a car's place is in the kitchen. And there's never been any such thing as distaff automobiles that couldn't vote or Chinese wire-wheel binding.

Automobiles have no unfortunate allegorical connotations. A man on horseback is a symbol of authoritarianism. But a man on a car roof is just silly.

There are no religious controversies among automobiles. Automobiles belong to no race and have no political opinions (though a Trabant, if it could, would probably wish it had been designed by somebody other than a drunk Communist).

Automobiles are free of egotism, passion, prejudice and stupid ideas about where to have dinner. They are, literally, selfless. A world designed for automobiles instead of people would have wider streets, larger dining rooms, fewer stairs to climb and no smelly, dangerous subway stations.

Indeed, we would lead better lives and be a wiser nation if we placed the automobile, instead of our own ambition and greed, at the center of our society. This should be taken into consideration the next time we amend our Constitution:

Article I

Congress shall make no law respecting the establishment of a boring old 55 MPH speed limit; or prohibiting the free exercise of performance cars on empty winding roads; or abridging the freedom to cruise around aimlessly; or the right of the people to remove those annoying voice boxes that tell you to buckle your seat belt.

Article II

Contented Yahoos being necessary for the amusement of a free state, the right of Texans (and people who act like Texans) to drive around with guns in the gunracks of their pick-up trucks and shoot varmints and critters out the window shall not be infringed.

Article III

No driver's education student or School Safety Patrol member shall, in time of peace, be quartered in any house if he won't shovel the driveway.

Article IV

The right of the people to be secure in their cars, trucks, vans and RVs against unreasonable nosiness shall not be violated, and no policemen with flashlights or irate parents shall come poking around country lanes or scenic overlooks while couples are parked and necking.

Article V

Excessive bail shall not be required, nor excessive fines imposed, nor cruel and unusual wisecracks by local traffic cops made just because somebody forgot to get their car inspected or was going 38 in a 35 MPH zone.

And so on. It would give us a federal charter that really has something to do with our day-to-day lives. And it would keep our legislators and Supreme Court busy with important things instead of school prayer and covert CIA antics. Plus—and this is very important—parking would be an unalienable right.

A CALL FOR A

NEW McCARTHYISM

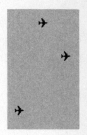

NOTES TOWARD
A BLACKLIST FOR
THE 1990s

Our era is supposed to be the 1950s all over again. Indeed, we are experiencing anew many of the pleasures and benefits of that excellent decade: a salubrious prudery, a sensible avariciousness, a healthy dose of social conformity, a much-needed narrowing of minds and a return to commonsense American political troglodytism. But there's one delightful and entertaining feature of the Eisenhower years which is wholly absent from the contemporary scene—old-fashioned red-baiting. Where's our McCarthyism? Who's our Tailgunner Joe? Why don't we get to look for Communists under our beds or—considering the social changes of the past thirty-five years—*in* them? ("Good night, honey, and are you now or have you ever been a member of the Committee in Solidarity with the People of El Salvador?")

God knows the problem is not a lack of Commies. There are more fuzzy-minded one-worlders, pasty-faced peace creeps and bleeding-heart bedwetters in America now than there ever were in 1954. The redskis have infiltrated the all-important exercise-video industry, not to mention movies and TV. Academia, too, is a veritable compost heap of Bolshie brain mulch. Beardo the Weirdo may have been laughed out of real life during the 1970s, but he found a home in our nation's colleges, where he whiles away the wait for Woodstock Nation II by pestering undergraduates with cultural diversity and collectivist twaddle when they should be thinking about better car stereos. And fellow travelers in the State Department? Jeeze, the situation is so bad at Foggy Bottom that we'd better *hope* it's caused by spies. If it's stupidity, we're really in trouble.

So how come the HUAC staff isn't returning my phone calls? Who's keeping "I Led Three Lives" from being remade starring Tom Selleck and Arnold Schwarzenegger? And why aren't we making sure that that Fidel-snuggler Ron Dellums never works again? Whoops, we already did that. We elected him to Congress. And, come to think of it, there are other problems with an up-to-date nineties-style witch hunt. For one thing, it's no use going after real, card-carrying Communists any more. Hard-core Party apparatchiks are already being persecuted by organizations more brutally efficient than anything we've got in the U.S., organizations such as the Union of Soviet Socialist Republics. Plus accusing somebody of being a "comsymp" just isn't the same since Gorbachev began his three-hankie *perestroika* performance. Even Margaret Thatcher said she sympathized with Ole Splotch-Top. And when it comes to the International Communist Conspiracy to Enslave Europe, Asia and the Third World— well, somebody's got to do *something* with those people. Good luck to the Patrice Lumumba University Class of '89.

No, a modern McCarthyism is going to have to concentrate on other things besides the Big Lie and the Red Menace. In fact, if we examine even a brief selection of people who should be tarred and feathered and run out of town on a rail (or, to be more contemporary, oat-branned and goose-downed and jogged out of the condominium complex on an exercise track), we see that they are not necessarily Marxist or even socialist in their thinking because that would presuppose thinking in the first place. Nobody is ever going to accuse us of being *thought* police for going after the likes of Kris Kristofferson, Phil Donahue, Marlo Thomas, Dr. Benjamin Spock, Yoko Ono, Dave Dellinger, Ben & Jerry's ice cream, the World Council of Churches, Ed Asner, Michelle Shocked, Lenora Fulani, Robert Redford and people who think quartz crystals cure herpes.

The distinguishing feature of this cluster of dunces is not subversion but silliness. If we hope to wreck careers, destroy reputations and drive holistic Ortega fans into exile in Sausalito and Amherst, Massachusetts, we're going to need tactics very different from those used by Roy Cohn, Bobby Kennedy and the distinguished senator from the great state famous for its La Follette and cheese. A traditional "black list" will never work. Put some *sandalista* on your black list and you probably guarantee him a MacArthur genius grant and a seat on the ACLU national board of directors. But maybe we can tear a page from the *Très Riches Heures* of Tipper Gore and insist upon a rating system for music, film, television and the *Boston Globe* editorial page. A warning would have to be prominently displayed: "OH-OH, A PERSON INVOLVED WITH THIS UNAPPEALING ITEM OF MASS COMMUNICATION HOLDS SILLY OPINIONS ON MATTERS ABOUT WHICH HE OR SHE IS LARGELY OR ABYSMALLY UNINFORMED." There'd be three ratings:

> S = Silly
> VS = Very Silly
> SML = Shirley MacLaine

Thus a rerun of "M*A*S*H" featuring Alan Alda would get an "S" rating. Any public pronouncement by a member of the innumerable Phoenix family, such as River, Leaf, Summer, Stump, Ditch or Pond Scum Phoenix, would get a "VS" rating. And the next Tracy Chapman album will get an "SML" with oak-leaf cluster.

No, this isn't going to work either. You can't shame or humiliate modern celebrities. What used to be called shame and humiliation is now called publicity. And forget traditional character assassination. If you say a modern celebrity is an adulterer, a pervert and a drug addict, all it means is that you've read his autobiography.

We have to come up with more clever ways to ruin these people. Perhaps we can spread rumors that they performed in South Africa before Nelson Mandela was released. I was in South Africa myself a few years ago, and I'm almost certain that was Sinéad O'Connor singing back-up for Frank Sinatra at Sun City. Or perhaps we can direct the wrath of the remarkably terrifying animal-rights activists against them. I'm going to write a letter to People for the Ethical Treatment of Animals about how Susan Sontag allows her intellectual ideas to be tried on innocent laboratory rabbits before humans are exposed to them. (As for the animal-rights activists, we can turn the animals loose on them later.)

But the worst punishment for dupes, pink-wieners and dialectical immaterialists might be a kind of reverse black list. We don't prevent them from writing, speaking, performing and otherwise being their usual nuisance selves. Instead, we hang on their every word, beg them to work, drag them onto all available TV and radio chat shows and write hundreds of fawning newspaper and magazine articles about their wonderful swellness. In other words, we subject them to the monstrous, gross and irreversible late-twentieth-century phenomenon of Media Overexposure so that a surfeited public rebels in disgust. This is the Burt Reynolds/Loni Anderson treatment, and for condemning people to obscurity, it beats the Smith Act hollow.

Anyway, I'm sure we'll find some way to chastise these buggers of sense, to bully, torment, harry them and generally make a workers' paradise of their lives. In the meantime, the fun part of McCarthyism is, as it always was, *writing out the enemies list.* * Heh-heh:

Sting
Gore Vidal
The Institute for Policy Studies
Tom Hayden (Hope you didn't give Jane your ideals in the divorce settlement, Tom.)
Victor Navasky
Angela Davis
William Sloane Coffin
Noam Chomsky
Abbie Hoffman (I guess we can cross him off; he was on God's list.)

*What follows was compiled in 1989 and is thus in dire need of amendment. Readers may use the endpapers and the inside of the dust cover.

Ralph Nader
Anthony Lewis
William "The Client Is Obviously Guilty" Kunstler
Jackson Browne
Allen Ginsberg
Norman Lear
Meryl Streep
Peter, Paul and Mary (Yes, they're still alive.)
The Christic Institute
Common Cause
Center for Constitutional Rights
Anybody whose last name is Cockburn
Anybody who inherited so much money and so little sense that
  her last name might become Cockburn
Cockburn wannabe Christopher Hitchens (Christ, who's check-
  ing the green cards around here?)
The Order of Maryknoll Nuns
Amy Carter
Susan Sarandon
The Redgrave family
Patty Duke
Casey Kasem
Daniel and Philip Berrigan (Yes, *they're* still alive.)
Jesse Jackson
The New York Review of Books
The New York Times Book Review
That poor man's Walt Kelly, Garry Trudeau
That poor man's Garry Trudeau, Berke Breathed
The Sandinista's Oliphant, Paul Conrad
The National Resources Defense Council
Lawyers Guild
The D.C. Statehood Party
Mayor of Burlington, Vermont, Peter Clavelle
The Berkeley City Council
Berkeley

Mother Jones
The Nation
The Village Voice
Any organization with "Peace" in its name
The English Department at Duke
The Law School at Harvard
The Liberal Arts faculty at Stanford
Any educator using the term "Eurocentric" (While we're at it, let's reintroduce corporal punishment in the schools—and apply it to the teachers.)
Salman Rushdie (Kick 'em when they're down is what I say.)
Martin Sheen
Charlie Sheen
The rest of the Sheen family plus Rob Lowe, Judd Nelson, Demi Moore, Molly Ringwald and all the other Brat Pack members (Which brings to mind another idea for a modified black list—this list would *require* left-wingers to write movie scripts, but only for Brat Pack movies.)

And let's not forget that most subversive of all organizations in America, the American government:

Senator Tom Harkin, D., IA
Senator Ted Kennedy, D., MA
Senator John Kerry, D., MA
Senator Chris Dodd, D., CT
Representative Pete Stark, D., CA
Representative Barbara Boxer, D., CA
Representative Ed Markey, D., MA
Representative Gerry Studds, D., MA
Representative Gus Savage, D., IL
Representative Barbara Mikulski, D., MD

And from Michigan—an improbable place to find a nest of Jacobin nogoodniks—these Not-the-Reagan-Democrats:

Representative George Crockett
Representative David Bonior
Representative John Conyers

And that's just a beginning. Let's make this a blood bath—well, a phlegm-and-bile bath anyway. Maybe we can reconquer our body politic. Maybe we can sweep the ideologically homeless from the streets of our Shining City on a Hill. Or maybe we can't. It might all backfire the way the splendid fifties backfired and led to the wretched and unspeakable sixties. Still, it's worth a try. At the very least "Red Scare—The Sequel" will rile the lefties and get them out demonstrating again so policemen can hit them on the head. The police have been having a rough time in recent years, what with crack and Miranda rights. They need some fun. And one other great good will have been accomplished. We will have found a job for J. Danforth Quayle. He's the perfect point man for Nouvelle McCarthyism, a Senator Joe Lite if ever there was one. Besides, I'm sure he'd much rather have a reputation for evil than the reputation he's got now.

SEX WITH
DR. RUTH

It's question-and-answer period at Central Connecticut State University, where Dr. Ruth Westheimer is giving a lecture to eighteen hundred students in a packed auditorium and I am dying of boredom in the audience.

A boy in the front row stands up. He's blushing hideously and surrounded by a half dozen seated, snickering pals. Maybe he's a fraternity pledge, or maybe he's just one of those kids who can be talked into anything. His friends have gotten him to ask a question about the most embarrassing sex act they can think of. A serious question, mind you, but embarrassing. He asks it.

". . . and, anyway," finishes the stammering youth, "why do some girls like that and some girls *hate* it?"

Dr. Westheimer is whatever the complete opposite of embarrassed is called, "antichagrined," perhaps, or "hyperconcerted." She doesn't, however, answer his question. She deflects it into one of her miniature homilies. Maybe it's "Most People Want to Have One Significant Other" or "The Need for a Sexually Literate Society" or "Don't Stint on Foreplay, Be Inventive!" There are dozens of these— obvious, pat and nearly irrefutable. And they are repeated endlessly, apropos anything.

More questions follow.

Student: "What about bondage?"

Dr. Westheimer: "Anything that pleases two consenting adults and doesn't hurt anybody is fine."

Student: "What's the most sexually stimulating thing you can do to a woman?"

Dr. Westheimer: "Love her."

Student: "Is the sponge a good method of birth control?"

I ask a question of my own. I tap the kid in front of me and ask, "Why are all these people here?" He says, "Everybody has boyfriend or girlfriend problems, or thinks they do." Or thinks they do?

Student: "What exercises can I do to improve my sex life?"

Dr. Westheimer: "The only exercises you can do are in your brain."

The questions continue. They are almost innocent enough to be exciting, but not quite. There are no questions about AIDS, not even any about herpes. None of the questions is antagonistic. Only a few are intended as jokes.

And Dr. Westheimer continues. She informs. She educates. She charms. She giggles. Dr. Westheimer is effervescently sincere. Her singsong voice burbles on, sensible, understanding, wise and just about impossible to shut up.

Weeks later I'm at the typewriter, circled by background material and notes, and I am plagued. Dr. Westheimer reminds me of something, something half-glimpsed, something partly remembered. I know it's significant. I go through her book and her bio sheet, through the articles about her in *Newsweek, Playboy, People, T.V. Guide,* the *New York Times Magazine* and, it seems, every newspaper feature section in the country. Then, while I'm watching *Terrific Sex,* her new how-to videotape, I see it:

Dr. Westheimer is standing in a mock living-room set, her clothing casual and homey. She is looking directly into the camera, speaking slowly. Her voice is soothing, perky and earnest all at once. She is saying, "How open can *you* be? Can *you* say to your partner, 'Look at my penis. Do you like it?'"

Yow! I jump away from the VHS. It's Mister Rogers run amuck!

And back there in the drab confines of Central Connecticut State

University, that's the Mister Rogers generation, isn't it? They want security even when they have their pants around their ankles.

I try to imagine my own generation putting up with anything like this. True, we did crowd the lectures of another Ph.D., one Dr. Leary. And, yes, he too said it was all right for us to take our clothes off and cohabitate. But he also said it was all right for us to paint our behinds Day-Glo orange and burn down our parents' summer homes. And he never said anything about "most people want to have one significant other." We would have hooted him out of the geodesic dome.

Anyway, what year is this? Aren't we too hip for "don't stint on foreplay, be inventive"? The sexual revolution is over and the microbes won.

But of all the sexual contagions rampant in our society, Dr. Westheimer seems to be the one most difficult to avoid.

This is a list of what Dr. Westheimer is doing or selling, though I'm a couple of hours out of date, and a line of perfume and a signature-model first-baseman's mitt may have been added by now:

- Private sex therapy practice at Bellevue Hospital and Kingsbrook Jewish Medical Center
- Teaching at Cornell University
- A weekly radio talk show, "Sexually Speaking"
- A cable television program, "The Dr. Ruth Show," nightly Monday through Friday
- Three books: *Dr. Ruth's Guide to Good Sex; First Love: A Young People's Guide to Sexual Information* and *Dr. Ruth's Guide for Married Lovers*
- The college lecture circuit
- The aforementioned *Terrific Sex* videotape
- A semiweekly syndicated newspaper column
- A monthly column for *Playgirl* magazine
- A board game called "Dr. Ruth's Game of Good Sex"
- Television commercials for Dr. Pepper, Smith-Corona and Lifestyles condoms

- A principal role in the Sigourney Weaver, Gerard Depardieu movie, *A Woman or Two*
- Frequent guest appearances on the "Tonight" show and "Late Night with David Letterman."

Maybe Dr. Westheimer is another spasm of celebrity, one more in the ten thousand such seizures which have wracked our nation. Maybe in six months she'll be as dimly remembered as H. Rap Brown. But, temporary or not, the public appetite for her chitchat must say something about the public. Backstage at Central Connecticut State a dozen mature, adult newspaper reporters were asking for her autograph.

Neither WYNY-FM, originator of the "Sexually Speaking" radio program, now heard in forty-eight markets, nor Lifetime cable network, syndicator of "The Dr. Ruth Show" to twenty-four million homes, had any idea what popular enormities they were about to commit. There is a vacuum in the lives of the great unwashed (but pretty well-deodorized). And Dr. Westheimer fills it. Says Michael Capes, Lifetime's Manager of Public Affairs, "There was such a void that no one knew it existed."

I go to see Dr. Westheimer do her cable television show. Two programs each week are live, three are taped. The viewer phone-ins are done by appointment. While "The Dr. Ruth Show" is being broadcast, an assistant takes the callers' numbers. Those with the most promising difficulties are phoned during future shows and asked if they still have problems and is there anyone home they shouldn't talk in front of.

There are also famous people who appear on the show. "These are pure entertainment, an audience builder," says Executive Producer Robert McBride. Tonight one famous person is David Huddleston, who plays Santa Claus in the movie of the same name. Another is jazz drummer Buddy Rich. As to what they're doing on the program, Huddleston looks slightly confused, Rich looks very. Dr. Westheimer does her best to tie it all in with sex somehow. "Drumming has a rhythm," she ventures. "Drums in primitive societies are often involved with sex."

"Yes," says Buddy Rich, "I've had some discussions about that and it's been very enlightening but we'll be off the air if I repeat them."

And he's right. After all, Dr. Westheimer's much-mentioned frankness is nothing but using the dictionary to call things what they're called. Neither the form nor the content of her language is anything compared to the dialogue in a typical one-act play.

Tonight, the first call-in is from a woman whose child has died. Now her husband is impotent and she's not interested in making love. The next caller's romance has disappeared with age and child-bearing. The next is worried her husband is homosexual. Their children's friends all call him "faggot." Only journalistic professionalism and thoughts of the mortgage payment keep me from running out the studio door. Is life so empty of solace and aid that these poor folk must call up a shrimpy TV personality and wail lamentations via satellite link?

There's nothing wrong with what Dr. Westheimer tells them, nothing that looks cheap or facile in the sympathy she shows, but it's like fighting evil with room freshener.

When she's on the telephone, Dr. Westheimer is frank, even adamant, that she's not a therapist. "Go to a professional," she says. She says, "I'm not a physician." "I'm not a psychiatrist." "I'm not a research scientist." "I'm not a rabbi." Until you wonder what it is she *is*.

Well, she is a conservative libertine:

> Human sexuality is best kept within the protection of a relationship.
>
> —*Dr. Ruth's Guide to Good Sex,* p. 242

She is an absolutist of moral relativism. It's all right to try unusual things, she avers, even really unusual things like being a devout Catholic or an Orthodox Jew:

I tell people . . . not to offend your family or religion if you can reasonably avoid it—and often you can.

—Ibid., p. 13

Her philosophy is what you'd get if Norman Vincent Peale and Hugh Hefner had a raging (but monogamous) affair:

You should like yourself, the special way you are and God made you—and remember that while you are alive you are a sexual being with sexual thoughts and feelings.

—Ibid., p. 12

She's giving us permission to do anything we want, now that we don't want to do anything much:

. . . being sure to have contraception and knowing the lady well enough, so you're almost sure she doesn't have herpes . . .

—Ibid., p. 309

But the annoying truth is, when you listen to Dr. Westheimer, you *do* learn something. For instance, I learned that women have a pubococcygeus muscle. Rest assured I won't describe the item. But it is a fascinating piece of biology. And Dr. Westheimer has nonfamous guests on her show, such as Dr. Mary Ellen Brademas, director of the Sexually Transmitted Disease Clinic at Bellevue Hospital, who discusses chlamydia. It's a malady I've never heard of that's not only double-horrible but also completely asymptomatic. I gather it infects all cute girls I'd like to fool around with.

Also, let's face it, listening to Dr. Westheimer's call-ins is awful but as compelling as eating Cheez Doodles—people with children who touch themselves, people who've never touched anything, wives who won't do something or won't stop, husbands who snooze *in flagrante delicto,* and teenagers thinking they can't get pregnant doing the only thing that can make them that way.

It can be hard for those of us with SAT scores exceeding our golf handicaps to remember that ignorance is a renewable resource. Dr. Westheimer has tapped into vast proven reserves of it. *Whatever* she tells these people is bound to be an improvement on what they think now.

Another call comes in on the studio phone. A thirty-two-year-old woman says she cannot have an orgasm without lesbian fantasies. She has never made love to a woman. She enjoys being with men. But she can't have an orgasm without her fantasies.

Dr. Westheimer says nothing but, "Fantasies are only fantasies. Don't worry about it."

"*Really?*" says the woman. There's a buoyant pause. "Okay!" she chirps.

Yet another call: A middle-aged woman has caught her husband masturbating in front of the television.

Dr. Westheimer: "What was he watching?"

Caller: " 'Wild Kingdom,' it was about rhinos."

Dr. Westheimer: "Did he know you saw him?"

Caller: "No."

Dr. Westheimer: "Don't tell him. For all you know, he was thinking of you."

(Actually, I don't believe Dr. Westheimer heard the part about the rhinos. She's usually not this funny on purpose.)

I try to get her to sit still for an interview. She is as overactive as her curriculum vitae would imply. But once you have her attention, you have a very great deal of attention indeed. The husband of one Lifetime Television executive has coined a word for her: "endearritating."

In person, Dr. Westheimer is not so easy to make fun of. Beneath an unflattering hairstyle and too much New York matron makeup, Dr. Westheimer is an attractive woman, a zaftig gamin. Not commonly pretty, perhaps, but she has perfect eyes, cute lips and a hint of the Tigris and Euphrates in the bones of her face. Thirty years ago she was a sniper in the Haganah underground during the Israeli rebellion in Palestine. I commend to your imagination her elfin figure on the rooftops, in khakis as adorably oversized as anything from Kenzo.

I ask her, "Is there any danger in treating humans as if they were rational?"

"I believe in that. I believe people basically know what's needed and what's good for them," she says. She will not tell me if she's found any good excuse for social reticence about sex. "It's only in the late stages of civilization that all this prudishness comes about." (So the clock is running backward for the Western democracies, I guess.)

"Isn't this subject intellectually limiting?"

"Yes. If the questions were only on sex, I'd be bored. But the questions are about relationships. The nice thing for me is this is all coming together with my doctorate, which is Interdisciplinary Study of the Family."

"What purpose does human sexuality serve?"

"Bonding," says Dr. Westheimer. "It needs two people to raise that gene. Monogamy is inherent in humans."

That's a truth this particular human has been known to fumble with. I blurt out, "Is it possible to be satisfied with just one partner?" (After all, the woman knows a lot and there's some information I'd like, just for personal reference.)

"We don't have another form," she says. And she's emphatic.

Dr. Westheimer interrupts the interview. A group of disabled teenagers have come to see the taping. Most of them are suffering from a genetic disease that has twisted their bodies. It's hard not to stare at them, also hard to really look. Dr. Westheimer talks merrily, patting shoulders and signing autographs, pleased with them as if they were Junior Olympians training for the synchronized swim or high hurdles. The kids beam.

When she gets back I ask her if she's familiar with Nathanael West's novel *Miss Lonelyhearts*. "No thank you," she says. "It won't happen to me." I tell her I detect a sense of mission. She backtracks to say sometimes she gets very sad. Then, "Mission?" she says. "I'm not sure about the sense of mission. Ten years ago I would have said yes."

For a quarter of a minute I feel I've escaped Dr. Westheimer's mental desktop filled with answer stamp pads. Then I ask for her utopia.

"People would have good communication with each other. Not *one* unwanted pregnancy. Abortion must remain legal." Her staccato becomes staccato now, "Prostitution should be legal. No person would ever be violent or rape another one. Homosexuals who do not want to be homosexuals, there would be a way we could help them. Peace, of course. No hunger. My program on a regular network," she giggles. "Sex education would be a combination of the efforts of parents, churches, community centers, schools and anybody who is interested in the next generation. The disabled would have satisfaction."

Reasonable enough, now try getting it through Congress.

I ask her, "How do you reconcile reason with the bigotries of deeply held faith?"

"To give successful advice I have to connect, give information within the realm of your values, hopefully with a grain of joie de vivre."

"But what about a clear-cut conflict between values and sense?"

"That's not my role. I have to know my limitations." She sighs, but not unhappily. "It's a cop-out but a cop-out I have to use or I'd be ineffectual."

Perhaps Dr. Westheimer has earned some intellectual half measures. She's been through the horrors of ideological extremes. She was slipped out of Germany and put in a Swiss orphanage when World War II started. Her parents disappeared in concentration camps. She was nearly crippled by an artillery shell in Palestine, lived the life of an impoverished student in Paris, then worked as a housemaid in Manhattan to put herself through graduate school. Now she has two grown children, a third husband, a B.A. in Psychology from the Sorbonne, an M.A. in Sociology from the New School for Social Research and her Ph.D. from Columbia University. She says she doesn't expect this limelight to last. She says she'll enjoy it while it does.

Her live broadcast begins. I page through my notebook. "Common sense," I've jotted. "Common-sensical attitude." "Philosophy is common sense." "Sensible." "Just applies good sense to things." "Sensible answers to questions."

I begin to feel myself mired in clearheadedness. There's a frightening rush of unbiased practicality. I am being overwhelmed by a great, gooey wave of prudent liberalism.

I go home and say to my own Significant Other, "No, really, dear, Dr. Westheimer is great. You'd love her. Do you know about the pubococcygeus muscle? It's right down . . ."

"Oh, wince," she says.

"And there are all sorts of really basic and straightforward things," I say, "that can be done for people if they're educated about it, for instance, if a man has a problem with premature ejaculation he can take his erect penis . . ."

"And get out of town."

The fog of common sense clears. I'm suddenly myself again. I put my pajamas on and fix a sandwich.

No, everything will not be all right if we just talk it over, face facts, use our noodles.

And you can't tell the truth and remain morally neutral. Religions have actual laws against doing the right and the reasonable thing. Clitorectomies are sacred in some parts of Africa, and contraception is a sin in a Catholic country, no matter if the children are stacked three deep. Stay within our own religious guidelines, says Dr. Westheimer. And get advice about Shi'ite suicide sex?

And maybe our inhibitions are not as otiose as they seem. Dr. Westheimer cites 1.5 million unwanted children a year as evidence of a need for education. But forty years ago young women were less educated in you-know-what, and there weren't 1.5 million unwanted children. It's not sexual ignorance making all those babies, it's sex.

Taboos have something to do with keeping human behavior in line. Given the record of human behavior lately, should we be throwing ancient restraints away? Is sexual modesty just a vermiform appendix of the conscience?

Life is not simple, let alone love. Maybe guilt and fear actually increase sexual desire. They did in the backseats of cars when I was younger. Or maybe the very obscurity of sex solders the bond between lovers. Maybe there's even something to that sublimation business. Errol Flynn slept around a lot and I notice he didn't come up with the Special Theory of Relativity.

Anyway, new inhibitions arise as quickly as the old ones wilt. I could never have brought myself to ask Dr. Westheimer how much she's making from this.

The physician Galen, in the second century A.D., said that man and nearly all other creatures feel shame and fatigue after coitus. Or maybe after talking about it for hours.

Please, Dr. Westheimer, go home and go to bed—on the couch.

THE DEEP THOUGHTS
OF LEE IACOCCA

Review of Iacocca: An Autobiography *by Lee*

Iacocca with William Novak, Bantam Books, 1984

You see the poor bastards at every airport in the country and all the Ramada Inns, Avis counters and Beef-and-Blank restaurants. They have shoes with metal dingles, vinyl briefcases, Seiko watches. They're dressed in poly-blend vested suits and don't know not to wear a belt with the vest. Horrible Yves Saint Laurent buckles peek out the bottoms of their waistcoats. They are America's young management meatballs. And every man jack of them has a copy of *Iacocca: An Autobiography* under his arm. It is the *New York Times* number-one nonfiction best-seller. It has overtaken *In Search of Excellence* as the nation's most popular business book. So far, 1.4 million copies have been printed, and each is being read by someone who moves his lips.

The secret is in there. The meatball knows it. If he can just read carefully enough he'll crack the code: "How I turned personal failure, corporate debt, the two-bit K-car and a goofy last name into glory, fame and worldwide respect."

Lee Iacocca is a hero for our time—a conceited big-mouth glad-handing huckster who talked the government into loaning his company piles of money. And *Iacocca: An Autobiography* is literature for our time. That is, it stinks. My copy looks like some origami-instruction manual, it is so dog-eared from marking idiocies.

Give War a Chance

First there is the beastly style—coarse, disorganized, repetitious and bulked with oatmeal filler:

During that time the factories were simply not operating, which meant that both the machinery and the workers were idle.

John Riccardo and his wife, Thelma, were two of the finest people I've ever met. Unfortunately, the crisis at Chrysler was so severe that I never really got to know them.

To say the least, testifying before Congressional and Senate committees has never been my idea of fun and games.

But then came the Depression. No one who's lived through it can ever forget.

Also, there's the earthy wit:

This was probably the greatest jolt I've ever had in my business career. When I thought about it, I was bereft. (That's a euphemism for feeling lower than whale shit!)

This much can be blamed on the amanuensis, William Novak, who knows better and ought to be held by his heels and shaken until his brains run out his ears and some more useful innard slides down and fills his skull.

The rest of the problems are Iacocca's own. He is a paranoid and an egomaniac. But those are not the terms. They are too clinical and blame-evading. We need older, stricter words. The man is consumed by pride and besotted with vanity. Every nitpick in his life must be of compelling interest to us, his co-adulators:

When I was in sixth grade there was an election for captain of the student patrol. The patrolmen all wore white belts with a silver badge, but the lieutenant and the captain got to wear special uniforms with special badges. . . . I loved the idea of wearing that uniform, and I was determined to be the captain.

A number of journalists have reported (or repeated) that my parents went to Lido Beach in Venice for their honeymoon and that I was named Lido to commemorate that Happy week. It's a wonderful story, except for one problem: it's not true.

There is persistent name-dropping done mostly with a degree of deftness thus:

Once, at a private dinner with Vince Lombardi, the legendary football coach and friend of mine . . .

And every now and then we are treated to a passage of the following kind:

Once [Henry Ford] and his wife, Christina, came to our house for dinner. My parents were there, too, and Henry spent half the night telling them how great I was and that without me there wouldn't be a Ford Motor Company. On another occasion, he took me to meet his good friend L.B.J.

Of course self-love cannot be displayed in full bloom without a leafy green background of hatred for others. Chapter 10 begins with the sentence, "In 1975, Henry Ford started his month-by-month premeditated plan to destroy me."

Darn that old Henry Ford, anyhow. And he'd just got done telling Lee's mom and dad what a swell kid they'd raised, too. Well, Lee is not going to take this lying down, not when he's got a whole book of his own to say things in. Iacocca launches a rhetorical assault the likes of which has not been heard since Cicero indicted Marc Antony. Rapier thrust follows rapier thrust: Lee wanted a signed photograph of Henry Ford, but Henry never got around to signing it. Henry sold the company plane to the Shah of Iran for five million dollars and "The company lost a bundle on the deal." Henry used tax shelters. Henry told his executives to "get off your asses and do what needs to be done for the black community," then later that day used the word "coon." And Henry Ford and women?

> Actually I always thought he hated women—except for his mother. When Henry's father died, Eleanor Clay Ford had taken over the family and put her son Henry in charge. She also kept him somewhat in line.
> But when she died in 1976, his whole world came tumbling down.

One sick puppy, that Henry Ford. What's more he likes to have a few shooters and get wide:

> Henry tried to be sophisticated and European. . . . But it was all a facade. After the third bottle of wine, all bets were off.

(With Iacocca in the next office, his head as large as a haystack and barbering from nine to five about what a big lasagna he is, who wouldn't need a drink?)

Anything can be excused by genius, and Iacocca has been called one. But where's this genius parked?

Iacocca's book is filled with managerial balloon juice. "The only way you can motivate people is to communicate with them." "The speed of the boss is the speed of the team." "In addition to being decision makers, managers also have to be motivators." "To sum up: nothing stands still in this world."

He exhibits general ignorance of business fundamentals. "A couple of months after I arrived [at Chrysler], something hit me like a ton of bricks. We were running out of cash!" He berates the Federal Reserve Board for being primarily concerned with banking. He blasts America as "a nation enamored with investing in paper," as though the cash represented by stocks, bonds and certificates of deposit were all jammed in a sock under Carl Icahn's mattress. He discusses the overseas retail prices of Japanese cars without reference to value-added tax, accuses the Japanese of exporting unemployment to the United States (How do they pack it? Does it spoil?), and he claims this for the United Auto Workers' reaction to his ballyhooed 1980 salary of one dollar a year:

> From that day on I was their pal. The union loved me. They said: "This guy is going to lead us to the promised land."

Moreover, Iacocca exhibits *specific* ignorance of the automobile business. He says, "Now, it's true that you can't make money on small cars—at least not in this country." But Honda does at its Marysville, Ohio, plant. And General Motors is investing 1.5 billion dollars in a new domestic small-car division, presumably not for kicks. Iacocca calls the Mustang II "a terrific design." It sucked. He says, "The K-car is a sensational product." It is adequate. He claims the Chevrolet Vega had a "pancake aluminum engine." It had nothing of the kind. And he proudly takes credit for the stupid seat-belt interlock ignition system that appeared on 1973 cars and disappeared as quickly as owners could unhook it.

Iacocca's idea of engineering:

> The [Mercury] Marquis had achieved . . . the softest, plushest ride in the world.

His idea of design:

> My plan was to create a new car using the same platform, engine, and even the roof, but to make enough changes so that the car really *looked* new and not like a spinoff of the T-Bird.

And the following explains better than John Stuart Mill himself could what it is Lee Iacocca does for a living:

> . . . on the island of St. Thomas, we unveiled the new Cougar. At a beach lit by clusters of brilliant torches, a World War II landing

craft pulled up to the shore and lowered its ramp. The audience was breathless as a shining white Cougar drove onto the sand. The door opened, and out stepped singer Vic Damone, who began to entertain.

But let's be fair. The man works hard. He took a risky job at a troubled company and managed to put it in the black. He . . . Oh, let's *not* be fair. This book is rubbish. The meatballs in the airports would be better off reading the phone book. Check under Brooks Brothers. A banker-gray two-piece chalk-stripe with a buttondown shirt and a pin-dot tie and at least you'll "really *look*" like you've got some sense.

As for Lee Iacocca, he's being bruited about as a Democratic presidential candidate. The man deserves no better.

THE VERY DEEP THOUGHTS OF JIMMY AND ROSALYNN CARTER

Review of Everything to Gain: Making the Most of the Rest of Your Life *by Jimmy and Rosalynn Carter, Random House, 1987*

Jimmy and Rosalynn Carter, who used to be employed as a live-in couple in Washington, have written a book. Actually, it's more than a book. Around my house *Everything to Gain* has become a complete home-entertainment center. Using the Carter opus, I've developed no less than five swell new parlor games. They are better than Trivial Pursuit, charades and nude Scruples combined. The rules are printed below. Try them yourself.

D-U-M *Dumb*

The object of D-U-M Dumb is to find the dumbest sentence in *Everything to Gain*. And, let me tell you, it's a toughie. The book is passed around and each player notes a passage. The winner is determined by the amount of laughter in the room when the quotation is read.

In the case of a tie, handicap points are subtracted according to the "dumbness potential" of the section of the book from which the quote was drawn. *E to G* is divided into little bits and pieces, some written by Jimmy and Rosalynn together, some by Jimmy alone and some by Rosalynn all by herself. Of course, the dumber the section, the easier it is to find a dumb quote in it. Professional help seems to have been applied to the parts written in duet. These get a handicap of −1. Dim Jimmy gets a handicap of −2. Learning-impaired Rosa-

147

lynn gets −4. Cover blurbs and dust-jacket copy, written by actual literate humans, get no handicap.

There are two game categories, "Form" and "Content."

Overall winner of the first D-U-M Dumb tournament and undefeated champion to date in the "Content" category is Ms. D.B., a New York TV executive. Even though D.B. was working with a Rosalynn quotation and, hence, a −4 handicap, no one has yet been able to top the gem she found on page 59:

> I have worked with the problems of the mentally afflicted for years, ever since I first became aware of the needs while campaigning for Jimmy for Governor.

D.B.'s victory was, however, marred by a rules protest. A fellow contestant held that this sentence properly belonged in a third, "Honest Confessions," category. D.B. replied to the challenge by offering an alternative Rosalynn quote, "We need people for shelving [which I learned was putting books back on the shelves] . . ."

I myself am a top competitor in the "Form" category. I won my last match with this topic sentence:

> Their search for a new life over the next few years led them eventually to Koinonia Farms, a nonprofit farm that uses its income to help the needy, not far from Plains.

That nosed out another −1 handicap entry backed by my lawyer:

> And having our mothers close by to call or visit every day was a particular joy.

D-U-M can be played with children, even preschoolers, since the Carter prose style makes advanced reading skills unnecessary.

Finish That Thought

The object of this game is to find a Carter thought (be sure to allow adequate time!) and take it to its logical conclusion. Examples are given below with the contestants' additional material marked in italics:

It was good therapy . . . to be able to go to my shop and design, cut, fit and finish a piece that was useful, permanent and sometimes beautiful—or just to bang on something *the way I used to bang on the economy.*

We savored the different seasons of nature and gathered wild fruits, such as plums, blackberries, mayhaws, grapes, blueberries, and persimmons that grow along or near the rural trails, *paths, pathways, tracks, walks, passages, bypaths, lanes, roads, and routes.*

I even surprised myself with some of the things I could write. *Words, for instance. All spelled out and everything.*

When together for meals . . . our family almost invariably had freewheeling political discussions or arguments on controversial issues of the day. Quite early Amy learned to join in and *that's how we figured out what to do about the Iran hostages.*

Sometimes an unpleasant or even catastrophic event can transform one's life and reveal opportunities that could never have been envisioned. *Take Hiroshima . . .*

That night when we called [Amy] to dinner and she didn't come, we found her outside in a tree *eating bananas with Abbie Hoffman.*

So often, the best therapy for a mentally ill person is just knowing that someone cares. *So Jimmy and I gave John Hinkley a call.*

Give War a Chance

Riposte

This is similar to Finish That Thought, but instead of adding material to different passages, a single passage is read and players compete to see who can come up with the most appropriate response. Examples:

> I had so much information written down about the earlier period of my life that I didn't have room to include much of it in my book. For instance, I learned that my daddy's mother climbed out the window at age sixteen and eloped with a traveling salesman named Mr. Smith, who was crippled and twenty-five years older than she was. I'm saving these anecdotes for our grandchildren.
>
> *Thank you.*

> Marriage was not seriously considered with girls known to "go all the way."
>
> *Which must have made for great honeymoons.*

> I've already mentioned that Jimmy also has an amazing capacity to sleep all night, even in times of incredible pressure.
>
> *Pressure on what, Rosalynn?*
> (or)
> *And the nation rested easier, too, knowing the son of a bitch was off duty for at least eight hours every day.*

> My wife has never been more beautiful than when her face was covered with black smut from scraping burned ceiling joists, and streaked with sweat from carrying sheets of plywood . . .
>
> *Okay, okay, we believe you.*

> We needed a lot more volunteers in 1980!
>
> *Pal, what you needed was votes.*

P. J. O'Rourke

You Don't Say

In this game selections of incredibly looney, puerile and ignorant prose are written on a piece of paper. Players then try to guess whether the selections come from *Everything to Gain* or from something else, such as an Andrea Dworkin tract or the *Washington Post* editorial page. Here's a sample game card:

On Japanese War Guilt

When I was young and in high school, during World War II, I thought Hirohito was the cruelest man in the world next to Hitler. I blamed the whole Pacific conflict on him. Years later . . . we went to Tokyo and called on a sweet little elderly man, who raised flowers in his hothouse at the palace. . . . This was Emperor Hirohito—as far removed from my conception of him as he possibly could be.
❑ The Carters
❑ Barbara Walters

On the Sandinistas and U.S. Central American Foreign Policy

A Habitat project was started in northwest Nicaragua in 1985. . . . Habitat volunteers are teaching the local people how to build good homes—without interference.
❑ The Carters
❑ *The Village Voice*

On Watergate and Its Aftermath

. . . we were joined by Chuck Colson, whom we had personally never met before, but for whom we had little respect because of his statements and actions during the Watergate years. . . . We were also somewhat cynical about his supposed religious "conversion." . . . We quickly saw that he was at ease about his past. . . . In just a short time our remaining doubts were removed by his enthusiasm and persistence.
❑ The Carters
❑ Tammy Faye Bakker

151

Give War a Chance

On the Need For an Expanded Federal Health-Care Program
By strict disciplinary measures, possible only in a totalitarian society, and using intensive educational programs and trained paramedics who work closely with village leaders, the Chinese have reduced their infant mortality rate, carried out a broad immunization program, practically eradicated venereal disease, and lowered the annual population growth rate.
❑ The Carters
❑ Mao Tse-tung

On Tibetan Buddhism, Not Heretofore Known to Be Polytheistic
I have memories of prayer wheels, large and small, which spin prayers up to heaven, and of prayer flags that flap their messages to the gods . . .
❑ The Carters
❑ Shirley MacLaine

On Soviet-American Relations
During the service different members of the Soviet delegation were called on to speak, and each said that though we have different languages, there is room for friendship and peaceful coexistence. The very conservative residents of this north Georgia community listened intently to the interpreter, and, when the speeches were over, spontaneously rose to their feet in a standing ovation.
❑ The Carters
❑ Tass

If you guessed "The Carters" on all six selections, you win.
I've also invented a great Carter Book Drinking Game. You just open the book at random and, boy, do you need a drink.

* * *

So that's *Everything to Gain*—a perfect icebreaker for any party and enjoyed by family members of all ages. But what—you may be asking—is the book *about*? It's about 193 pages. Ha. Ha. Ha. Excuse me. Spend a couple hours with Jimmy and Roz and you get silly. I don't know what the hell the book's about. I mean, I read it and everything, but I haven't got the faintest idea. It just sounded to me like a couple of prissy old ratchet-jaw hicks yammering away about nothing until you wanted to stuff them headfirst through the outhouse seat.

Maybe we'd better ask the *New York Times*. After all, the *New York Times* is so much smarter than the rest of us. Let's see . . . here we go, the May 31, 1987, issue of the *NYT Book Review*. Therein a certain Letty Cottin Pogrebin casts an overeducated eye made wide by thought provocation upon the Carter tome and concludes it's "autobiography that is part confession, part pep talk and part handbook for activism . . . an inspiring account of the creation of a meaningful life." I don't know if we should listen to a woman from a family so obviously bad at spelling, but, what the heck, let's take Letty Cottin Pogrebin's word for it. Any questions? I don't want to keep seeing the same hands.

You know, the Carters may be onto something here—autobiography/confession/pep talk/handbook for activism *and* blueprint for meaningful life. I'd like to try one of those myself and give Jimmy a little of his own back. Let's see if I can do it in twenty-five words or less:

> I was born in Ohio. I drink. Hooray for the Red Cross. Send contributions to 17th and D NW, Wash., 20006. Get a job, Goofy-tooth.

We didn't really elect this hamster President of the United States, did we? Naw, get outta here. It was *Gerry*, Gerry Ford. That was the one we elected. Jimmy, Gerry—easy to get the two mixed up. And you know how vague we Americans are about history. We've just plumb forgot which fellow we voted in.

Whoops. I looked it up. We *did* elect Jimmy Carter President. Although, I notice, we unelected him as soon as we possibly could.

So now what are we going to do with him, him and his nitwit wife? We can't go on letting them write books. It's too embarrassing. This is an industrialized, Western nation. We can't have things like this in our bookstores. We'll get drummed out of the English-Speaking League. We've got to find some other line of work for these two before they, oh God, write again.

> Television evangelists
> Permanent guest hosts on "Hee Haw"
> Carnival sideshow attractions
> Goodwill ambassadors to Sri Lanka

Those possibilities leap to mind. But I have a better suggestion. Let's put them back in the White House.

All right, it sounds insane. But think about it for a minute. We've got all our seventies' debts paid off with cheap eighties' dollars. We've got low mortgage rates locked in on our houses. Now, if we could just get T-bills to yield twenty percent again, we'd be fixed. We're *ready* for double-digit inflation.

Then there're the Russians. Carter would keep them worried and off balance. When you've got a guy as dumb as this in the White House, hell, he might *sit* on the button. The Soviets would be shaking.

And Carter has this remarkable peace-making ability. Reading *E to G* makes it suddenly clear how he managed the Camp David Accord. Begin and Sadat were so bored by the blubber-skulled Carter family that they were willing to do *anything* to get out of Camp David. It might just work again with Syria or Jordan.

Plus there's the matter of kick-ass patriotism, which has been slipping in the aftermath of the Iran-contra hearings. With J.C. at the helm, there'd be another disaster such as the hostage crisis. That might be what we need to put some lead back in the national pencil and get us started whooping on creepy foreigners again.

Furthermore there'd be no obnoxious big-government activism in a new Carter administration. This is because of the people Carter would appoint. As soon as they were in office they'd run down to the South African embassy to protest apartheid. And they'd get thrown into jail and wouldn't be able to cause trouble.

The country's editorial cartoons would become hilarious again because Carter is funnier looking than Reagan. Indeed, as Jimmy gets older, he's funnier looking than *anyone*—a sort of Don Knotts of the undead.

And here, *here,* is the kicker. If Jimmy comes back, Billy comes back. Damn it, don't we all miss Billy Carter!*

So run right out and buy a copy of *Everything to Gain,* and write and tell Jimmy and Rosalynn just how much fun you had with it. (I've found my copy is also great for playing fetch with the dog.) Do everything to encourage the fellow. Maybe he'll make a comeback.

It's increasingly clear that nobody in his right mind wants to be President of the United States. Therefore let's, as Rosalynn doubtless says, "go with the flow" and put somebody in the White House with no mind at all.

---

*Almost all the predicted benefits of a Carter presidency have been, amazingly enough, provided by the Bush administration. The exceptions being twenty percent T-bill yields and, of course, a return of Billy Carter to the public eye. (Also, Bush's political associates tend to run afoul of the law for reasons other than protesting apartheid.)

MORDRED HAD A POINT—CAMELOT REVISITED

Review of The Kennedys: An American Drama *by*

Peter Collier and David Horowitz, Summit Books,

1984

This is a wonderful hater-of-Kennedys guide, an assemblage of ugly facts and rude anecdotes about this large and dirty family. It is not, of course, a complete collection. Deforestation of North America would be needed to print a book that size. But it will suffice.

Here, for those who have forgotten or just love to hear it all again, is the fulsome scurvy truth: Old Joseph P. Kennedy was a liar and a greedy thief, an ignoramus, adulterer, vile anti-Semite, coward, and pompous ass. His wife, Rose, was a frigid martinet, unashamed to suckle at the teat of shabby lucre, awash in pietism and Tartuffery, filled with the letter of Catholicism and empty of its spirit. They raised their nine whelps in an atmosphere of brutal pride and stupid competition. When the hapless Rosemary turned out to be retarded, they had her lobotomized and parked her with the nuns. The remaining eight turned out foolhardy, arrogant, unprincipled, and wholly lacking in sense of consequences. This last trait caused Joe Jr. and Kathleen to die in airplane crashes and allowed Jack to get his PT boat T-boned by a Japanese destroyer. (A tale of heroism was manufactured from that incident. The family wasn't so lucky with Teddy's Chappaquiddick skin-diving efforts three decades later.)

The Kennedys, however, continued to wax. Elections, intellectuals, and press adulation were purchased. One family member rose, briefly, to great political power and almost unlimited sexual excess.

Some others nearly achieved the same results. Two were shot, but under the most romantic circumstances and not, as might have been hoped, after due process of law. A third remains a fat dog in a Senate manger that's overdue for mucking out. Thus the Kennedys excelled in every Irish vice and learned others strange to the sons of Erin, such as simony and lust.

Then comes the morally satisfying third act, when the last generation of Kennedys reaps the trust-fund dividends of sin. They wallow in drugs and indolence, perform wild acts of self-destruction and roll in social manure. At Studio 54, Xenon, and Danceteria, they fritter away the advantage and wealth gained by their loathsome ancestors. They overdose and get arrested and, best of all, disappear from the public eye. Just desserts! Just hors d'oeuvres! A just main course of crow!

What fun this book is, what a storehouse of chortles and gloatings. It satisfies the streak of mean self-righteousness in us all. But that is just the problem. After reading *The Kennedys* one feels a little guilty for wasting the time and even a bit embarrassed at watching such manful thwacks being given to this dead equine. Why bother? The Kennedy pitchmen have folded their tents. The bogtrotters' circus has left town. Everywhere, except perhaps in benighted Massachusetts, the Kennedys are defeated and gone. What's the point of hating them anymore? Well, there are several points.

The Kennedys were more than a rich, bad family who gained temporary political power. They were demagogues of oligarchy. Disguised as populists, they championed the definitely privileged and supposedly enlightened few. These few, when ensconced in the offices of government, would decide what was best for the many. The Kennedys saw political office as the source, rather than the result, of social order. They held government to be the fountainhead of all privilege, responsibility, benefit, and constraint. They did not know and probably couldn't understand the idea of a free people chartering a government for the sake of convenience and paved roads. It never occurred to a Kennedy that the proper role of federal administration might be to guard the coasts and let UPS deliver the mail. And only in the vaguest, election-fixing way did any Kennedy realize that public officials serve at the people's sufferance.

What's worse, the Kennedys not only believed in the primacy of government but believed it to be good. With the exception of the disgusting Joe Sr., there was genuine idealism in the tribe. The rotting leftovers can still be whiffed in Teddy Kennedy's speeches. There is something more horrible than hoodlums, churls and vipers, and this is knaves with moral justification for their cause. The Kennedys thought the world would be a better place for having them run it. And thus their every excess and corruption could be excused as contributing to a larger good.

Peter Collier and David Horowitz are not as alert as they might be to this idealistic evil. Collier and Horowitz have abandoned the leftism of their youth, but they retain something of a social-activist point of view. They see the Kennedys as doomed figures who failed to accomplish noble objectives because of moral shortcomings. But the Kennedys didn't have a tragic flaw. The Kennedys were themselves a tragic flaw of ours. And, in fact, they accomplished lots. They changed the nature of electioneering forever with thespian talents and piles of cash. They expanded executive power to do things like make war without Congressional permission or even public knowledge. They helped bring on the age of truly elephantine government programs. And they nearly established America's first hereditary political dynasty. To the extent the Kennedys succeeded, they did so precisely because of their unscrupulousness, never in spite of it. By having us hate the sinners rather than the sins, Collier and Horowitz distract us from the proper vein of bile.

Collier and Horowitz also fail to explain how these sewer trout managed to swim upstream into our body politic. The authors attribute the Kennedy rise to the family's pet intellectuals. This is giving the American public too little credit. We may be dumb, but we're not so dumb that we ever spent a minute listening to Theodore Sorenson. Neither were lick-spittle journalists at fault (though not through lack of trying by the likes of Joe Alsop and Philip Graham). We have no one to blame for the Kennedys but ourselves. We took the Kennedys to heart of our own accord. And it is my opinion that we did it not because we respected them or thought what they proposed was good, but because they were pretty. We, the electorate, were smitten with this handsome, vivacious family.

> *It's always tempting to impute*
> *Unlikely virtues to the cute.*

We got a mad crush on the lot of them. They were so stylish, so charming, and—at least in their public moments—so gracefully behaved. We wanted to hug their golden tousled heads to our dumpy breasts.

This may be the stupidest thing that has ever happened in a democracy. And certainly it shows an emptiness at the center of our idea of government, if not at the center of our lives. A desire to adore a head of state is a grim transgression against republicanism. It is worse than having a head of state who demands to be adored. It is worse even than the forced adoration of the state itself. And this puts the Collier-Horowitz book in another light. It's ourselves we should be flailing. Trust hubris to bring such trash as the Kennedys to their knees. They are but few and a passing evil. We are another matter. There are 230 some million of us, and we'd better start talking sense to ourselves soon. The President of the United States is our employee. The services he and his legislative cohorts contract for us are not gifts or benefices. We have to pay for every one of them, sometimes with our money, sometimes with our skins.

If we can remember this we'll get a good, dull Cincinnatus like Eisenhower or Coolidge. Our governance will be managed with quiet and economy. We'll have no need to go looking for Kennedys to love. And no need to boil over with hatred for them later.

GIVE WAR A CHANCE

Dispatches from

the Gulf War

JORDAN

August 1990

War! War! Blood-red savage war! Cry havoc and loose the dogs of ditto. Saddam Hussein—he's worse than Hitler, worse than Stalin, worse than waking up wearing a wedding ring next to Roseanne Barr. He invaded Iran. He invaded Kuwait. He even invaded some parts of the country he already lives in, that's how crazy Saddam Hussein is. He's got chemical weapons filled with . . . with . . . *chemicals.* Maybe he's got The Bomb. And missiles that can reach Riyadh, Tel Aviv, Spokane. Stock up on nonperishable foodstuffs. Grab those Diet Coke cans you were supposed to take to the recycling center and fill them with home heating oil. Bury the Hummel figurines in the yard. We're all going to die. Details at eleven.

It's lots of fun being in the panic industry. If you can't convince the world to love you, then scaring everyone out of their Bart Simpson Underachiever-and-Proud-of-It T-shirts is the next best way to get attention and feel needed. My fellow members of the news media and I have been pursuing this strategy with zest since August 2nd. "Horror Show," "Talk of War," "Must This Mean War?," "Should War Come: A Scenario," read the headlines. *Time* ran a cover bannered "Is the World Ready for This?," showing a photo of what looks like a cellular phone wrapped in a table napkin wearing Ray-Bans and a shower cap but which was labeled "U.S. soldier testing chemical warfare gear in Saudi Arabia." The daily papers and the

163

nightly news are festooned with maps—arrows going every which way, little silhouettes of tanks and planes and proposed casualty figures that look like long-distance phone numbers.

The U.S. government has also been pretty good at spreading alarm—not to mention money and guns—all over the place. We are sending 250,000 troops, six hundred fighter planes, three naval carrier groups and twenty-six B-52 bombers to the Persian Gulf, a little late to save Kuwait, maybe, but just in time to rescue the U.S. defense budget. One well-placed ICBM and Saddam Hussein would get the message, but that wouldn't prevent Congress from taking all our Stealth Bomber money and giving it to naked NEA performance artists to rub on their bodies while denouncing male taxpayers.

Everybody's been cashing in on Hussein Hysteria. The Soviet Union is accumulating points in the civilized-nation lookalike contest. The U.N. thinks it might finally have found something to do for a living. My own fiancée plans to make a fortune selling "FUQ IRAQ" bumper stickers. Literary agents are lining up hostage tell-alls and sending faxes to Baghdad instructing trapped Americans to have poignant thoughts and spiritual insights and to get tortured a little, if possible. So many TV camera crews have descended on the Middle East that Arab authorities are rushing to tourist hotels to check the Gideon Bibles—Exodus, chapters 7 through 12—on the subject of plagues: blood, frogs, lice, flies, dead cattle, boils, hail, locusts, darkness, firstborn sons and, yep, network anchormen. Of course, Jesse Jackson is on hand, warning the world in *vers de société* couplets about a situation "Where the price of oil would go up / And the price of blood would go down." The occasion being too solemn for rhyme.

So I figured I'd better get over there. I've been to the Middle East three whole times before and know several words in Arabic, including *la* ("no") and *Ayna akrab mal'ab golf?* ("Where's the nearest golf course?"), therefore I'm an expert, too, and can put things into perspective, give you a clearer picture of unfolding events and maybe relieve some of the unnecessary fears and needless anxieties stirred up by cynical, sensationalistic journalists like me.

* * *

I know what you readers are saying to yourselves. You're saying, "P.J., P.J., how can you possibly tell us what these people are going to do? Here they are gadding about in their mothers' nightgowns, playing with pop beads and going, 'Muhammad this' and 'Muhammad that,' when they've got to know Ali is pushing fifty and has Parkinson's disease and couldn't go half a round with Razor Ruddock."

Well, that just shows how ignorant of Arabic culture you readers are. Ali could go the distance with Ruddock any day of the week standing on one foot, I don't care whose disease he's got. Besides, the Arab peoples possess an ancient and highly developed civilization that is in many ways more sophisticated than our own. For instance, they invented algebra. And this is why we have to go to war with Saddam Hussein this minute and bomb the shish kebab out of him before he invents trig and chemistry and the whole of America flunks high school.

Sending everything we've got short of Dan Quayle in a National Guard uniform to the Middle East to keep Saddam Hussein from doing whatever it is that he hasn't managed to do already is called "being the world's policeman." There's a lot of argument about this, mostly from American newspaper editorial writers who like to begin paragraphs with, "America isn't the world's policeman." But you'll notice that when Kuwait got invaded, nobody called Sweden.

So here we are, running around armed to the eyeballs in the same kind of weather you can get at the laundromat by putting two quarters in the dryer, while our domestic economy deflates like a cheap beach toy. And do we hear any thank yous?

I hadn't even gotten out of the Kennedy Airport Royal Jordanian

Give War a Chance

Airline first-class lounge (a windowless room with two bottles of Johnnie Walker, no ice, a bowl of pistachios and a television permanently tuned to "Wheel of Fortune") before a Jordanian started in on me: "When Israel invades Sinai, did America send troops? When Israel invades the West Bank, did America send troops? When Israel invades Lebanon, did America send troops?" Of course he was being very unfair. We didn't send troops but we *did* send arms, materiel and a great deal of financial assistance. Albeit we sent them to Israel.

At the baggage carrousel in Amman, a Jordanian-American businessman, when asked where the *bureau de change* was answered with an impassioned defense of Saddam Hussein. "Again and again and again Iraq asked Kuwait to quit violating OPEC guidelines. Again and again and . . ."

I bought a copy of the *Jordan Times*. They wanted the Cold War restarted:

> . . . it is most unfortunate that the Soviet glasnost and
> perestroika policy has meant giving the Americans more leeway
> to do what they want with the smaller countries in the world . . .

Like, you know, save their butts.

At my hotel an organization called the Child Welfare Committee of the General Union of Voluntary Services was handing out press releases about a "Women's and Children's March" to protest the trade embargo on Iraq:

> Such a blockade constitutes no less than an act of savagery,
> unprecedented in recent history . . .

The march was organized by the same kind of earnest wholegrain busybodies we have in the States, wearing Birkenstock sandals and primitive jewelry and arriving at the demo in their husbands' Volvos. They were trying to get seven or eight hundred kids under twelve to quit dropping, losing and smacking each other over the head with printed signs reading, "ARAB WORLD IS MY WORLD,"

"IRAQI CHILDREN = ARAB CHILDREN," "HOW MANY KIDS' LIVES FOR A BARREL OF OIL?" and "DO NOT KILL MOM."

Do-gooders are always hard to figure, but watching the Women's and Children's March was—considering the porky guy with the poison gas who stands to benefit—like being a spectator at an Earth First! spotted-owl shoot.

And one more thing I discovered on my first day in Jordan: The Jordanian American Friendship Society has been dissolved. (Though its president, Mohammad Kamal, admitted, "The organization . . . has really been dormant since its establishment.")

America is the world's policeman, all right—a big, dumb mick flat-foot in the middle of the one thing cops dread most, a "domestic disturbance."

To the uninitiated, what Iraq did to Kuwait seems like regular war: Country A whacks Country B, which screams bloody murder, dragging Countries C, D and E into the fray. But within the large, noisy and exceedingly fractious family of Arabs, it's not that simple. Iraq, Kuwait, Jordan, Syria, Saudi Arabia and so forth are hardly nations as we understand the term. They are quarrels with borders.

Until 1918 the Arabian peninsula was ruled by the Ottoman Empire, so called because it had the same amount of intelligence and energy as a footstool. When the Turks backed the wrong horse in World War I, the French and English divvied up the region in a manner both completely self-serving and unbelievably haphazard, like monkeys at a salad bar. The huge, senseless notch in Jordan's border with Saudi Arabia, for instance, is known as "Winston's Hiccup" because the then head of the British Colonial Office, Winston Churchill, is supposed to have drawn this line on a map after a very long lunch.

The British were fans of one Hussein ibn Ali, the Grand Sherif of Mecca, who led the Arab revolt against the Turks that Lawrence of Arabia claimed to be such an important part of. The British wanted to make members of Hussein's Hashemite family kings of what-all and which-ever. They crowned Hussein himself King of the Hejaz, the Red Sea coast of the Arabian peninsula. They put his son Faisal on the throne of Syria. But the French threw a fit, so the Brits moved Faisal to Iraq. And Faisal's brother Abdullah—grandfather of the King Hussein we've got these days—was given the booby prize of Transjordan, an area previously known as "to-hell-and-gone-out-in-the-desert" when it was called anything at all.

In the 1920s, Ibn Saud—the man who put the "Saudi" in Saudi Arabia—chased Hussein ibn Ali out of the Hejaz. This is why the Jordanians hate the Saudis.

The Jordanians should hate the Iraqis, too, because the military government that Saddam Hussein now runs killed every available member of the Iraqi branch of the Hashemite family in 1958. But Jordan and Iraq are both too busy hating Syria for Syria's attempt to achieve Arab hegemony by allying with Iran, invading Lebanon and trying to gain control of the Palestine Liberation Organization.

The PLO, meanwhile, nearly toppled King Hussein in 1970, whereupon the king, with Iraqi support, exterminated thousands of Palestinians. Thus the Palestinians should hate the Jordanians and vice versa, but since sixty-five percent of Jordanians *are* Palestinians, it's easier for everybody to hate Israel.

Which still doesn't explain why the people in Jordan are furious at the United States for coming to the aid of Kuwait. Unless it does.

Amman is a pretty dangerous place for an American to go—you wouldn't believe the traffic. Everybody in Jordan drives everywhere at top speed. They parallel park at sixty miles an hour. And Jordanians never touch the brakes, turn signals, dimmer switch or even the steering wheel. All driving is done by horn.

Amman's street layout was designed using the splatter technique popular with action painters of the post-abstract expressionist school. The idea of numbering buildings and naming streets has been taken up, but in a grudging, desultory manner, the way baby boomers practice dental flossing.

There are no major intersections in Amman. Instead there are roundabouts, from which radiate four, six, eight, twelve or thirty avenues. There's really no telling because, although it's possible to enter a roundabout from virtually any street in the city, it's not possible ever to exit again.

This is why I missed a special Rotary Club of Jordan meeting called to protest America's unfairness to Iraq. I had been eager to see the results of backslapping Rotarian boosterism applied to Islamic *jihad:* "Okay, fellows, any member who hasn't drunk the blood of an infidel dog since the last meeting has to stand on his chair and sing 'I'm a Little Teapot.' "

Rotary International is just the thing for Amman, a bland, clean, busy, humdrum, commercial city, a kind of Arab Brussels, although perched on spectacular hills.

The buildings are all cement block made to look like limestone, except for some made of the limestone the cement's supposed to look like. By day the whole town is the color of those afternoons at the beach when you can't tell where the sea ends and the sky begins, and by night it's alive with the headlights of drivers lost in roundabouts. All the modest one- and two-floor cement homes have metal rebars left sticking up from their roofs like whiskers—a Third World symbol of hope, meaning the residents are planning to make enough money to add another story to the house. Even the poorest parts of the city are tidy and unodoriferous, thanks, in part, to huge subsidies Jordan receives from the oil-rich Gulf states such as Kuwait.

But subsidies or no, pictures of Saddam Hussein were beginning to appear on the smaller and shabbier storefronts and in the rear windows of taxicabs. Copies of that old anti-Semitic forgery *The Protocols of the Elders of Zion* were stacked next to the cash register in an expensive bookstore. And, according to the *Amman Star,* University of Jordan students "from all political trends" were condemning "Arab traitors, Saudi Arabia and Kuwait, for inviting foreign troops into Arab and Islamic lands," and calling for "a battle of honor against the United States, the Zionists and all other treacherous forces."

Give War a Chance

The students had formed something called the Preparatory Committee for the General Union of Jordanian Students. One of their spokesmen said the Gulf crisis "pushed us to political extremism that hopes for an Arab-American confrontation that will lead to re-drawing the map of the Arab world." In which case I hope they get New Jersey.

I did manage to find—by just leaving my car in a roundabout and walking—the University of Jordan, a handsome, shady campus filled with polite kids. The members of the infelicitously acronymed PCGUJS said, however, that only the head of their Information Sub-Committee was authorized to make statements to the international press. To my relief, they couldn't find him.

Most of the students at UJ were dressed like students anywhere, or better than that, Jordan being more or less a Mediterranean country and quite stylish. But about a third of the women students were wearing no makeup, scarves covering all their hair and drab ankle-length dresses. This in adherence to fundamentalist Muslim rules of decorum which mean, basically, dressing the way middle-aged dads with teenage daughters think girls should. To judge by the amount of fiddling, tugging and adjusting of the scarves, it was a fashion that had just come in. It's been a long time since I was in college, so maybe I've forgotten how these things work, but a campus fad for looking like a Russian cleaning lady and acting like a nun seems odd.

When I got back to my hotel Saddam Hussein was on the English-language TV news, pestering a group of British expats he had stuck somewhere in Baghdad.

"Your presence here and in other places is best to avoid the scourge of war," said Saddam through a not very competent translator. "Are you having recreational facilities?" Not waiting for an answer, he suggested they take a group photograph "about preserving the memory of this time," then said, "Let's put this on TV!" as though struck with a remarkable inspiration having nothing to do with the video cameras, soundmen and lighting crews in the room. Saddam reached out with a beefy mitt and petted the head of a freckled little English kid later identified as Stewart Lockwood. "Are you playing volleyball with Iraqis?" asked Saddam, pawing the youngster's face, kneading his cheeks and playing with his nose. Young Stewart—sturdy chap—bore it all with more disgust than fear. A week later I was in Abu Dhabi, watching English-language news again, this time about Jesse Jackson's return from putzing around in Iraq. And there was poor Stewart, now gripped by Jesse like a pet being taken to the veterinarian and giving Jackson exactly the same look he'd given Saddam. If we're serious about achieving world peace, we could start by getting international political leaders to leave Stewart Lockwood alone.

I drove out to Ruwayshid, the Jordanian checkpoint where the refugees from Iraq and Kuwait were beginning to arrive in large numbers. It's 250 kilometers through desert waste. Those of us brought up on Disney "The Living Desert" films expect time-lapse blooming century plants and lizards with funny tongues pursuing bugs all over the place. But in fact this desert looks like house plants do after six months in a bachelor's apartment. It's flat and featureless with nothing sentient visible. At noon the temperature is in the hundreds. Dust devils slop back and forth in dirty spirals across the plain. And the whole is bathed in a nasty shimmy of mirage. Mirage being not an optical illusion of a palm-fringed oasis, but the constant glare of hot sunlight reflected by an even hotter layer of air along ground that's too hot to talk about.

There is one real oasis 100 kilometers from Amman, Al Azraq, a nasty littered collection of concrete-block buildings with a salt marsh and about fifteen half-dead date palms. This was Lawrence of Arabia's headquarters and, for five dinars, an ancient worthy will tell you, "This was Lawrence of Arabia's headquarters."

Beyond Al Azraq the desert gets worse, all covered with small chunks of basalt that absorb and compound the nauseating heat. This is the Black Desert, where even Bedouin caravans wouldn't go, because the sharp, heated stones destroyed the feet of their camels. After another 75 kilometers the desert gets worse yet. Solid lava flows with the texture of piles of razor blades are interspersed with lumps of basalt now big as chairs and sofas. And if you roll down your car window swarms of tiny flies cover every part of your exposed flesh.

Lawrence called Al Azraq a "luminous silky Eden," and by the time you get back from Ruwayshid it actually looks that way.

This two-lane asphalt highway across the desert is the only ground link to Iraq, and there was plenty of blockade violating traffic on it. The Iraqis seemed to be running every old tanker truck they could get started, trying to get cash for their oil in Jordan. But the return traffic was not exactly a good-buddy, that's-a-big-10-4 version of the Berlin airlift. Many of the trucks headed toward Baghdad were empty, very few seemed to be carrying food and a number of them were loaded with two-by-fours or immense rolls of pulp paper, playing what part in the war effort I'm not sure.

The road is straight and paved in a sort of folk-craft blacktop. The truck drivers go right down the center crown to avoid as many potholes as they can, and nobody dawdles out here. It is a memorable experience to roll head-on with a closing speed of 240 kilometers per hour at a fully loaded eighteen-wheel gasoline truck being driven by somebody dressed like Yasir Arafat.

The rest of the traffic coming toward me was made up of refugees. I guess I'd expected them to be pushing all their belongings in baby carriages or something, the way movie newsreel refugees always were when I was a kid. That type of refugee would sizzle and pop open like a weenie on a grill in this climate. Besides, these were affluent refugees—at least they had been until recently—in Chevrolet Caprice Classics, 200-series Mercedes, Peugeots and BMWs. And they were very modern refugees, people making a run for it not because Stukas were strafing their villages but because their bank cards wouldn't work in Kuwaiti cash machines anymore.

Every refugee car carried suitcases tied on the roof, the immense vinyl suitcases of the underdeveloped world, big as folded-up rollaway beds. Each car was more splendidly loaded than the last, bearing huge swollen stacks of luggage, and every moment that these stacks stayed in place was a tribute to Middle Eastern knotwork. But now and then some vast baby-blue portmanteau would pitch loose and go vaulting down the highway berm like a rectangular Olympic gymnast, until it exploded—an underwear bomb.

Less affluent refugees were packed into buses. And refugees less affluent than that were standing in the back of open trucks. You'd see one of these trucks pulled to the side of the road for a piss break, its occupants scattered across acres of featureless landscape, squatting in their *disdasha* robes to preserve some modesty during the call of nature.

At the Ruwayshid checkpoint thousands more refugees were arguing with officials and one another, standing in petrified lines, wandering around bedraggled or patiently hunkering in whatever shade they could find. They were contained in a five-acre barbed-wire space with a dozen smelly cement buildings between two border-guard posts that looked like turnpike tollbooths. The compound was covered with shit and litter and aflutter with the Oriental mania for making copies of documents in triplicate and stamping everything with rubber stamps six or seven times. There seemed to be some food and water available, and a mosque where, when the *muezzin* made the midday call to prayer, nobody went.

These were the lucky refugees. Out in the desert toward Iraq, beyond the Jordanian border guards who refused to let me pass, were thousands and thousands more people with no shelter at all—thirsty, hungry and desperate to get into Ruwayshid, the first-class section of hell.

I talked to a Jordanian named Abnan abu Sherke who'd waited two and a half days out there. He owned a store in Kuwait that he had abandoned and had five thousand dinars in a Kuwaiti bank which were gone forever, and he'd driven 1,750 kilometers so far trying to get back to his family in Jordan.

"We are Arabs," said Mr. Sherke in a pleasant and conversational tone of voice. "We are very happy because Iraq is face-to-face with the U.S. I have the admiration for Saddam Hussein. I lose everything but I am happy."

* * *

The next day I drove the new four-lane desert highway out to Aqaba, Jordan's only port and a would-be Red Sea tourist resort that looks like a Bulgarian's idea of Fort Lauderdale.

This is another crucial chink in the international cordon that's supposed to convince Saddam Hussein to act like Václav Havel. At the quays I counted two ships loading Jordanian phosphate, one rusty tramp steamer from Bombay and a grossly overloaded car ferry full of Egyptian refugees headed for Suez. If Saddam is going to feed a nation of eighteen million people by way of Aqaba, they'd better start eating Egyptians and their automobiles.

In an absolutely empty souvenir shop downtown the doddering owner told me, "Jordan is a friend to all nations." His thirty-year-old son said, "You know almost all the taxes you pay in America go to Israel, eighty percent." He said he wasn't anti-Semitic, either, because he'd gone to college in Romania and had a Jewish girlfriend there for six months.

I drove back to Amman by the old mountain route, 360 kilometers of goats in the right of way and spectacular cliff-top views of the Dead Sea that will kill you in a second if you take your eyes off the road. I passed through Wadi Musa, the Springs of Moses, where he struck the rock with his staff and brought forth water; and past the picturesque Bedouins with their flocks and tents and dreams of running a grocery store in Detroit.

I traversed the ancient lands of Ammon and Moab and Edom and viewed the sites of King Solomon's Mines and the Palace of Herod where Salome danced for the head of John the Baptist. The mountain highway follows the same path that the Roman road took two thousand years ago, beside the ruined line of Crusader castles with remains of Byzantine, Ottoman and British forts in between. It's a kind of Grayline Tour of failed foreign policy initiatives.

These heights above the Jordan valley, along the great rift that runs from Africa almost to Europe, are the home and hearth of the entire world's culture. The oldest remains of fixed human habitations—houses from eleven thousand years ago—have been found here in Beida and Jericho. These people buried dead children in jars under their living-room floors. No kidding. I checked up on it at the Archeological Museum in Amman—evidence that not only the Arab world but our entire civilization was founded by crazy people.

Near Wadi Musa, about 95 kilometers north of Aqaba, I stopped for a few hours to look at the ruins of Petra. This was the great stronghold of the Nabataean Arabs who flourished from the fourth century B.C. until the first century of the Christian era by straddling the caravan route from Arabia Felix to the Tigris-Euphrates valley. They made their money by helping themselves to some of everything that went by—a previous example of vast, unearned wealth in the Middle East.

The Nabataeans used their swag to build Petra, which can be reached only by traveling down the floor of an unnerving canyon called the *Siq*—three hundred feet deep and barely wide enough for three people to walk abreast. At the end of this passage is a two-square-mile city of tombs, temples, houses and public buildings all carved into the face of living rock in the most elaborate Greek and Roman styles. It is a monumental hidey-hole, a thing done by mad children with unlimited resources.

Trade routes shifted. Petra lost its livelihood. The very location of the place was forgotten, and it wasn't rediscovered until the early nineteenth century. Bedouins were still building their cooking fires in the palaces of Petra until a few years ago, when the Jordanian government's Department of Antiquities shooed them out. They come back to water their flocks and lead tourists around. A kid of about fourteen was showing me a spectacular Doric cavern with a strong smell inside. "Is here was the great temple," I said in profound and solemn pigdin, "and now is used to pen goats." The Bedouin kid looked at me like I was a big dope. I had some better idea what to use it for?

UNITED ARAB EMIRATES

September 1990

The situation down in the Gulf States is, of course, very different from that in Jordan. For one thing, the guy who stamped my passport at the Abu Dhabi airport was wearing a wristwatch worth more than my car. Also, we've got a quarter of a million troops around here keeping the locals from being pounded like cheap veal, so they're very pro-American. Well, sort of pro-American. "The foreign forces will leave the area as soon as the reasons for which they came are ended," said United Arab Emirates Defense Minister Shaikh Mohammed bin Tashid in an interview with the U.A.E. *Khaleej Times,* which also ran an editorial blaming the whole Gulf crisis on "big powers":

> The big powers have only themselves to blame for what is happening now. Greedy for money they and unscrupulous arms dealers in Western countries have supplied Iraq with all the weapons now being pointed at themselves.

So maybe they're not very pro-American, but they're very pro–not getting pounded like cheap veal. The exiled Defense Minister of Kuwait told the *Gulf Times* that he'd order an immediate attack on Iraq if he were commanding the U.S. troops in Saudi Arabia, and as I got into the elevator to go to my room at the Abu Dhabi Sheraton, a Kuwaiti in a perfectly pressed *disdasha* and carefully draped *ghutra* headdress began to speak to me in high-speed Arabic, "America something-something-something-something." I shrugged and he held up an admonishing index finger. "Quickly! Quickly!" he said.

The Gulf is a place that does not surrender itself easily to mere description. The weather, to begin with, is so bad in September that people *long* for the interior of Saudi Arabia. When I was there the temperature was over 110 degrees every day, but with a dampness that can't be possible under skies as blue as a vinyl swimming-pool liner. The windows of my hotel room were frosted like an iced-tea pitcher. One afternoon the humidity was actually 100 percent, at which point air isn't even vapor. I was breathing soup. A poison gas attack would be wholly redundant here.

Everything is air-conditioned, but not for comfort. An air-conditioned car is like a space suit. Step outside it for more than a few seconds at midday and you get dizzy, sick and as wet as if you'd been flushed down a toilet.

And there's the architecture. Abu Dhabi is new, really new, with a half million people packed into an unrelenting pre-post-modernism worse than Epcot Center. I've seen a photograph of old Abu Dhabi. There was a mud fort, of exactly the kind used as the set of *Beau Geste*. There was a mud mosque. There was the home of the British Colonial Officer and a few Bedouin tents. That was it. That was the whole town. The picture was taken in 1966.

Now buildings tower, ooze and mushroom in every shape that concrete can be poured. Some are trimmed in chrome and smoked glass like the coffeetables in time-share condos, and others make a daffy nod to Islamic tradition with pointless pointed arches opening to nowhere or senseless spreads of mosaics on ceilings instead of floors. My hotel was supposed to evoke, with rounded crenelations and brown tints, the mud fort in the center of town. But it only succeeded in looking like a grain elevator.

The city is laid out in an uncompromised grid which should make it easy to get around in even during the twilight 500SEL Benzlock. But, instead of a few numbered addresses like Amman, there are none, and no concept that a street, once named, should keep that name for any length of its existence. Thus in a downtown as simple as a tic-tac-toe board, I lost the whole Saudi embassy, and two street maps, the concierges at three hotels, the Avis rent-a-car girl, the Marines on duty at the U.S. embassy, several shopkeepers, an Iman at a mosque and the guards at the ambassador of Saudi Arabia's own residence were unable to direct me there.

When I did find the Saudi embassy, two days later, it was a big and obviously expensive building with not only no style but no discernible front. The reception room was bare except for chrome and Naugahyde conference-room chairs, one dusty formica-topped table and a standing ashtray. The floor was cheap terrazzo, the walls shabby stucco, but the ceiling was covered with rococo plaster work painted in pink and aqua and highlighted with gold leaf. On the wall was an official Saudi government map of the Arabian peninsula, which—in case you think the Kuwait fracas is the last we're going to hear from this neck of the woods—indicated disputed borders with the U.A.E., Oman, Qatar and Yemen.

There is no charm in Abu Dhabi. As the *Economist Business Traveler's Guide to the Arabian Peninsula* puts it, "There are virtually no 'sights' as such." And the only place I've ever seen with worse aesthetics or a greater taste for flash and fake was Jim and Tammy Bakker's Heritage Village USA. To which place the U.A.E. bears other similarities as well. "Oil wealth has also reinforced the religious basis of society in the Emirates," says a locally printed tourist booklet. "Today, in the cities, no one need walk further than half a kilometer to the mosque."

There are beautiful gardens, however, along all the streets and in every open space, all brought to blooming, verdant life by that thing which, in the desert, is more precious than gold—money. Even the superhighways have gardens. The road that runs 130 kilometers to the oasis of Al Ain in the mountains on the Oman border is irrigated and landscaped the entire way, sleeved in date palms and tamarisk trees and flowering shrubs, the plants tended by brown, sweating people from Pakistan, Bangladesh, India and Egypt. Only here and there can you see what's behind the mask of greenery, which is nothing, the true, complete nothing of the sand desert. There are not only no plants or animals but not even any objects, just creeping, blowing, red-blond sand in dunes that rise as high as three hundred feet.

I went, in the early mornings when I could almost stand the heat, to the *suqs,* the open-air markets in Abu Dhabi and Dubai. Though almost nothing is manufactured in the Emirates, or, really, anywhere in the Arabian peninsula, shops were stuffed with goods, a barbaric splendor of merchandise—truly barbaric. That is, synthetic fabrics of astonishing ugliness, shoddy housewares, bad appliances, every kind of electronic gimcrack known to East Asia, a million overpriced Rolexes, garish nylon carpets in lampoons of Persian designs, gold necklaces with medallions bigger than salad plates, gems cut and set like carnival prizes, furniture to make a Mafia wife wince and table lamps Liberace wouldn't have owned.

We think of a barbarian as somebody with a bone in his nose. But, in fact, a barbarian is more likely to have his nose full of a Hong Kong Shalimar knock-off. I wonder if all the polyester and highway beautification will weather as well as the ruins of Petra.

But, never mind. World peace and international order must prevail, so we're going to sacrifice ourselves and our treasure . . . Well, not actually our own personal selves. More like eighteen- to twenty-year-old selves who couldn't find worthwhile civilian jobs. And the treasure is borrowed, like the rest of the national debt. But you know what we mean. We're going to make the same brave, selfless sacrifices to save the Arabs from Saddam Hussein's crazed aggression that we made to save the Jews from Hitler's death camps, the Cambodians from Pol Pot's massacres and the Poles, Hungarians and Czechoslovaks from Stalin's terror . . . That is, the same brave, selfless sacrifice that we were going to make as soon as the Jews, Cambodians, Poles, Hungarians, and Czechoslovaks struck oil.

"SOMEWHERE IN EASTERN SAUDI ARABIA"

January 1991

This is the first globally broadcast, real-time, live, on-camera, televised war. It's so televised, in fact, that increasing CNN's Nielsen share seems to be an allied war aim only slightly less important than degrading Saddam Hussein's command-and-control capability. However, what you're reading at the moment is, as you may have noticed, print. This report is not electronic, maybe not even electric—to judge by the sound of this rented typewriter, I've got one of the early IBM diesel models. These words are thus as out-of-date as the U.S. State Department's tilt toward Iraq in the last Gulf war. By the time you read this we may be up to our Kevlar underpants in the kind of bloody trench warfare not seen since the French got their crêpes folded at the Somme. Or we may be drinking Saudi near-beer out of the open-toed slippers of Saddam Hussein's harem concubines in liberated Baghdad. Who knows? Truth is the first casualty of war, but, in this particular conflict, print journalism took the second hit.

What you're reading is not only out-of-date, it's hastily written and disorganized, too. This is war, for chrissake. At least that's my excuse. Actually, the best thing about this war has been all the new excuses generated by the Pentagon briefing officers. These will doubtless prove handy to Americans in all walks of life, especially school kids who haven't done their homework:

My book report impacted harmlessly in an unpopulated area.

I can't tell you what happened in 1066, we're waiting on the bomb-damage-assessment reports.

I'm sorry but units of elite Republican Guards were dispersed and dug in around my algebra problem.

I arrived in Saudi Arabia thirty-two hours after the war began having taken a sixteen-hour flight in the cargo hold of an Air Force C-141 Starlifter. There were 126 other journalists on the trip. Now that 2 Live Crew has been arrested, the C-141 Starlifter is the single noisiest thing on earth. The journalists couldn't hear themselves think. Of course there's nothing unusual about 127 journalists not thinking, but the Starlifter was so loud that the journalists couldn't even talk. And 127 journalists silent for sixteen hours is another first for this war.

We had a brief stop in Frankfurt, where we received what the Air Force called "a hot Italian food meal" followed by everybody's last Scotch until the war is over. We landed "somewhere in eastern Saudi Arabia," which means the port area of Dhahran on the Persian Gulf about 180 miles south of the Kuwaiti border—as Saddam Hussein has surely figured out by now. Then we were herded into a U.S. military briefing where it was explained to us that we could do absolutely nothing as journalists without U.S. military permission to do it, and whatever it was that we got permission to do, we might not be able to do that either.

In fact—as of this writing—the military has been reasonably helpful in dragging journalists out to places of moderate discomfort and/or mild danger and letting those journalists ask Oprah Winfrey–quality interview questions. But the military press office—the Joint Information Bureau, or JIB—has a strictly grade-school field-trip mentality with much posting of rules, schedules and little lists of things reporters are expected to bring along. The JIB will be requiring notes from our parents next.

Reporters used to covering "low-intensity conflicts"—where we took taxis to the fighting and it was the U.S. military advisors who weren't supposed to be there—are, in a word, bored. But, in an *un*-low-intensity conflict, bored is the way to be. It means you're still alive. Besides, what's really hurting journalism around here isn't military censorship, it's military jargon. Spend more than an hour at the JIB and you begin calling the staircase "a foot-impelled bi-directional vertical transport asset."

I haven't been to the front yet. There are more than seven hundred journalists here—far more newsmen than there is news—and there's only room for about one hundred of them on the military "pools" covering the troops. Also, I'm here as a radio journalist but am not even sure which part of a tape recorder takes the pictures.

I'd been trying to get a Saudi Arabian visa since Iraq invaded Kuwait last August, but when the name of your magazine means "a large rock that moves around" and its pages are filled with pictures of Madonna wearing cookie tins on her chest, you don't get taken as seriously as the guys from *Time*. John Lyons, an old friend of mine at ABC Radio, got me a slot as an emergency incompetent broadcast correspondent, and I'm left in the rear manning the phones and explaining the Gulf Crisis to Blitzo Bob and Rocket Jaw Jim on the WONK morning drive-time zoo.

That's all right. The rear is where the action's been. We call it "Club Scud." We've had missile attacks almost every night. When the first attack came, ABC-TV producer Derwin Johnson and I got in a car and began driving around Dhahran looking for missile damage. We heard sirens and saw flashing lights on one of the main roads. We rushed to the scene and discovered a car wreck. Then we heard more sirens and saw other flashing lights. We rushed to that scene and discovered another car wreck. We saw four or five smash-ups that night, including one involving a police car. When the air-raid sirens go off everybody starts looking at the sky instead of the road, and

Saddam Hussein's most fearsome weapon of the war's first week was the unguided Chevrolet Caprice Classic sedan.

The first sign of a Scud attack is a deep, vibrant *whoosh* from the Patriot anti-missile missile being fired. Then there's a *crack* when the Patriot breaks the sound barrier, followed by a light in the sky and a huge *boom* from the Scud being destroyed. After that there's a brief pause followed by an incredibly loud air-raid siren which our hotel sets off to let us know that the Scud attack that has just happened is expected soon. This sends the Filipino waiters and Indian busboys into a panic. They go running down the stairs to the air-raid shelter, colliding, on the way, with journalists running up the stairs to see the Scud fireworks from the hotel roof. Getting out on the roof is the third most dangerous thing about the Scuds—after car wrecks and falls on the staircase. You have to go through the blacked-out kitchen of the Chinese restaurant on the top floor, and there's considerable danger of falling into a big pot of stewed cat.

A Scud only carries about 250 pounds of explosives which—assuming the Patriots don't get it first—would create a blast a hundred yards wide at the most. These missiles are being lobbed into an area of eastern Saudi Arabia that's roughly fifty miles long and thirty miles wide. That's 4,626,400,000 square yards. The actual chance of taking a direct Scud hit is two in a million. Don't tell CNN this, however. Their nightly Scud watch—called the "Range-Finder Show" for its comments on where the missiles seem to be headed—is about all we have in the way of entertainment here.

Not only is this the first live televised war, it's also the first war ever covered by sober journalists. There is nothing available in Saudi Arabia with more "command-and-control capability" than Moussy. Which explains why a lot of the coverage from here seems a bit, well, sober. (Some of us journalists have discovered, by the way, that what we'd thought for years was the pain of genius was, in fact, a hangover.)

Coverage from here has been sober and—as sobriety often is—uninformative. After five months of the United States being about as involved with another country as it's possible to get, most folks back home still don't know what Saudi Arabia looks like. Sand and camels, they think. Sand and Marlboros and Pepsi would be more like it. Eastern Saudi Arabia looks like Arizona would if Arizona had beautiful beaches. There's the same big sky, the same sparse vegetation and the same modern architecture—most of it ugly, just like in Phoenix.

Local mores do not, however, allow for much in the way of beach-blanket bingo or *Sports Illustrated* swimsuit-edition photo ops. And there are no movie theaters, night clubs, discos or rock concerts either. And no Victoria's Secret catalogues or even lingerie ads from the *New York Times Magazine*. But there are superhighways, supermarkets and malls. Most of the power shoppers are men. What few women you see are all in black, veiled up past the forehead and draped down to the ground. When the women want a better look at things in the market, they pull the hems of their veils out and over the merchandise like nineteenth-century photographers taking tintypes.

Saudi Arabia is perhaps the richest country on earth, and there are some big houses here and some Mercedes-Benzes that aren't much smaller. But it's not an ostentatious nation. Saudi men all dress the same no matter their wealth or importance. They wear sandals and a long nightshirt of a *disdasha* or *thobe,* in white cotton or brown wool according to the season. They wear white or red-checked *gutra* headdresses held in place by the *igal* headband, a cord that was once used by Bedouins to hobble their camels. Status is told by the details—a Rolex watch, a Mont Blanc pen, a gold Dunhill lighter.

Saudi mansions are built close to each other. The two- or three-story houses are always plastered white and usually roofed in red tile. The architecture is grand in scale but austere in form—a sort of cousin-on-steroids of the Spanish colonial style. Each home is enclosed in a small garden. You don't see that slew of leisure toys with which rich Americans clutter their yards. There are no ski boats, ATVs, dirt bikes, camper vehicles, ultralight airplanes, hang gliders or whatnot. The desert comes right up to the garden walls.

Not that Saudi Arabia is all desert. There are large oases along the Persian Gulf coast. These contain thousands of date palms in a landscape so ripe, wet and buggy that it could come out of central Florida. Except that these groves of palm trees have been occupied by the same clans of strict and pious Arabs for fourteen centuries. Imagine Disney World without the Disney and without the world.

Most native Saudi Arabians adhere to the orthodox Sunni Muslim Wahabi sect. Wahabis are strict like old-fashioned American Baptists are—no drinking, dating, mixed dancing or movie going. But the Wahabis are not looney televangelist-with-a-gun fanatics of the Ayatollah Khomeini stripe. The religious practices and attitudes of Saudi Arabia are no more peculiar than those of Billy Graham. A church-going, small-town American from forty years ago would be perfectly familiar with the public morality here. Only the absolute segregation of the sexes would seem strange. And I'm not so sure about that. At O'Rourke family Thanksgiving dinners in the fifties all the men were in the living room watching bowl games and the women were in the kitchen washing dishes.

During the nine days that I've been here I have, of course, spent most of my time watching CNN to see what's happening to me. But I've also managed to visit the markets, or *suqs,* in the various towns along the Gulf coast—Dammam, Al Khubar, Qatif, Tarout. It's nice for an American to be someplace where people love the country they come from—a big change from being in America.

I've tried to get some "man in the *suq*" radio interviews but without much success. People are shy of the tape-recorder microphone. But they're eager to shake hands, say *"Marhaba"* ("Hello"), buy me a cup of coffee and ask about the war. "You are the journalist but now we will interview *you*," said a wholesaler in the Dammam fruit and vegetable market. I asked why he wanted to do that. "Because you have talked to too many people"—an accurate solecism if ever I've heard one. The people in the market wanted to know how dangerous the Scuds were, how the air war was going, when the ground war would start. They said they didn't trust the information they were getting. They wanted to talk to a newsman and hear the real story. I asked where they were getting this information that they didn't trust. "From the news," they said.

People in eastern Saudia Arabia are still worried about poison-gas attacks. Nobody here goes anyplace without a gas mask. The masks come in imitation leather shoulder bags. Every man on the street has one. Dhahran looks like it's hosting an international convention of purse-snatchers. Nothing could be further from the truth. There is virtually no crime in Saudi Arabia. You can leave the key in your car ignition here and leave your wallet and watch on the car roof, for that matter. This is one of the most honest places on earth and for good reason. Under Shari'ah religious law murder is considered a mere civil matter, involving monetary compensation of some kind, but theft can be punished by amputation of a hand. There's also no begging or importuning or wheedling of any kind. I don't know what they amputate for this offense, but whatever it is, I suggest we start cutting it off in New York City.

The Dhahran area seems a bit empty and, at the same time, over-populated with foreigners—sort of like Paris in August. Many local residents have decided that Scud month is a good time to visit relatives down around Yemen somewhere. But other than light traffic and everpresent gas masks, life is normal. Food prices have actually gone down and the only notable shortage is of AA batteries. This tells us that the U.S. troops are moving up to the front. As the troops leave, they empty the battery racks, stocking up to keep their Walkmans running. This is—one more first—the first war where everybody gets to pick his or her own theme music.

In case you're wondering, a gallon of premium gasoline costs 58¢, and, no, you don't get your windshield washed. The gas stations are just like ours, including the bathrooms. Most bathrooms in this part of the world are Turkish style—you put a foot on either side of a hole in the floor and hunker down. But Saudi Arabian gas stations are equipped with American facilities. Some of the local people are unaccustomed to using these, however, which leads to one little problem—footprints on the toilet seats.

U.S. troop morale seems to be ridiculously good. I ran into some members of the 101st Airborne Division buying art supplies in downtown Al Khubar. I'd say that indicates confidence (not to mention a previously little-suspected creative bent among our nation's paratroopers). The soldiers, sailors, marines, airmen, coast guarders and whatever in Dhahran are cheerful. Maybe they're cheerful because they're not off in hell's outhouse somewhere sleeping in sand holes and eating MREs ("Meals Ready to Eat" or, as they're called, "Meals Refused by Ethiopians"). But from what we've been seeing in the "pool" reports and hearing from the reporters who've been to forward positions, the troops up there are in a pretty good mood, too.

It's important to remember that the 1991 U.S. military is not made up of Oliver Stone and his hootch-torching platoon of hopheads. These young men and women were barely born then. They're the Reagan Kids. They took one look at the sixties leftovers which littered their childhoods and said, "Give me a haircut and a job." They've got skills, training, education, and if they'd just quit calling me "sir" and telling me, "You're the same age as my mom," they'd be the salt of the earth.

*　*　*

Give War a Chance

One more thing about this generation of soldiers—they grew up in video arcades. It's no coincidence that watching the Gulf War's high-tech weapons on our TV screens is so much like watching computer games. This war is the daddy of all Mario Brothers, the Gog and Magog of hacker networks, the devil's own personal core dump. And our soldiers have an absolutely intuitive, Donkey Kong–honed, gut-level understanding of the technology behind it. Thank God they do. It's why we're winning. So here's what you folks back home can do to help with the war effort. If you happen to have any kids and they're outdoors exercising in the healthy fresh air and sunshine, give them hell: "YOU GET IN HERE RIGHT NOW AND PLAY NINTENDO!" The future of our nation may depend on it.

GULF DIARY

January 28 through February 8, 1991

MONDAY, JANUARY 28, DAMMAM SUQ It's supposed to be a male-dominated society in Saudi Arabia, but I'm not so sure. There are amazing dresses for sale in the stores here—loud-colored silks and violently patterned satins with gold embroidery and gem-stone trimmings. Under those black *abayas* Saudi women are wearing some important fashion statements. There are also a lot of jewelry stores with big gold necklaces and big ruby bracelets and diamond rings so large that you'd practically have to wear them on both hands at once just to lift the things. I'm a married man. You can't fool me. If this were *really* a male-dominated society, the jewelry stores would be stocked with plastic pop beads and the only thing the dress shops would be selling is aprons.

Since the time of the Crusades we in the West have been using so-called "Arabic numerals." But the numerals actually used in Arabia are different from ours. The 1's are the same, but an Arabic 2 looks like a backward 7. An Arabic 4 is a backward 3. A 7 is a 6. A 0 is a 5. And a little dot is a 0. I don't know why the two systems of numbers are different, but I can guess. I'll bet if we went back and examined the Crusaders' expense-account receipts, we'd find out that Richard the Lion-Hearted got skinned.

TUESDAY, JANUARY 29, HALF MOON BAY Oil is so important in Saudi Arabia that thoughts of "Liquid MasterCard" seem to pervade everything. The U.S. Consulate in Dhahran hands out a pamphlet to visiting Americans. The pamphlet gives tips on tourism and recreational activities. But a suggested picnic outing is described by the U.S. Consulate in these terms: "The beaches nearby are open to the general public and afford a good view of the oil terminal."

WEDNESDAY, JANUARY 30, AL KHUBAR One of the pleasures of going someplace where people don't speak English is making fun of the English the people don't speak there. Many of the commercial signs in Saudi Arabia are printed in English—more or less. I've seen the "Decent Barber Shop" and the "Meat Cow Fresh Butcher Shop," also "Wow" brand toilet paper, a fast-food restaurant advertising "humburgers" (ham being illegal) and a fancy model of running shoe called, in all innocence, the "Crack."

Of course, when it comes to truly not speaking English, it's impossible to top the U.S. Department of Defense. The DOD calls a metal nut—the metal nut that goes on a bolt—I'm not kidding about this—a "hexaform rotatable surface compression unit."

One peculiar feature of Saudia Arabia is intersection art. There are lots of traffic circles, and in the middle of each traffic circle is . . . something. Devout Muslims don't approve of statues of people, so there aren't any of those. But, just in the Al Khubar area alone, there is a giant cement Arab coffeepot (a symbol of hospitality), a scale model of the Space Shuttle (because a Saudi Prince was a crew member on one mission), a real, twenty-foot-long fishing boat mounted on a concrete plinth, a large jet airplane engine in a glass case and an entire mosque, utterly isolated and unreachable on its island in the highway. There's also a lot of abstract stuff, such as a huge metal spiral (representing oil prices?) and two immense stucco triangles flanking what appears to be the robot vacuum cleaner from "The Jetsons." What I have not seen in a traffic circle—and don't think I will see—is a monument to the first Saudi Arabian who learns how to signal a turn or a lane change.

THURSDAY, JANUARY 31, INTERNATIONAL PRESS HEADQUARTERS, DHAHRAN There don't seem to be a lot of celebrities protesting against this war. New Kid on the Block Donnie Wahlberg did wear a "War Sucks" T-shirt at the Grammy awards, but that's about it. In fact, I've heard that Jane Fonda has decided to maintain public silence on the subject of Desert Storm. Getting Jane Fonda to be quiet—this alone makes fighting Iraq worthwhile.

The Saudi Arabian beach resort of Khafji has been retaken. Which leaves us with the question: what do Saudi Arabians do at a beach resort? The women are dressed in tents, you can't get a beer to save your life and it's hard to play beach volleyball in robes that drag on the ground. As much as I can figure, the only amusement that's ever been available in Khafji is the one we've just witnessed—shooting Iraqis.

You may wonder what the job of being a Gulf War journalist is like. Well, we spend all day broadcasting on the radio and TV telling people back home what's happening over here. And we learn what's happening over here by spending all day monitoring the radio and TV broadcasts from back home. You may also wonder how any actual information ever gets into this loop. If you find out, please call.

FRIDAY, FEBRUARY 1, INTERNATIONAL PRESS HEADQUARTERS, DHAHRAN Dogs are considered "unclean" in Saudi Arabia. Which, if you think about it, is true so far as it goes. Sport does like to get mud on the bedspread and roll in stuff on the lawn. But camels are *not* considered unclean in Saudi Arabia. This leads me to believe that the Saudi Arabians know something about house-training animals that we do not.

Give War a Chance

* * *

Members of the press corps have been trying to figure out what the U.S. military means when it talks about "air supremacy." We think it means that American Air Force pilots bombing Iraq are the only people in the world who can take a long trip by air and not have to change planes in Atlanta.

The so-called "pool" system of reporting the war is causing a lot of frustration. The U.S. military puts together groups, or pools, of reporters—one reporter from each kind of media. Then the military takes these pools on little trips to see things. This is like not being able to go to a football game unless Joe Montana invites you personally. If the pool system were used in dating, two hundred people would all . . . well, it would be the 1960s all over again. If we got our news at home the way we're getting it here, the only time you'd know about a fire would be when kids playing with matches phoned the local newspaper before they lit the living-room drapes.

SUNDAY, FEBRUARY 3, DHAHRAN AIR BASE I was interviewing some British Tornado pilots who've been flying missions deep into Iraq— missions that sometimes take four or five hours. And I asked them the question that was foremost in *my* mind: "Isn't that a long time to go without taking a leak?"

It turns out the pilots do have "relief sacs." But they're wearing so much clothing—flight suits, G-suits, chemical-weapon-protection suits—that it takes them ten minutes just to get ready to use these aerial bedpans. So they avoid liquids for a couple of hours before they fly, and, so far, only one Tornado pilot has actually relieved himself over Iraq. And, no, he did not target civilian areas.

MONDAY, FEBRUARY 4, THE ROAD TO ABQAIQ Out in the Saudi desert I came across one of the strangest road-hazard signs I've ever seen. I was driving through a region of huge sand dunes, and every mile or so there would be a triangular sign—the kind that says "SLOW, CHILDREN" or "DEER CROSSING" in the States. But these signs said "SAND DUNES!" Sand dunes drift at a rate of about thirty feet a year. Saudi Arabians are fabulously bad drivers, but even they should be able to avoid something that's moving at less than one millionth of a mile per hour.

WEDNESDAY, FEBRUARY 6, KING FAHD AIR BASE I was with a couple of U.S. Air Force officers, and they were complaining how everything has to be shipped in here—food, water, even the most primitive construction materials. While they were grousing I was looking around at all the bunkers, gun emplacements and air-raid shelters built out of sand bags—thousands and thousands of sand bags. "Well," I said, "I bet there's one thing you guys can get locally . . ."

"You're *wrong*," said the Air Force officers. "We know what you're going to say, but the sand here isn't the right kind of sand to make sand bags—too powdery." So the U.S. military is buying sand in Saudi Arabia.

Because of the time difference, we get the late-night TV talk shows here early in the morning. Arsenio Hall by himself is plenty alarming enough at 8:00 A.M. but this morning he had Sandra Bernhard on and, whoa, talk about something that doesn't go with breakfast. At least she makes the troops feel a little better about there being no USO shows here.

We've been having an informal competition to come up with the worst movie idea based on this war. Here's a strong contender:

A group of American war correspondents somehow gets trapped behind enemy lines, and they have to complain and exaggerate their way out of Iraq.

Give War a Chance

THURSDAY, FEBRUARY 7, HOFUF This is an ancient oasis town a hundred miles off into the Saudi desert, and it's one of the few places in this country which retains any character or visual charm. It has narrow-roofed streets in the *suq*. There's a bit of Ottoman Empire architecture left mid the concrete-block modernism. And Hofuf has one of the world's largest mud forts, a place that looks like . . . one of the world's largest mud forts.

It must have been interesting to live here. I guess when you grow up in a mud fort, Mom yells, "You kids take your shoes off before you leave—I don't want you tracking our house all over the outdoors."

FRIDAY, FEBRUARY 8, INTERNATIONAL PRESS HEADQUARTERS, DHAHRAN I watched Secretary of State Baker's speech to the House Foreign Relations Subcommittee the night before last, and I actually heard the secretary say that America will help rebuild the economy of Iraq after this war. Mr. Secretary, I just can't tell you what enthusiasm your plan has inspired here in Saudi Arabia. First, let's donate the American savings-and-loan industry to the Iraqis. Then we'll give them Michael Milken so he can set up a Baghdad junk-bond market. And, when we're done with that, we'll send in Michael Dukakis for a repeat performance of his Massachusetts Miracle.

As everyone knows, the U.S. military censors our news "pool reports." We're not supposed to tell specific locations—cities, military bases, etc. We're only allowed to name the country or, at most, the general region of that country. Hence, "somewhere in eastern Saudi Arabia."

One of my radio pool-report tapes came back from the censors with a so-called red flag and a note saying, "You cannot mention 'Thumerate' in Oman." I'd never heard of Thumerate. In vain I searched the map of Oman for Thumerate. Finally I played the tape back. What the military censors were sure was a city or vital base—

Thumerate—was an Air Force colonel from North Carolina saying, *"The Emirate* of Oman."

We keep hearing about Iraq's "elite Republican Guard." Well, if they're so elite why don't they have better jobs than sitting around getting the stuffing bombed out of them in Kuwait? And what are they guarding anyway—big charred wrecks of buildings and blown-up bridges? And one more thing—how many of these elite Republican guards are really still Republicans?

AT THE FRONT

Early February 1991

Halfway through a ninety-minute flight to the front lines aboard a C-130 Hercules cargo plane, Colonel Clay Bailey, Commander of the U.S. Air Force's 317th Tactical Airlift Wing, began explaining that this particular Hercules was patched together from two other C-130's which had crashed. "The crew calls it 'Franken-Herc,' " said the Colonel with the large smile that military men get when they're scaring civilians.

The inside of a Hercules is like an airborne basement, with wires, pipes and ductwork covering whatever you call an airplane's walls and ceiling. There's room for 42,000 pounds of cargo. Colonel Bailey wouldn't tell me what this cargo was, a secret which made me sincerely hope his crew would avoid air turbulence, let alone enemy anti-aircraft fire.

The cargo was in wooden boxes held in place by what looked like women's hairnets. That is, if a woman had big wooden boxes for a head and was wearing a hairnet, she'd look like this. Each netful rested on a metal plate as wide as the plane, and the plates sat on a wheel-covered deck—a kind of reverse skateboard or roller-floor which allows the cargo to be rapidly shoved out the back when the plane lands or even when it doesn't land, if parachutes are used.

We were flying at 6,000 feet with fighter planes somewhere above and below us so that we were the tuna fish in a giant airlift sandwich. There was nothing to see from the cockpit except winter desert haze—endless murky gray-brown ground and murky gray-blue sky with a smudge of horizon in between. We seemed to be inside a bad Mark Rothko painting. But if I looked straight below us and concentrated, I could pick things out, things that looked like random scatterings of runes or Arabic letters—wiggles and dots in the sand. The wiggles were berms—bull-dozed ridges of sand pushed up around the tents, tanks, guns and trucks, which were the dots. Berms are this war's trenches. You get dug in, but first you get bermed up. There was nothing actually random about the wiggles. This was a modern front with soldiers and weapons carefully spread around thousands of square miles. It is to the front lines of past wars as today's pro football defense is to the way football was played in the 1950s. The troops don't just line up and crouch anymore.

At first a modern front didn't seem impressive, and then I realized how long I'd been looking at wiggles and dots while flying by at 300 miles an hour. This is a big, but uncrowded, war. The sky isn't black with airplanes. The ground isn't honeycombed with bunkers. Everything in this war is so powerful, so fast and has so much range and reach that a roomy bloodbath is required.

The C-130 landed on a mile-long blocked-off section of two-lane highway about fifteen miles from the Iraqi border. The plane came in at the same angle that's used for bobsled runs. The pavement was only twenty feet wider than the landing-gear track. This is not a large margin of error when crosswinds are blowing, and they always are. Outside the scenery was similar to that photographed on Mars by the *Viking* spacecraft—so similar as to be identical and I think a NASA audit is called for.

The land was hard-packed grit the color of blood and diarrhea. It was strewn with mud-pie-looking rocks and was so awful in its perfect flatness that I thought I could see the curvature of the earth. Anywhere I stood I seemed to be standing on high ground. The horizon fell away in every direction. I got dizzy when I stared into the distance.

A cold and arid wind seemed to come from every direction at once. A few tents had been pitched. They had grit all over them and drifts of grit coming in under the tent flaps. A few soldiers were there, grit all over them, too. One of the Air Force officers had just come back from a year-long tour of duty in Greenland. "When I got off the airplane in Greenland," he said, "I thought, 'I've found the end of the earth.'" I asked him what he thought now. "I've found the other end."

Army Specialists Forest Chester of Aberdeen, Washington, Michael Lindstrom of Reno, Nevada, and Sherrie Murry of Lyons, Georgia, were using a tent pole to scratch a map of the United States into the dirt, making the outline as nearly life-size as they could. They'd been five months in Saudi Arabia without leave, and they'd been a month in this particular Satan's parking lot. The fact that I was from *Rolling Stone* magazine was the most interesting thing they'd heard in days, although that wasn't saying much. They wanted me to please tell John Prine to do another album, quick.

Listening to Walkmans is about the only fun American troops are having in a place where there's no booze and most of the women either are covered with the front-hall rug or they outrank you. By now every American soldier has listened to every cassette and C.D. in Saudi Arabia at least twice. I was talking to a sergeant in a Dhahran record store, a black woman from Chicago. She said, "Who's that girl who's got the song that goes 'da-da-da-da-da' forever?"

I said, "Suzanne Vega?"

"Yeah," she said, "I'm even going to listen to her."

Peacenik types say there would be no war if people truly understood how horrible war is. They're wrong. People don't mind a little horror. They can even be enthusiastic about it if the horror is happening to somebody else. But everybody hates to be bored and uncomfortable. If people truly understood how much sleeping on rocks, how much eating things rejected by high school cafeterias, how much washing small parts of the body in cold water and how much sheer sitting around in the dirt war entails, we might have world peace after all.

The dirty little secret of this war is that we all privately hoped the Israelis would get fed up with being Scud-whipped and break down, drop the big one and fuse the sands of Iraq into one vast sheet of glass so we could go in there and finish this thing with Windex. That isn't going to happen. And so the war drags on—a whole three weeks now. Jeeze, this thing is turning out to be longer than the Civil War miniseries on PBS.

Boredom aside, U.S. troop morale seems to be fine, whatever that means. You'll notice that the term "morale" is never used except in reference to soldiers or people in analagous positions, such as employees of large corporations or prison inmates. Even educational institutions have "school spirit" or "the mood on campus" rather than "morale." Nobody ever talks about the morale of participants in a passionate love affair, nor does the word come up in discussions of wild drinking sprees, marathon poker games or visits to whorehouses in Bangkok.

"Morale" apparently means "how well people are doing when they're not doing well at all." In that sense, U.S. troop morale is, as I said, fine. Nobody has painted a peace symbol on his helmet. And nobody—except journalists dealing with the military's Joint Information Bureau—has threatened to frag an officer. Everybody has a pretty good idea why he's here. And just about any Pfc. can articulate it better than President Bush: A whole bunch of U.S. citizens are facing a tin-pot dictator with the fourth-largest army in the world so that the tin-pot dictators with the fifth-, sixth-, seventh- and eighth-largest armies in the world won't dis Uncle. Or anybody else. One of the war's favorite T-shirts bears a takeoff of the *Ghostbusters* logo with Saddam Hussein in place of the ghost. "Who Ya Gonna Call?" it says, and below that are the numbers 001, the international telephone-access code for the United States.

Morale is particularly fine in the air. Airforces own the franchise for this war so far. Even the crews from the British Tornado fighter-bomber wing which has had four of its planes shot down were full of smiles and sang-froid. A half dozen Tornado fliers were trotted out to endure the press. When asked the inevitable age-of-sensitivity "How does it feel?" question, the crew members gave answers better suited to a gardening column than the Phil Donahue show.

"One of the things that obviously you can't train for and get used to is the amount of flak and missiles coming up," said pilot Richard Goodwin. "It does look very, very spectacular."

"I'm still amazed at the sort of sparkling lights of the anti-aircraft fire and the missiles and so forth," said Goodwin's navigator Dave Chatterson, "and I stupidly enough still find them quite pretty."

A lieutenant colonel in the Kuwaiti Air Force—who'd managed to escape to Saudi Arabia in his A-4 jet last August—was even more cheerful. "It's, kind of, happy feelings to get into Kuwait," he said. "After six months we didn't see Kuwait. And then we fly inside Kuwait. You see the country. At the same time, you know, we bomb our country." Though this didn't seem to upset him. After all, anybody who's been a bored schoolboy has fantasized about doing that. "But we try to avoid to bomb which is populated areas," he added.

Morale is fine and boredom is preferable to getting shot, but Saudi Arabia is off the hit parade. Very few people who came here for Desert Storm will be coming back on vacation. It's not that the Saudis aren't fighting. Saudi troops—uncouth-looking fellows who seem to be from the boonies of Asir and the Yemen border—fought well if not wisely at the battle of Khafji. (The Saudi brass have explained to everyone who will listen that they didn't allow the Iraqis to slip into Khafji and they won't do it again, also it wasn't their fault and furthermore it was part of a plan.) But the drab sanctimoniousness of Saudi Arabia is getting on everybody's nerves. There's no noise, no fun, no movies, no Christmas and our military chaplains have to be called—that word again—"morale officers."

Our Father, who art in . . . um . . . the gym at the Y. . . . Give
us this day our daily hobby- and leisure-time activities. . . . And
forgive us if we get in a bad mood.

And civilian Saudis themselves aren't acting much like American
civilians would if the fourth-largest army in the world were massed
on the Canadian border. Nobody is up in the master-bedroom window with his duck-hunting shotgun or out fixing punji sticks in the
herbaceous borders. The Saudis aren't doing much of anything,
which is par. They pray five times a day and everything shuts down
for about five hours at every prayer time—you figure it out. All real
work in Saudi Arabia is down by dark-skinned poor people—from
India, Egypt, Thailand and the Philippines. (Of course, you could
make a somewhat similar argument about the U.S. military, but don't
make it in front of General Powell.) There's a standing wager in the
press corps, a free bottle of postwar champagne to the first person
who sees a Saudi lift anything heavier than money.

The entire Saudi civilian war effort in Dhahran has consisted of
half the Saudis leaving town, even though Dhahran is separated from
the front by 180 miles of desert and all the U.S. Army, Air Force and
Marines in the world. I talked to an Indian who was managing a
Dhahran sportswear store. About two-thirds of the shops on the
block were closed. I asked when they'd shut. "From the beginning of
the war," he said.

"Was it the Scud missiles that scared the shopkeepers away?"

"Oh, no," said the Indian. "Just the war. They never know what
is going to happen."

"Where'd they go?" I said.

"Maybe some went to Jiddah. Maybe some are sleeping at
home. All the stores open here, they are open by Indians and Filipi-
nos."

I said, "I guess it's too far for you to go back home?"

He frowned and shook his head and said it wasn't too far at all.
"My sponsor has my passport." He couldn't leave.

So far no pejorative term has been coined for Iraqis. There's no

"Gook" or "Kraut" or "Nip" for this war. And the only Iraqi jokes I've heard, I've heard on the telephone from back home. As a matter of fact there's only one war joke going around in Saudi Arabia:

> What's the name of the Saudi national anthem?
> "Onward, Christian Soldiers."

GULF DIARY

February 11 through February 25, 1991

MONDAY, FEBRUARY 11, DHAHRAN One thing all of us here sincerely regret is that John Tower was not confirmed by the Senate as U.S. Secretary of Defense. You can bet we'd be able to get a drink in Saudi if Good-Time Johnny Tower were in charge of Desert Storm. Either that or we'd be fighting this war someplace where we could—New Orleans during Mardi Gras, for instance.

TUESDAY, FEBRUARY 12, DHAHRAN AIR BASE Ever since bombs were invented it's been customary to personalize them with messages written on the shells: "Stick this in your mustache, Saddam," that sort of thing. We've been trying, however, to improve the quality of bomb graffiti, make it a little more clever. Not that we've had much success so far:

STEALTH PILOTS DO IT IN THE PLACE WHERE YOU LEAST EXPECT THEM TO DO IT

IF YOU CAN READ THIS, YOU'RE DEAD

MY OTHER BOMB IS ATOMIC

Anyway, we're open to suggestions.

Give War a Chance

WEDNESDAY, FEBRUARY 13, DHAHRAN An Iraqi air-raid shelter was hit by American bombers. Initial estimates from Baghdad of the casualty figures ranged from 40 to 1,500. This illustrates a persistent problem in the Middle East. The zero was invented by the Arabs, but so were the next six or eight zeros after that. Americans should be warned that you will hear a lot of numbers coming out of this part of the world, but don't count on them.

THURSDAY, FEBRUARY 14, DHAHRAN It's Valentine's Day, time for romance. And what could be more romantic than sex toys? We've been trying to figure out what Saudi Arabian sex toys would be . . . edible veils? Inflatable plastic airline tickets to Europe? But in a country where a man may have as many as four wives, the most popular marital aid is probably ear plugs.

Have you noticed Saddam Hussein's furniture? You can see it in the background in his CNN interview or when he's having a photo opportunity with international peace-pest diplomats. Is this stuff Cosa Nostra Rococo, or what? Now we know why the Iraqi Air Force disappeared—they didn't want to get the white velvet upholstery in their MIG cockpits messed up flying combat missions.

If we want to demoralize the population of Iraq and sap their will to fight, we ought to show them videotapes of the South Bronx, Detroit City and the West Side of Chicago. Take a look, you Iraqis—this is what we do to our own cities in peacetime. Just think what we're going to do to yours in a war.

FRIDAY, FEBRUARY 15, DHAHRAN Maybe Kuwait really *was* a threat to Iraq. I talked to a Kuwaiti Air Force colonel who thought it had been. He explained that Kuwait was using all its oil money to buy things for its citizens while Iraq was using all its oil money for military hardware. "Iraq," the colonel said, "either had to bring its

204

citizens up to the Kuwaiti level or bring Kuwaiti citizens down to the Iraqi level." In other words, Kuwait caused the war by shopping too much. This leaves us with little hope of overall world peace as long as wives are allowed to hold credit cards in their own names.

I passed a Saudi bus on the highway last night. U.S. soldiers had written in the dust on the back and sides. "Iraq sucks," said one message, but most of the graffiti was home towns—Mobile, El Paso, Detroit, Des Moines. And way up in the corner of the bus's back window one soldier had written the name of that quintessential home town of almost all us Americans—"Suburbia."

SUNDAY, FEBRUARY 17, RIYADH I came to the Saudi capital to attend a couple of the military briefings in person.

The journalists in Riyadh are even more earnest, whiney and weenie-like than the journalists with the troops in Dhahran. One long-haired worrywart who was with either the *Village Voice* or National Public Radio was concerned that we were bombing every one of the government buildings in Baghdad. "Are we going to leave Iraq without *any* government departments?" he asked the briefing officer indignantly. Not all the reporters in Riyadh are like that, of course; the British newspaperman sitting next to me said, "We'll leave them the Department of Tourism—'See the Ruins.'"

We're used to not getting much information during the question-and-answer periods at the military briefings. But the Saudi briefing today won the prize. A reporter asked the Saudi general in charge, "What's the weather like in Saudi Arabia in March?" Said the Saudi general, "I will try to find this out for you."

MONDAY, FEBRUARY 18, WADI AS SAHBA I got stuck out in the desert. I pulled off the road to take a leak and my car went down in the sand like the *Andrea Doria*. I didn't have a shovel. I tried to dig the car out with a hubcap—the car went in deeper. I tried to put brush and rocks under the wheels—the car went in deeper. I had the car in sand up past the doorsills by the time the Saudi police happened by. They almost got their car stuck in the sand, too. They didn't have any rope so they flagged down a trucker. He didn't have any rope either so we used one of the canvas straps from his freight load. We got my car out, but the canvas strap became completely snarled in my front bumper and tangled in the police car's back axle and none of us had a knife. We spent the next half hour sawing at the cargo strap with the edge of a flattened soft-drink can.

America has all the guns and Saudi Arabia has all the money, but it's no wonder the Japanese are ruling the world.

WEDNESDAY, FEBRUARY 20, DHAHRAN I read today on the A.P. wire that our loyal NATO ally Turkey is sending two generals and three colonels to Saudi Arabia. No soldiers or anything, just generals and colonels. "Forward, me!" "About my face!" "Self, I am hereby recommending that a medal for heroism be awarded to me for saving the life of everyone under my command—which action was accomplished by my sitting myself down right here in a Riyadh hotel room."

Between 350 and 400 Iraqi soldiers just surrendered to U.S. helicopters flying hundreds of feet in the air. Not long before, another group of Iraqi soldiers had surrendered to three *Life* photographers. The Iraqis seem willing to surrender to anything. The Saudis have promised that all prisoners of war will be given adequate food and shelter, kept away from the fighting and released when the war is over. Adequate food and shelter? Kept away from the fighting? Released when the war is over? The press corps must have surrendered months ago.

THURSDAY, FEBRUARY 21, DHAHRAN Personally, I'm coming back to the United States as a big supporter of atomic power. It's worth the risk just to make sure that this part of the world *never* has any political, strategic or economic significance again. That done, we can use the Middle East for the purpose to which it is so ideally suited—dumping nuclear waste. Watch out for the nine-legged camels.

Every time I look at American TV I see these "defense experts"—former generals now being paid large fees to go on "Nightline" and talk about the Gulf War. Well, I'm a former hippie. Maybe I can get a job as a "protest expert."

Ted Koppel will say: "P.J., does your expertise as a retired long-haired butt-head lead you to think that the protesters will continue to beat drums outside the White House or will they begin chanting 'No Blood for Oil'?"

And I'll say, "Well, Ted, I believe that we will see continuation of a primarily drum-focused activity here although we cannot rule out the possibility that the protesters may eventually utilize 'Draft Neil Bush' signs. We know they have the capability."

FRIDAY, FEBRUARY 22, DAMMAM I've mentioned before that Saudi Arabia is an incredibly honest country—as well it might be, since they cut your hand off if you're caught stealing. But although there seems to be no theft here, there are enormous padlocks on all the shops and offices—sometimes four or five of them on a single door. Maybe there's a side to Saudi Arabia I don't know about. Whatever, I've decided to stay out of neighborhoods full of one-handed men.

MONDAY, FEBRUARY 25, DHAHRAN One terrible problem confronting Iraqi troops is finding something white to wave when surrendering. They've run out of pocket hankies. The Iraqi army doesn't issue bedsheets. And, since the Iraqi soldiers have been at the front lines for a long time without adequate supplies, their underwear is, frankly, gray and dingy. So, if anti-war organizations back home want to stop the fighting in the Gulf, they should send some Clorox to Iraq, quick.

Give War a Chance

*   *   *

We hear the Iraqi army is systematically blowing up buildings in downtown Kuwait City. If the architecture in Kuwait resembles the architecture in Saudi Arabia, the Iraqi army will have done one good deed, anyway. As soon as the Iraqis have all surrendered, let's send them to New York and let them take a whack at Trump Tower.

RIYADH AND THE DESERT

Late February 1991

Certain of the ancient moral philosophers—Norman Mailer comes to mind—hold that every man should experience war because war, like love, is one of the central mysteries of life.

Central? Let's hope not. Mysterious? And how. Even the most modern and baffling romances, with their diseases, divorces, custody battles over the dog and years spent afterward in therapy and Woody Allen movies are not more mysterious than combat. For example, during the past week and a half we've been facing the worst threat of this war so far—peace. Giving the Iraqi armed forces a chance to go home, simonize their tanks and think up new ways to amaze the world is the most terrifying imaginable outcome to the Gulf conflict.

But we were reasonably confident that bloody, murderous peace wouldn't break out. We'd managed to survive Saddam Hussein's first call for a cease-fire, "The Dog Ate Kuwait" peace initiative, which he presented last week. Then there was the Soviet-brokered "I'll Pull Out in Time, Honey, Honest I Will" peace plan. We endured that. So we figured we could get through George Bush's noon on February 23rd deadline.

And, indeed, as I write this, on Sunday, the 24th, word comes that the ground war has started. Word also comes that we're going to learn nothing about that ground war. The secretary of defense tells us we are entering a period of "media blackout." Thus war grows more mysterious still. And so does war reporting. Here I sit scribbling trivia while the most serious events of a generation take place so close that I can see the haze from the oil-well fires in Kuwait.

War is mysterious but never more so than when it involves two of life's other big mysteries, Saudi Arabia and the U.S. military mind.

Nothing about the U.S. military—except killing bad guys—makes sense. The military mind is unfathomable even in the most minute and specific details of its operation. Inside each MRE field-ration kit there's a pouch containing salt and pepper, gum, napkins, other odds and ends and a pack of matches. The matchbook cover is plain olive drab and bears the message:

> These matches are designed especially for damp climates but they will not light when wet.

As for Saudi Arabia, the English-language newspaper here, *Arab News,* has an Islamic agony column where readers can write in with the kind of questions Ann Landers would get if she were a Muslim scholar:

> Q. What lesson do we draw from knowing that a certain person died in the toilet?

The answer being no particular lesson to speak of. But some of the replies in the *Arab News* leave a westerner feeling that he has encountered a mentality almost as foreign as the one which produced the MRE matchbook:

> A. The rule is that when you put your socks on in the morning you should have a full ablution, washing your feet. Then before that ablution is invalidated, you put on your socks. . . . If you need to do ablution again that day, you need not take off your socks. You simply wet your hand and, using your fingers, you pass them over the top of your feet.

Simply as a physical locale Saudi Arabia is incomprehensible. It's not a matter of, "What are we doing in this place?" It's a matter of, "What is this place doing in existence?" The two-hundred-mile stretch of desert between the Persian Gulf and the Saudi capital of Riyadh is so scruffy, flattened-looking and devoid of physical features that it hardly seems to be part of nature. The land appears to have been cleared by a bulldozer the size of the Hoover Dam. It's God's Vacant Lot. There's a whole section of Saudi Arabia called the Rub al Khali, the "Empty Quarter," and the frightening thing is, this isn't it. The Rub al Khali is somehow emptier yet.

An ugly four-lane highway runs through the ugly desert from Dhahran to Riyadh. Junk is strewn all along it—rusted mufflers, empty water bottles, waste paper, lengths of cable, old truck tires, construction detritus and a thousand bright pink and yellow plastic shopping bags floating like jelly fish on the breeze.

We Americans are long trained in highway citizenship. It's been thirty-five years since I threw something out a car window without guilt. I'd forgotten the pure exhilaration of littering and found myself heaving Coke cans and half-eaten sandwiches into the ether at every opportunity.

The other signs of human life along the Riyadh road are oil wells and oil storage tanks, a few plumber's nightmare petrochemical factories and an occasional gas station.

The Saudi landscape, when there's a landscape at all, is utilitarian, industrial and dumpy—grimly practical stuff. But what is the practical result of all this practicality? There's no clue in Riyadh. It is a city with two million people and uncountable wealth, and there is no reason on earth to go there. A large, glossy picture book, *The Kingdom of Saudi Arabia,* commissioned by the Saudi government itself, says of Riyadh:

> With its flyovers and tree-lined boulevards, its first-class hotels
> and . . .

Here is a glowing official description of a nation's capital, and the first thing that the first sentence mentions is highway overpasses.

Rightly so. Riyadh is almost all new, with the worst kind of urban newness—a grid of lifeless streets in a cage of freeways, and every little rectangle is filled with modern architecture. There are miles of the usual high-rise concrete and steel self-storage-in-the-sky buildings. But the Saudis can afford the creative kind of modern architecture, too. You can always tell when modern architecture is being creative—the rest of the thing looks like the same old curtain-wall rabbit hutch but the roof is nutty. Lumpy roofs, wavy roofs, roofs in curlicues and roofs puckered in the middle like assholes—Riyadh has them. Also, like Abu Dhabi and Dubai, it has modernism that gives a nudge and a wink to Arab traditions—giant cement Bedouin tent shapes serving no purpose and enormous onion-shaped arches in the middle of nowhere. And there are all the other varieties of contemporary design: Havatrail Modern, Brobdingnagian Lego Block, Behemoth Tinker Toy, Cheese Grater of the Titans, plus some of those buildings that are wider at the top than they are at the bottom, who knows why?

The Saudis are guaranteeing the safety of all surrendering Iraqi troops, and they're also providing asylum to everybody who ever got kicked out of architecture school.

Only a few of the traditional mud houses of the Nadj, or central Arabian highlands, are left in Riyadh, and the Saudis are tearing these down as fast as they can. The flat-roofed buildings are reddish-beige, the color of a frostbitten nose. More vertical and austere than American adobe homes, each is a sort of private tower keep with only a few small, deep-set and shuttered windows. The floors are made of palm-trunk beams covered in layers of thatch. Simple pie-crust and pinking-shear patterns are traced around the edges of the roofs. By watching the demolition work I acquired a sort of X-ray vision. Where walls were toppled, I could look inside the houses and see the steep switchback staircases with their rounded mud steps leading to snug rooms all white-washed, with borders around the windows and doors painted in brilliant blues and greens.

Around the corner from the demolition site I found several dozen Filipino construction workers shoveling wet dirt and straw into a cement mixer. They were building a brand-new mud structure. This, I was given to understand, would be ready for tours in a month—the traditional architecture of Old Riyadh painstakingly reconstructed within two hundred yards of Old Riyadh being torn down.

I drove southeast out of the capital, following a line of oasis towns in the riverless riverbed of the Wadi as Sahba. Each town was a miniature of Riyadh in its up-to-date ugliness and sat in a nasty little tangle of date palms that looked like the cat had gotten into the potted plants.

The road was two-laned here and the driving was, as it is everywhere in Saudi Arabia, horrific—conducted at absolute top speed with no thought for consequences. Though there were plenty of consequences to be seen. Amazing car wrecks lay beside the road, sometimes a dozen of them in a mile, things you would never know had been cars if a couple of car wheels weren't sticking up out of them. Whole Chevrolets were crumpled like gum wrappers. And these wrecks had taken place without collision on a perfectly straight and level road that is absolutely free of obstructions. Cars just somehow go blooey and wind up in a wad beside the highway.

Running parallel to the road was a railroad track that was also perfectly straight and level and absolutely free of obstructions. And— sure enough—amazing train wrecks lay beside the rails, things that you would never know had been trains if a couple of train wheels weren't sticking up out of them.

* * *

I stopped in one of the oasis towns to get gas and some more Coke cans to throw out the window. There was a Bedouin kid about fourteen years old at the little store there. Most Saudis are—whether they take their socks off during ablution or not—fastidiously clean, and they are polite to the point of cold formality. But this kid was pesky and dirty and determined to practice his nonexistent English. "Riyadh? Riyadh? Riyadh?" he said. Yes, I'd come from Riyadh. "Is seeing George Bush?! George Bush?! George Bush?!" George Bush is a president. Riyadh is a capital. Naturally I'd seen him there. Then the kid tried to sell me something. It was a photograph of a girl—with her veil off. I've been here so long I blushed.

Turning back toward the Persian Gulf, I drove northwest through the 150-mile-long Ghawar oil field. The whole way I could see an immense natural gas burn-off flaring on the horizon like the pillar of fire that guided the Hebrew tribes by night when they were fleeing from Egypt. Above the flame was a huge vertical cloud like the pillar of smoke that guided the Hebrew tribes by day. But the Hebrew tribes wound up in Israel and the oil wound up here. Those Hebrews took a serious wrong turn.

Is this empty, dusty, cheerless, oily, fun-free place making the American military crazy? Here's another mystery of war—no. Even being in the American military isn't making the American military crazy. I visited an Army motor pool where the soldiers had—with the exceptions of a few forays into the shockingly dull local town—been confined for five months to one vast expanse of asphalt surrounded by razor wire. Specialist Hefner of St. Mary's County, Maryland, and Specialist Jonas of Bay City, Texas, both streaked with grease like zebras, were happily wrenching on a large truck. "She's our best mechanic," said Specialist Hefner of Specialist Jonas, who had left a baby behind in the States to come do this. Specialist Jonas gave a shy smile of nondenial. "We don't like it here too much—nothing to do," said Specialist Hefner. But that was all I could get out of them in the way of complaints, although Specialist Hefner did allow that the Saudis "drive like fools."

At Saudi Arabia's main Persian Gulf port facilities in Dammam, I talked to Captain Johnny L. Sawyer from Detroit, Michigan, Commander of the 551st Transportation Company. His job is to unload boats. Captain Sawyer said, "When we initially arrived here, we worked the soldiers eighteen hours a day, gave them four to six hours rest, at most, and put them back to work. There weren't any complaints whatsoever. That's seven days a week, and we've been doing that for the past six months. They're down to a twelve-hour schedule now but we still have soldiers that are willing to work extra hours without being told. They stay behind just to finish a job." Captain Sawyer had been in the Army for thirteen years and had come up through the ranks. "The quality of the soldiers, from then to now," he said, "has improved drastically. I don't think that a soldier that we would have called standard then would be allowed to join the Army today."

I talked to a medical officer at one of the British field hospitals. He'd been in Vietnam and this was his first contact with the American military since. "I was astonished when I got here," he said. "Every American soldier I met was tidy, cheerful, eager to help, glad to be here—well, not precisely *glad,* but you know what I mean. This had not been my experience in Vietnam. It is as if the American soldiers here come from a different nation."

And that is one last mystery of war—where did the addled, sniveling, pointless America of the past quarter century go? There's no trace of it in these parts. The catch phrases of this war are "I'll make it happen," "not a problem," "good to go" and "hoo-ah!," a sort of all-purpose noise of enthusiasm. When the chairman of the Joint Chiefs of Staff visited here, the soldiers asked him for his autograph. A sense of doing something worthwhile and important has even infected a few members of the press corps. Some reporters were ready to check into the local clinic after experiencing a strange and frightening choked-up feeling when looking at the American flag.

At the King Fahd Air Base, west of Dhahran, there's a small sign posted in one of the buildings taken over by the U.S. Air Force:

GIVE WAR A CHANCE

MISSILE ATTACK ON DHAHRAN

February 25, 1991

We couldn't go to war, but war came to us. Two days into the ground assault on Iraq the majority of the press corps was stuck, as usual, in the press headquarters at the Dhahran International Hotel. There was a Scud missile attack on Monday night, one of dozens since the war began. We didn't think much about it. Some of the technicians on the outdoor TV platforms—where you see correspondents stand with the foolish blue-domed roof of the hotel's pool cabana in the background—watched the Scud go down. They thought it hit near the local shopping center and we joked that Saddam Hussein was targeting Dhahran's only decent record store. Then we went back to the work of pretending we knew more about this war than people watching television in Cleveland.

The missile had, indeed, struck right behind the record store, going through the roof of a warehouse that had been converted to a billet for U.S. troops. We heard nothing about this at the press headquarters. Almost two hours later I was driving to Dammam and I saw hundreds of blue police lights blinking in clusters around the shopping center. A half dozen helicopters hung in the sky with their searchlights moving back and forth like blackboard pointers. And ambulances were rolling away in long and frighteningly silent convoys.

Saudi police blocked the road. I parked and followed a crowd of robed Saudi onlookers, some of them holding hands, most of them speaking in whispers. They moved across a half mile of open fields toward the shopping center. It didn't seem like a disaster scene. What had been the warehouse with more than one hundred Americans inside didn't look like a building that had been blown up. I thought I was staring at a construction site. The framework of steel girders was mostly still standing. Some of the I-beams were twisted or collapsed, but the ventilation ducts and the electrical conduits remained in place. What I didn't understand was that there had been a roof and walls. And these were utterly blown away.

There was really nothing else to see except slightly panicky Saudi police and very serious American troops. Twenty-seven soldiers were killed and ninety-eight were wounded—more American casualties caused by one unlucky Scud strike two hundred miles behind the lines than had been suffered in the whole rest of the war so far.

KUWAIT CITY

March 1991

As befits a short war, it didn't take me long to readjust to peace—three minutes and forty seconds to be exact, the length of one Billy Idol music video. I was drunk and lying on a hotel bed in Rome. In the previous forty-eight hours I had managed to get myself out of the reeking, scrambled mess of Kuwait, back to the ugly, sterile, unwelcoming Saudi capital of Riyadh. From there I'd driven across hundreds of miles of stupid desert in a disposable diaper of a Korean rental car and finagled a ride out of Dhahran on an airliner chartered by an English TV company to take its people and gear to the next place foreigners decide to get killed.

It didn't seem like it had been a short war at that particular moment, not after two months with the arrogant, lazy Saudi Arabians and nothing to drink. We charter passengers were into the Johnnie Walker miniatures before the plane cleared the runway, and grown men, adult broadcasting executives with serious jobs in a large corporation were kneeling in their seats, trying to swill from three or four little Scotch bottles at once and screaming out the windows at the diminishing landscape, "FUCK YOU, YOU MOVING TEA TOWELS."

Anyway, as I was saying, I was lying on a hotel bed in Rome, and I flicked on the television, and there was MTV showing a Billy Idol video. Billy was really going at it, running around the stage in a most histrionic way, thrusting his fist into the air, stamping his feet and making violent and emphatic faces at the camera. It was a dramatic performance but confusing to my woozy intellect. What, I wondered, was Billy Idol being dramatic *about?* I'd just spent the past week in a burned-up, blown-up, looted city where there was no food or water, seeing mangled bodies and hearing stories of murder, rape, abduction, etc.—pretty dramatic stuff. It made me get drunk and lie on the bed without taking my shoes off. But Billy Idol seemed to have experienced something much more dramatic, so much more dramatic that it made him strip half-naked, dye his hair platinum, wear a bunch of jewelry and jump around like an ape.

"Billy Idol concerts are," I thought, "obviously worse than war."

Kuwait did have a better light show. There is nothing else in the world (I'm glad to say) quite like four or five hundred burning oil wells casting a lambent glow upon a nighttime desert landscape. The flames come up out of the wellheads in soft, thick, billowing shapes like clouds or turds or cake batter. The fires are scary when you glance at them but terrifying if you keep looking. That is, the fires seem to be big and close. Then you stare into the perspectiveless desert and realize they are fifteen or twenty miles away and are therefore enormous beyond comprehension. You can hear them across all that distance. There's no reassuring, ordinary crackle and roar in the noise the fires make, and no blast of heat. Instead the sound is a steady, sucking rumble of the whole atmosphere being dragged toward the conflagrations. And beyond the fires that you see are the fires you can't see, brightening the horizon on all sides like a dozen simultaneous dawns breaking on one very bad day.

I had a lot of time to look at the oil-well fires because on the third night of the ground war I spent six hours with forty-five other journalists and a half dozen British army officers being held at gunpoint in the middle of the Kuwaiti desert.

Not by Iraqis, of course. The Iraqi army was in high-speed

rewind. We were under arrest by a Saudi colonel who was furious that the British didn't have the correct paperwork for escorting a convoy.

Our mission to bring pool journalists from Dhahran to Kuwait City was not moving with the same efficiency and precision as the rest of the allied Gulf War operations. The British military escort, an affable but clueless bunch—"The Desert Squirrels"—did not have two-way radios or even maps. They put the eighteen-vehicle convoy together with the slowest things at the back so that the trucks all lost sight of the cars within minutes. The main purpose of the convoy was to get the British Independent Television Network's satellite dish into Kuwait. The first thing the British officers did was leave that dish behind. The second thing they did was take a wrong turn leaving Dhahran and head south toward Qatar instead of north toward Kuwait City. It took us eight hours to reach the Kuwaiti border, a three-hour drive.

It was dark by the time we passed through the well-shelled town of Khafji and its abandoned Saudi customs post. We could hear artillery fire in the distance now, and every few hundred feet we'd pass a burned Iraqi tank or personnel carrier. Saudi troops moving north had pushed these derelicts to the side of the road, and they sat like the cars up on blocks in front yards in certain parts of America. We seemed to be driving through a neighborhood of ultra-militant hillbillies.

Shrapnel was scattered everywhere on the road, causing a half dozen blowouts. And more time was wasted when young journalists—members of that generation so handy with keyboards, modems and electronic what-all—had their first encounters with screw jacks and lug wrenches. Then we got arrested.

The Saudi colonel, who looked like a cross between Omar Sharif and Mr. Potato Head, had a platoon of soldiers line up across the road and level their rifles at us. "YOU DO NOT HAVE THE PERMISSIONS! HOW CAN YOU BE COMING HERE WITHOUT THE PERMISSIONS WHEN I AM THE PERSON WHO IS MAKING THE PERMISSIONS FOR YOU TO COME

HERE?! YOU MUST GO BACK TO DHAHRAN AND GET THE PERMISSIONS FROM ME THERE TO COME HERE AND GIVE ME PERMISSIONS!!!" shouted the Saudi colonel.

In vain it was explained to the colonel that this was an official British military convoy, that the British were Saudi Arabia's allies, that this was Kuwait and not Saudi Arabia anyway and that we could hardly go back and get permission from him in Dhahran when he was here.

The electronic-minded young journalists fetched a Peter Arnett–style satellite phone out of their luggage and set it up in the middle of the road and phoned the Kuwaiti Minister of Information at his exile home in Tarif. The minister told the colonel the convoy could proceed, whereupon the colonel hung up on the Minister of Information and threatened to shoot the satellite phone with his submachine gun.

In the midst of this argument a metallic-blue Ferrari 328 came humming through our convoy, its thousand dollars' worth of tires and its three inches of ground clearance apparently immune to jagged metal fragments. This was just a couple of Kuwaiti refugees determined to get home before the liberation rush. They didn't even slow down for the gun-pointing soldiers, who jumped like quail to get out of the Ferrari's way.

In the end it turned out what the Saudi colonel wanted was a sufficiently abject and humiliating apology from the British officers for, I guess, failing to fill out, in triplicate, the Request for Permission to Help Keep the King of Saudi Arabia from Getting the Holy Kaaba Stuffed up His Butt by Saddam Hussein Form or something.

Apology delivered, the Brits led our convoy directly into downtown Kuwait before realizing that the city had not actually been reconquered.

Iraqi jeeps, trucks, armor and artillery pieces were lying on their tops and sides all along the Kuwait City expressways as though somebody had spilled Saddam's toy box. The Iraqis who'd been inside all seemed to be gone, in one sense of the word or the other. In place of the Fourth-Largest Army in the World we saw cruising teens. This was the Kuwaiti Resistance. One group of five pulled up in a Buick Park Avenue, happily brandishing AK-47's out the windows of dad's car. They were dressed just like teenagers would dress if the cool kids at the high school got to form their own partisan army—one guy favored the Rambo look, another was dressed like Little Steven, two others were got up in Mutant Ninja Turtle garb and one fellow, who wasn't quite with the program, seemed to have stepped out of a J. Crew catalogue. They were hunting for Iraqis or people who looked like they might be Iraqis or people who had collaborated with Iraqis or had thought about collaborating. And I wouldn't be surprised if they were also keeping an eye out for the algebra teacher who gave too many pop quizzes. Small arms fire could be heard coming from various places in the lightless city. It was a teenage dream come true: Bad guys invade your neighborhood and you and your best friends get to stay out late, kill them, skip school and impress girls. The Kuwaiti Resistance fighters welcomed us effusively. But when teenage dreams start coming true, sensible adults get out of town.

The Brits decided we should go to the International Airport even though we'd been hearing on the shortwave radio about a tank battle there. Fortunately, this was over but lots of jumpy U.S. Marines were patroling the airport perimeter, and it was a shock to their systems when they came across us, totally lost, in eighteen civilian vehicles packed with camping gear, foodstuffs, bottled water and people in Banana Republic clothes. It must have looked like the Adventure Tour travel business had gotten completely out of hand.

Going back into the city at 6:00 A.M., we could see that the Iraqis had left in brainless panic. All their wrecked military equipment was pointed in the same, Baghdadward, direction. Allied air strikes had caused some of the destruction but traffic accidents had caused more. Jeeps had smashed into tanks. Tanks had rammed bridge abutments. Armored personnel carriers had rear-ended ambulances. A truck towing a howitzer had jack-knifed and collided with itself. And a T-55

Soviet tank came a cropper on a highway divider and wound up high-centered, three and a half feet in the air.

Iraqi defenses had been abandoned with the same comic haste. Guns, ammunition, canteens, helmets, even shoes were left behind. Tea kettles were still sitting on paraffin burners. I found somebody's uneaten dinner—a pot full of chicken and rice, or rice and cat maybe, white meat anyway. The defenses themselves were pathetic. The Iraqis had built miles of low dirt berms across the main road from Saudi Arabia. These were little more than speed bumps, and were supposed to . . . to what? . . . signal allied armor, "Slow, War Zone"? In Kuwait City every highway overpass had a little pillbox built on it—four feet square and three feet high with no roof or back wall. These tiny redoubts were made of crumbly local bricks pasted together with a few dabs of mortar. Hundreds of them pimpled the city in places the Iraqis had, by some mysterious thought process, decided were strategically important. Thus the roofs of all the hotels had pillboxes but the roofs of other tall buildings didn't, and while expressways were defended, roads with two-way traffic were not.

Iraqi soldiers had made sad little nests in these emplacements—lined them with stolen blankets, chunks of foam rubber, old clothes and canned goods taken from local homes, pictures of pretty women torn from magazines and other bits of unmilitary junk. The local soccer stadiums and Kuwait's only ice-skating rink had also been fortified, the fortifications consisting of one row of sandbags placed in front of each principal entrance. The Iraqis must have thought that General Neal began every press briefing in Riyadh by saying, "In excess of two thousand combat air sorties were flown in the Kuwaiti Theater of Operation yesterday, targeting continues to be travel and leisure facilities and small mounds of dirt."

Members of the Kuwait Resistance showed me a twenty- by thirty-foot model of Kuwait City in the basement rec room of a mansion that had been occupied by Iraqi staff officers. The model was made of sand with blue-dyed sawdust for the Persian Gulf. Roads were indicated with gift-wrap ribbon and the principal buildings and military installations were represented by Lego blocks. Handsome navy-blue construction-paper arrows showed U.S. forces coming ashore into conveniently located minefields, while much larger and more festively lettered red arrows showed Iraq's reinforcements arriving from somewhere in the direction of the rec room's projection TV. It seemed Saddam Hussein had let the defense of Kuwait be planned by the prom decorations committee.

The Iraqis were better at destroying Kuwait City than they were at keeping ahold of it. But they weren't really too good at this either. Again their first concern was with the hotels, as if allied forces would never be able to effect a real conquest without room service. The Iraqis tried to set all the hotels on fire, but in many cases they used diesel oil, which is not the best of arson accelerants. The hotel where I found a room had survived pretty much intact except that a thick layer of greasy and insoluble oil soot had settled on every chair, table, towel, bedsheet and toilet seat. After a couple of days, all the reporters staying there looked like they had passed out in a tanning booth.

Downtown there was evidence of plentiful random artillery fire, like children had had tantrums with tanks. But the big cocktail onion–looking pointy water-tower things that are the symbol of Kuwait City proved too sturdy for Iraqi gunfire, or maybe just too hard to hit when whole sides of city blocks offered themselves as targets. The *suqs* with their flammable jumbles of shops had been successfully torched. And anything complex and vulnerable, such as power stations, desalinization plants and the main telephone switchboard, was thoroughly ruined.

But what the Iraqis were really good at was looting. Every store and office and an enormous number of homes had been sucked clean of all possessions. Nothing was left behind except the trash of deliberate vandalism and, in some cases, piles of human shit. The Hilton Hotel had been taken to pieces room by room. It looked like all the worst rock bands in the world had stayed there at the same time.

The city was not, however, extensively booby-trapped. The Iraqi soldiers were evidently so stupid and eager to leave that it was hard to imagine them having the forethought to wire up surprises. "All boobies, no traps," was the consensus. And most of us quit worrying about dirty tricks. Besides, there was so much untricky dangerous stuff lying around the city—live bullets and artillery shells, loose mortar rounds, unexploded American cluster bombs and so forth. An NBC camera-crew member lost some fingers fondling a land-mine detonating cap he'd picked up as a souvenir. And mines were going off on the city beaches with fair regularity, turning some unwary Kuwaitis into what the GI's call "pink mist." I was helping dismantle one of the small pillboxes on the Hilton's roof, getting bricks to level a satellite dish. There was a wooden carton sitting in the pillbox. I lifted the lid and found enough RPG—rocket-propelled grenade—rounds to put me, bricks and satellite dish in permanent earth orbit. I closed the lid carefully and extinguished my cigar.

The Hilton is next-door to the American Embassy, and a couple days later U.S. Special Forces came and "swept" the hotel to make sure a small thermonuclear device wasn't hidden in the basement or anything. I saw one of the Special Forces guys later in the hotel lobby. "Hey, we found a booby trap!" he said in the perky, enthusiastic, pumped-up way nineteen-year-old Special Forces guys have of saying these things.

"Good for you," I said. "Where was it?"

"In a big box of RPG's, in that first gun emplacement on the edge of the roof. You know, the one with some bricks missing off it. There was a hand grenade with the pin out in there. Man, if anybody had jiggled that box . . ."

I briefly got religion. "God spared me for a special reason," I thought and felt very good about myself. "I must be going to accomplish something very important in life, something that will benefit all mankind." It was a couple of days before it occurred to me that there had been two dozen other people on that roof, also spared for a special reason by God. It's probably one of them who's going to invent a vaccine to prevent Jim Morrison revivals or whatever.

On Thursday afternoon, February 28th, about six hours after the U.S. declared a cease-fire, the victorious armies began to roll into Kuwait City. The Arab contingents were firing their guns in the air and the Kuwaiti Resistance fighters responded by firing *their* guns in the air and then the other Kuwaitis picked up all the leftover Iraqi guns and started firing these in the air, too. People were singing, dancing, clapping their hands and beating on car horns. The women began their eerie ululation, that fluttering liquid animal sound made somewhere in the back of the throat, and the women's kids joined in with a more familiar plain screaming of heads off. An impromptu parade was begun past the American embassy, but there really wasn't anyplace else that the crowd wanted to parade to so the parade turned in ever tightening circles in front of the embassy and finally just stopped and became a crowd. The crowd yelled, "George Push! George Push! George Push!" Someone had already spray-painted "Thank you for George Push" across the American embassy wall, and the "P" had been carefully crossed out and the spelling corrected. A donkey was led down the street with an Iraqi helmet tied on its head and "Saddam Hussein" painted on its flanks. The first American soldiers showed up and everyone had to kiss them and shove babies into their arms and get the soldiers to autograph Kuwaiti flags. Kuwaiti flags were everywhere and at least a dozen little girls wore Kuwaiti-flag dresses—one red sleeve, one green sleeve, white down the middle and a black triangular yoke at the neck. Their mothers must have been stitching these all through the war. There were plenty of American flags, too, one with a picture of Marilyn Monroe sewn over the stripes. And across one intersection downtown a thirty-foot banner had been strung, reading—in answer to the U.S. and European anti-war protestors' "No blood for oil" slogan—BLOOD FOR FREEDOM.

Then there was a great noise and wind, and descending from the sky into this melee came a huge American Army helicopter down onto the roof of the U.S. embassy. The helicopter disgorged a squad of Army Rangers to roaring, stentorious cheers. It was the fall of Saigon with the film run backward.

A lot of people were crying, and I was one of them. A young Kuwaiti came out of the crowd and he was crying, and he grabbed me by my notebook and, with that immense earnestness that you only have an excuse for two or three times in your life and usually that's when your mother is dying, he said, "You write we would like to thank every man in the allied force. Until one hundred years we cannot thank them. What they do is . . . is . . ."—words failed him— ". . . is *America*."

Not everything was quite so saccharine as that in Kuwait City, of course. Earlier in the day, on the other side of the Hilton Hotel, some scores had been settled. Kuwaiti Resistance kids shot up an apartment building that was supposed to be full of Iraqi collaborators. The Kuwaitis dragged out three ordinary-looking middle-aged men, one howling for mercy and two looking deeply bummed. "They are Sudanese Intelligence," said one Resistance kid. Though any review of Sudan's recent history would render that phrase oxymoronic. The suspects were shoved into a Toyota Supra sportscar and taken off to I'd-rather-not-think-where. Later I saw another alleged collaborator arrested at bazooka-point. Let me tell you, that was a quick give-up.

Palestinian guest workers, many of whom had had the bad taste to chortle over the Iraqi conquest of their Kuwaiti employers, were a particular target of the Resistance. Roadblocks were set up all over town to ferret out the Pals. The roadblocks were manned—boyed, to be exact—by nervous kids with automatic weapons. It was like being back in Beirut in the mid-eighties except these militants wanted to hug you for being American instead of shoot you for it. Considering how sloppy the Kuwaitis were about gun safety, getting hugged was probably as dangerous.

Some of the Palestinians weren't playing things too smart. I found one of them standing in line with a jerrycan at a gas station. He was being insulted by the Kuwaitis on either side of him. Instead of making excuses or becoming suddenly Syrian, he jumped out of line and started shouting at me: "Why you Americans come here and do this, why you don't come to the West Bank as we have been waiting for since 1962?!" I presume he meant '67 but, whatever, it didn't seem like the most politic tack to be taking at the moment. The

Kuwaitis apologized to me and pulled the Palestinian back into the gas line so they could insult him some more.

As joyful as the Kuwaitis were, they were just that furious. It was a difficult frame of mind to understand at first, though happy anger is probably more common and less contradictory than it sounds. Every Kuwaiti I spoke to had had members of his or her family beaten, killed or simply taken away. The hospital morgues were filled with the remains of tortured Kuwaitis, many unidentifiable. Every cemetery had a swath of new graves, mostly filled with men, the birth dates on the tombstones painfully contemporary and the death dates beginning August 2nd, 1990.

I visited a mass grave where two-hundred-some Kuwaitis were interred and these were only the bodies that family members had been able to retrieve and bury by stealth. In another cemetery I found a man tending the graves of his uncle and his uncle's son-in-law. Each tomb had an improvised wooden marker and a bottle stuck neck-down into the dirt with a verse of the Koran rolled inside. The man stood between the bare-earth mounds with his hands at his sides and spoke very quietly. His expression was of enormous, almost hysterical resignation, a kind of smile of grief. He said his uncle's body had burns from a clothes iron and from cigarettes. There were marks of electrical wires. His fingers had been chopped off. His eyes gouged out. Finally he had been shot in the head. The son-in-law had been tortured with an electric drill, then scalped, then shot in each eye.

"They were taken away on January 17th," said the man in the cemetery. That was the day the air war began. "The bodies were left at hospitals on January 19th," he said. "These people were not resistance." He paused and then said in the same quiet voice, "Iraqi occupying soldiers should be given back to the Kuwaiti people."

When the Iraqis tried to leave Kuwait City, early on the second day of the ground war, they headed en masse up the road to Basra using both sides of the six-lane highway. About thirty-five miles north of

the city, near a low rise called the Mutlaa Ridge, this bug-out was
spotted by U.S. Navy A-6 attack planes. These Navy pilots must fly
New York City traffic helicopters in civilian life, because they knew
exactly what to do. They went right to the spot on the crest of the
ridge where the road narrows from six lanes to four and plugged that
bottleneck with cluster bombs.

> We've got a real tie-up, outbound on the Basra Road this morning
> due to explosion, incineration, mutilation and death . . .

The panicked Iraqis tried to drive around the burning wreckage
and became bogged down in the sand. The traffic jam spread out and
backed up until it was nearly a half mile wide, more than a mile long
and contained at least fifteen hundred vehicles. Then all the airplanes
that the U.S. Navy, Marines and Air Force could muster came in and
let loose with everything they had. One Navy pilot called it "shooting
fish in a barrel," but it was more like sticking a 12-gauge shotgun into
a goldfish bowl.

The wreckage was still smoldering four days later. It didn't look
like a battlefield. There were some Iraqi army vehicles in the mess—
tanks opened up like bean cans and armored personnel carriers
turned into giant hibachis. But most of the transport had been stolen,
stolen in a perfectly indiscriminate frenzy of theft that left the ground
covered with an improbable mixture of school buses, delivery vans,
sports coupes, station wagons, tank trucks, luxury sedans, fire engines, civilian ambulances and semi–tractor trailers. I saw a motor
scooter, a Geo Tracker and—the vehicle that would be my personal
last pick for something to escape in—a cherry-picker crane. It looked
like a bad holiday traffic jam in the States except charred and blown-
up, as though everybody in hell had tried to go to the Hamptons on
the same weekend.

Allied burial details were moving through the wreckage, but
some bodies were still lying there crispy and twisted in agony. I felt
sorry for the poor dead bastards, but it was a reasonable, detached
kind of sympathy that came from the went-to-college part of the

brain. I was intellectually obligated to feel sorry for them, but after seeing what they'd done in Kuwait City, I had more of an Old Testament feeling in my heart:

> Then did I beat them as small as the dust of the earth, I did stamp
> them as the mire of the street, and did spread them abroad.
> —II Samuel 22:43

Of course I didn't do this personally, but my tax dollars helped. I caught myself giggling at the carnage. This supposedly formidable and certainly ruthless army had not only run from a fight like a flock of broiler hens, it had also tried to carry with it every item of portable swag in the Emirate. The killing field here was littered not so much with corpses as with TVs, VCRs, Seiko watches, cartons of cigarettes, box lots of shampoo and hair conditioner, cameras, videotapes and household appliances. School desks, tea sets, stuffed animals, silverware, an accordion and a Kuwaiti family's photo album were all being dragged back to Iraq. I saw a pickup-truck bed full of women's ball gowns and another truck stacked with Pampers. A hot-wired camper van sat with two cans of club soda resting in the dash-mounted drink gimbals. The camper bunks were filled with men's boxer shorts, the price tags still on them, and the whole—camper van, club sodas, underpants and all—was punched full of tiny holes like a cheese grater from cluster-bomb shrapnel. What we had here was the My Lai of consumer goods.

Six days after the liberation of Kuwait the Kuwaitis were still celebrating outside the U.S. embassy, firing every available weapon in the air, including the .50-caliber dual-mount machineguns on the Saudi and Qatari personnel carriers. It's one thing to get plinked on the head by a falling pistol bullet, but a .50-caliber slug plummeting from the sky at terminal velocity could go right through you to the soles of your feet. One American marine told me that sixteen people had been killed by "happy fire" so far, but a U.S. Army officer said it was more like a hundred and fifty. All the press corps' telephone and television satellite up-links were on the roof of the Hilton and rounds were beginning to land up there. One bullet came down between the feet of ABC executive Neil Patterson, who started handing out helmets and battle gear to everybody on the ABC payroll. The most dangerous thing I did during the entire war was cook spaghetti sauce on a camp stove on the Hilton roof without wearing my flak jacket.

Finally, one of the ABC satellite technicians—a Brit and a veteran of the Special Air Services—could stand it no more and leaned over the roof parapet and bellowed at the trigger-crazed Kuwaiti merrymakers, "STOP IT! STOP IT! STOP IT! PUT THOSE FUCKING GUNS AWAY AND GO GET A MOP AND A BROOM AND *CLEAN THIS COUNTRY UP!"*

I went out to the Kuwait International Airport, or what was left of it, to try to get home. While I was sitting out there next to the burned ruins of the International Terminal, a Saudi business jet arrived guarded on all sides by U.S. Cobra and Apache helicopters. The Crown Prince of Kuwait was returning home after a comfy exile in Tarif.

The next thing I knew the tarmac was covered with sleek Kuwaitis in perfectly draped *disdashas*. They were shaved and scrubbed and their gold wristwatches sparkled in the sun. A U.S. Air Force enlisted man, sitting next to me on a broken couch that had been dragged out of the rubble of the first-class lounge, said, "When the fat guys in the bath robes come back, you know the war is over."

I hitched a ride back to Saudi Arabia on a New Zealand Air Force C-130. The members of the flight crew were all in their twenties and filled with leftover joy of combat. They let me stand on the flight deck as they brought their 132-foot wingspan, 100,000 pounds of an airplane down to a hundred feet and began chasing camels and goats across the desert at 300 miles an hour. The scattered tamarisk bushes were coming at us like uncountable fastballs in a batting-cage nightmare. The camels gave out pretty quick but the billies and nannies and kids were inspired to remarkable sprints of terror—turbo goats. The vast destitution of the Dahna Sands spread out in an infinity around us. "Wall-to-wall fuck-all, eh?" shouted the Kiwi pilot. He and his crew mates had smiles as wide as their skulls. This was the stuff that made it all worthwhile, to be in absolute charge of 17,200 horsepower, to have, gripped in your fists, the whole might of science, of industry, of civilization's mastery of the world—*our* civilization's mastery of *this* world. "HOOOOO-AH!!!" as the Gulf troops say.

We popped over the top of a little ridge, and there was a Bedouin camp on the other side. I watched a boy about nine or ten years old come running out from one of the goat-hair tents. We were so close I could see his expression—thrill and fear and awe and wonder combined. His whole life he'll remember the moment that sky-blackening, air-mauling, thunder-engined steel firmament of war crossed his face. And I hope all his bellicose, fanatical, senseless, quarrel-mongering neighbors—from Tel Aviv to Khartoum, from Tripoli to Tehran—remember it too.

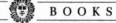